THE VENTNOR WEST BRANCH

BY

PETER PAYE

WILD SWAN PUBLICATIONS LTD.

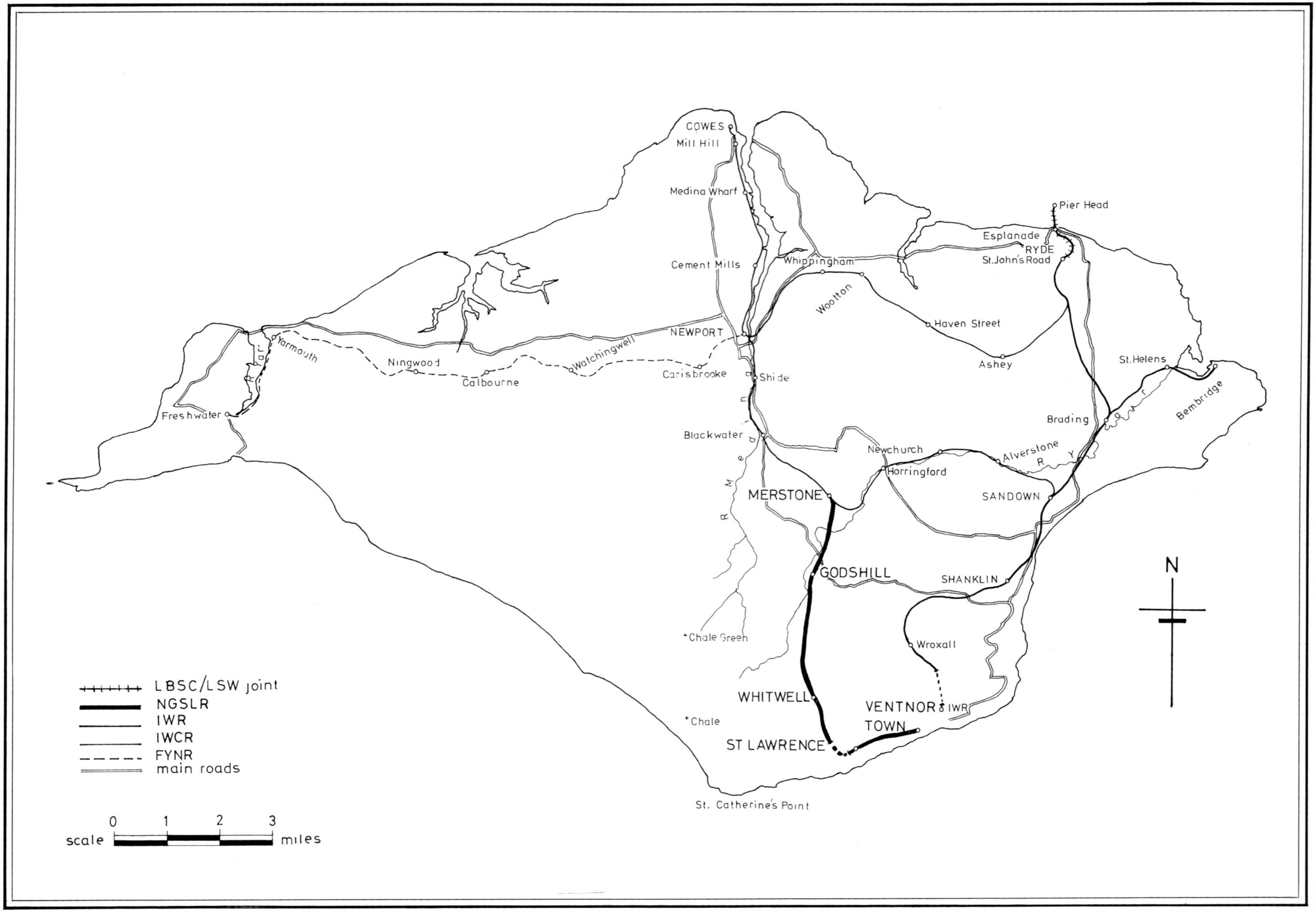
COWES
Mill Hill
Medina Wharf
Cement Mills
Whippingham
Wootton
NEWPORT
Pier Head
Esplanade
RYDE
St. John's Road
Haven Street
Ashey
St. Helens
Bembridge
Brading
Yarmouth
Ningwood
Calbourne
Watchingwell
Carisbrooke
Shide
Freshwater
Blackwater
Newchurch
Alverstone
Horringford
SANDOWN
MERSTONE
GODSHILL
SHANKLIN
Wroxall
Chale Green
WHITWELL
VENTNOR
IWR
TOWN
Chale
ST LAWRENCE
St. Catherine's Point
R Medina
R Yar
R Yar
N
LBSC/LSW joint
NGSLR
IWR
IWCR
FYNR
main roads
scale 0 1 2 3 miles

INTRODUCTION

THERE can be few railways in Great Britain that can lay claim to the distinction of having totally changed the direction in which the line was to be built. Such was the Newport Godshill and St Lawrence Railway, the last line to be built on the Isle of Wight, which was completed in two stages – from Merstone to St Lawrence in 1897 and then on to Ventnor three years later.

Originally authorised in 1885 as the Shanklin and Chale Railway, the intention was to build a line to run from east to west to serve the south-western part of the Island which was devoid of railways. Disagreement with the Isle of Wight Railway, which had initially offered running powers to Shanklin, forced the promoters to seek alternative arrangements. In 1887 the company gained parliamentary powers for additional junctions and a connecting line going north to Merstone on the Isle of Wight (Newport Junction) Railway in the hope of attracting to Ventnor the lucrative through traffic from Newport, Cowes and indeed the mainland. Once again the IWR succeeded in stopping the competitive venture entering Ventnor. The only destinations left available were a rural junction with no road access between Shanklin and Wroxall, or the small village of Chale and there appeared little hope for the scheme.

A significant change in the Island railway affairs in 1887, however, proved beneficial. The IW(NJ), Cowes & Newport and Ryde & Newport companies amalgamated to form the Isle of Wight Central Railway. After joint talks between the directors of the S&C and IWCR companies, the old route was abandoned in 1889. The NGSLR was born out of the ashes of the old S and C, with an authorised route to run north to south from Merstone to St Lawrence. Subsequent Acts authorised the short extension to Ventnor and thus a route competing with the IWR.

From the outset difficulties were experienced. The promoters were constantly short of capital and the contractor went into receivership. After the line was opened the IWCR worked the railway but traffic never came up to expectations. Experiments with steam railcars to reduce operating expenses met with failure and by 1910 affairs were in a parlous state. Two of the directors sued the NGSLR for unpaid debentures and the chairman instituted proceedings for the appointment of a receiver. The IWCR threatened to terminate the working agreement and it was rumoured the line would close. On 1st October 1913 the IWCR assumed full responsibility for the railway but unfortunately could do little to attract traffic away from the IWR route to Ventnor.

When the Southern Railway took over in 1923 the Ventnor Town branch was a backwater of the Island railway system, still laid with lightweight flat-bottom track. The new regime, whilst improving the track, instituted a number of economy measures in the late 1920s, removing the crossing loop at Whitwell, switching out the signal box at Ventnor West, destaffing the stations and introducing push-pull trains with the guard issuing the tickets. The outcome was a basic railway and, except for a few through workings, passengers were required to change to or from the branch train at Merstone for forward journeys. Possibly because of this action the branch survived the spate of closures which affected mainland branch lines in the 1930s.

The population of the area was sparse and passenger-travel minimal. As roads and motor vehicles improved, so passenger traffic declined, attracted to local bus services which offered an almost door-to-door service. The branch survived World War Two but then declined rapidly. After 1948 British Railways found the branch an expensive luxury they could ill afford to maintain, for many trains carried no passengers at all. All services were subsequently withdrawn on and from 15th September 1952 and the line closed.

Now all is silent, most fixed assets are gone and the track formation in many places reverted to farmland. I have attempted to trace the history of the branch and details have been checked with available documents, but apologies are offered for any errors which may have occurred.

P. PAYE

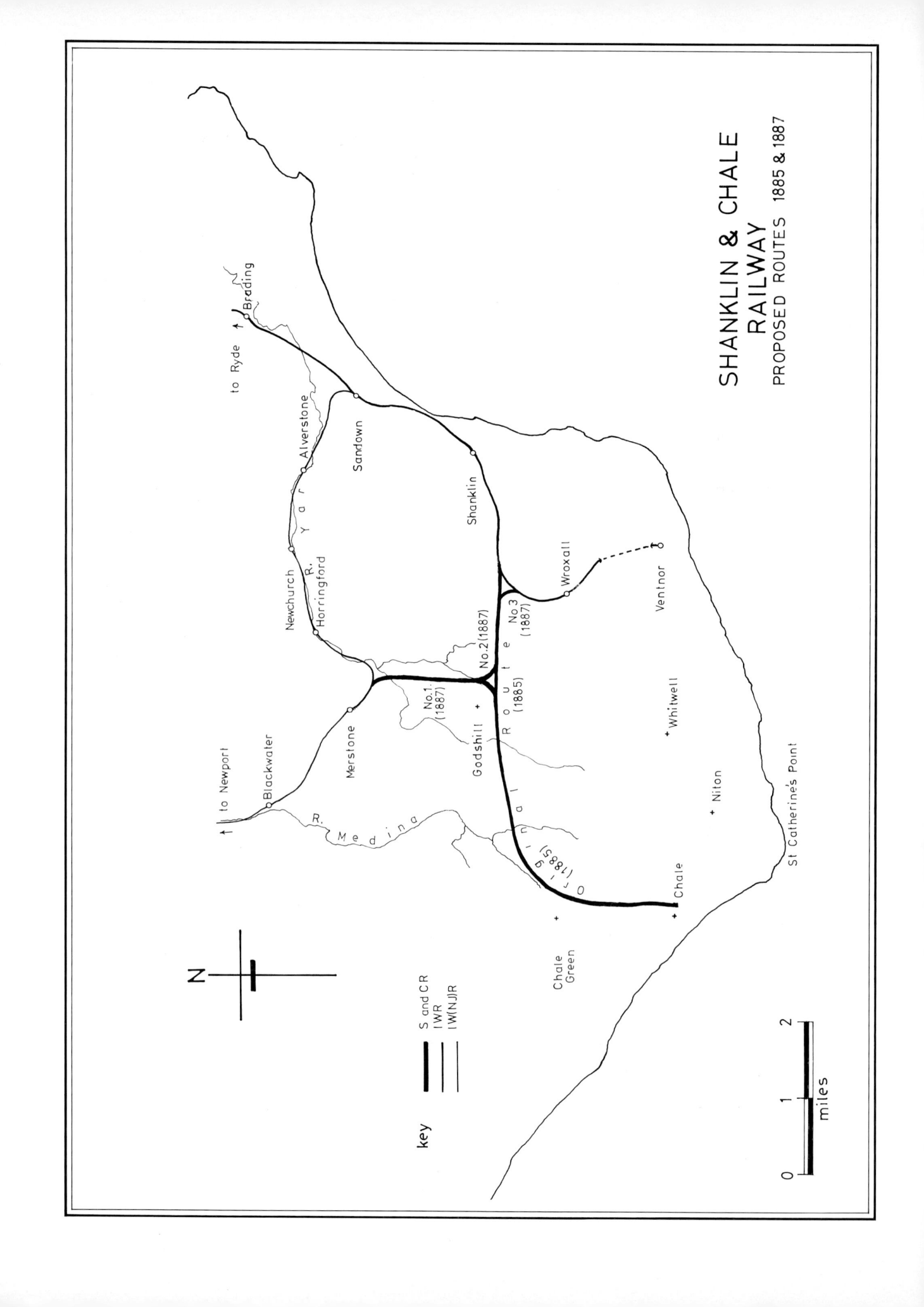

CHAPTER ONE

THE SHANKLIN AND CHALE RAILWAY

THE Isle of Wight, measuring some 23 miles from Bembridge Foreland in the east to the Needles in the west, and 13 miles north to south at its broadest from Cowes to St Catherines Point, has long been renowned as a holiday resort. Few could afford the visit across the Solent until the advent of a regular ferry service linking the island with the mainland from 1820 gradually brought changes. By far the largest upheaval came with the building of the railways on the Isle of Wight, as the population increased and holidaymakers swelled their ranks to sample the delights of downland scenery and sandy beaches. In 48 years, the 60 miles of coastline guarding 147 square miles of land became host to $55\frac{1}{2}$ miles of railway serving 33 stations and 2 halts. Their advent, however, was far from being smooth.

The first serious interest in railways for the island appears to have been stimulated in 1845, the Railway Mania year, when an attempt was made to enlist support for a line some 20 miles in length from the seaport and yachting centre of Cowes along the banks of the River Medina to Newport, the county town, and thence via Blackwater and Godshill to Ventnor, famous for its mild climate. A branch line was planned from Newport to Ryde and the undertaking known as the Isle of Wight Railway Company was provisionally registered with a share capital of £300,000. The whole scheme aroused intense local opposition headed by the Earl of Yarborough and Sir John Simeon, Bart., and other prominent landowners, which resulted in the plans being abandoned.

Thereafter many railways were projected but the first step towards the construction of the Island network came with the opening on 16th June 1862 of the $4\frac{1}{4}$-mile Cowes and Newport Railway, operated with two 2-2-2 well tank locomotives and some second-hand four-wheel coaches. Two years later the Isle of Wight Railway opened between Ryde and Shanklin on 23rd August 1864. Ventnor, the final objective of the IWR, was reached on 10th September 1866 by way of the inland route via Wroxall and a tunnel under St Boniface Down, the heavy earthworks south of Shanklin delaying completion of this latter section.

In 1868 a third company – the Isle of Wight (Newport Junction) Railway – obtained authority to construct a $9\frac{1}{4}$ mile line from Sandown to Newport. Since this route served only a rural part of the island with no towns en route, it received little financial support, and initially opened only between Sandown and Shide (one mile south of Newport) on 1st February 1875. Monetary difficulties and the necessity to build a brick viaduct to gain entry to the town of Newport effectively delayed construction of the final sections, which were completed from Shide to Pan Lane on 6th October 1875 and thence to Newport on 1st June 1879. Whilst the IW(NJ)R was struggling with its problems the Ryde and Newport Railway had meanwhile constructed a line connecting the IWR in Ryde to the county town, opened on 20th December 1875. The Cowes & Newport and Ryde & Newport companies were then governed by a Joint Committee until July 1887 when they absorbed the IW(NJ)R to form the largest pre-grouping company on the island, the Isle of Wight Central Railway.

From 1871 passengers bound for the mainland arriving at Ryde were conveyed by horse tram from the station at St John's Road to the Esplanade and then down the pier to the boats. With the opening of a new pier in 1880 both IWR and IWCR trains ran through to the Pier Head station over a railway jointly owned by the London Brighton and South Coast and London and South Western Railways, replacing the inconvenient street tramway. On 27th May 1882 the IWR commenced working the $2\frac{3}{4}$ mile branch connecting Brading and Bembridge. The line was originally authorised in 1874 and built by the Brading Harbour Improvement and Railway Company across the reclaimed harbour. After sixteen years of contract working the IWR purchased the line outright in August 1898.

The western part of the island remained devoid of railway accommodation until 10th September 1888 when the Freshwater Yarmouth and Newport Railway commenced working freight trains between Freshwater and Newport. Such was the poor condition of the works and finances that it was 20th July 1889 before passengers were conveyed and even then under an arrangement with the IWCR which worked the line.

All these plans left the south-western part of the island devoid of railways. After the failure of the Cowes to Ventnor venture of 1845, the scheme was revived in 1852. Another Isle of Wight Railway, sometimes known as 'Fulton's Line', named after the promoter, was proposed in three parts, with Cowes to Newport and Ryde to Newport as the most important sections, whilst the third route suggested was Newport to Niton via Godshill. Bills were promoted in Parliament but failed the following year. Another scheme mooted was a coastal line from Ryde Pier Head via Brading, Sandown, Shanklin and Bonchurch to Ventnor, St Lawrence and Niton, but this also failed to reach fruition. For almost two decades promoters and speculators left the area alone but in 1871 there was a proposal for a Yarmouth and Ventnor Railway, Tramway and Pier Company to build a line running from Ventnor via Whitwell, Chale, Atherfield, Brixton (now Brighstone) and Freshwater Bay to Yarmouth. Associated with this scheme was a southern extension of the IW(NJ)R from Merstone via Godshill to join up with the proposed railway by triangular junction at Whitwell. This sparsely populated area of Vectis held little hope of making such a venture viable and saner counsels decided to withdraw the proposals.

Evidently the lessons learned went unheeded for in 1884 various interested parties had informal discussions with the IWR authorities hoping to entice them to build a railway into the area. Lucrative agricultural traffic was the alleged attraction, as well as an over optimistic forecast of passenger flows. The IWR was, however, consolidating its position after taking over the operation of the Bembridge Railway and had no wish to be involved in speculative schemes. The promoters were informed, however, that no opposition would be raised if the railway was built as an independent concern. To protect their interests the IWR gave permission for running powers into Shanklin station from an intended junction at Winstone, between Shanklin and Wroxall. Thus the Shanklin and Chale

Railway was born, and the advocates of the scheme (having received the backing of the IWR) advanced their promotion to the Parliamentary Private Bill Office.

The Bill duly received the Royal Assent on 14th August 1885 as the Shanklin and Chale Railway Act 1885 (48 & 49 Vic Cap CXCII). This authorised the making of a railway 6 miles in length commencing in the Parish of Newchurch by a junction with the Isle of Wight Railway at a point $28\frac{1}{2}$ chains or thereabouts north-east from the 9 mile post at Winstone between Shanklin and Wroxall and terminating at or near the southernmost corner of field No 326 in the Parish of Chale. The proposed railway was to pass through the parishes of Newchurch, Godshill and Chale. The act authorised the company to raise £60,000 in £10 shares and granted borrowing powers of £20,000 after the complete capital was promised and £30,000 actually paid up. Three years were allowed for the compulsory purchase of the necessary land and five years for completion of works. Henry Francis Giles, A. Curzon Thompson and Philip Powter, with two others, were the first directors of the company. The statute also granted running powers over part of the alignment of the curve to the IWR, and working powers thence, and the use of Shanklin station were removed.

Unfortunately, as the Bill passed through the several stages of the Lower and Upper Houses, the promoters realised they had no hope of ever operating independently and would require the IWR to work the line. This decision was confirmed when the IWR forced the withdrawal of the clause granting running powers into Shanklin because of the cramped nature of the track layout. Further urgent talks were held with IWR officers. Horace Tahourdin (General Manager of the IWR) subsequently visited the area and travelled over the proposed route, after which the promoters were advised that it was impossible for the IWR to operate the new line without an extension of the route from Chale to Freshwater. The Ryde-based company was seeking further lucrative pastures and hoped for a share of traffic from West Wight by inducing the Shanklin and Chale directors along this path – a fact which was later denied. Approaches were also made to the IW(NJ)R but with their insecurity, the company showed no interest in the scheme.

Giles, Thompson and Powter were in a hapless position, for the passage of the Bill through Parliament had almost exhausted resources and this, combined with the demands made by the IWR, meant no shares had been issued. It was now imperative to extend their objectives and introduce a Bill for the extension to Freshwater. At that time William Bohm, who was later to take up shares in many of the island railways, was taking an active interest in the affairs of the Chale company. He contacted a close friend – Harry Magnus of Ingatestone, Essex – who agreed to finance the new Bill in return for shareholdings and a possible position on the board. The necessary plans were formulated and papers passed to the Parliamentary Bill Office on 30th November 1885 although, as expected, opposition was registered by the Freshwater, Yarmouth and Newport Railway and Mr G.T. Porter. The latter was a solicitor with offices in Westminster who specialised in Railway Law. He also acted at other times for the R&N Joint Committee and IWCR.

The objections to the Shanklin and Chale (Freshwater Extension) Bill were considered by a Select Committee of the House of Lords on 12th March 1886, under the chairmanship of Lord Balfour of Burley. Balfour Browne put the case for the FYNR, but the Committee found that the Freshwater company had insufficient cause to object to the Bill, which was accordingly referred back to the Chairman of the Committees.

Despite this satisfactory outcome, the Bill subsequently foundered at the third reading, and the company was left to develop as best it could the 6 mile section between Winstone and Chale. The IWR was also hardening its attitude and announced the terms for working the line would be on the basis 55 to 80 per cent of the net receipts provided annual receipts were not less than £3,900. If the takings were below this total, all earnings were to be taken by the IWR leaving nothing to the Chale company. These terms, with other stipulations, were totally unacceptable and left the promoters no alternative but to seek an outlet through the IW(NJ)R and thereby attract traffic from Newport, Cowes and beyond.

The alternative certainly offered an agreeable solution, for the Newport Junction Company was then party to an amalgamation with the Cowes & Newport and Ryde & Newport companies which together would supersede the IWR as the largest railway on the island. Further afield the Swindon, Marlborough and Andover Railway, which had running powers over the LSWR, had in 1882 proposed to build a branch line from Totton to Stone Point on the Hampshire coast opposite Cowes. From there it was proposed to ply steamers to the Isle of Wight with a sailing time of ten minutes, and thus create a more direct route from the Midland and Western counties of England, obviating the longer journey via Ryde. Another factor in the railway politics of the day was the animosity in Ventnor and surrounding villages against the IWR for its exorbitant fares and charges, which directly affected the commodity prices in the town. Here then was an opportunity to introduce a competitive influence against the IWR by offering a second and shorter route to Ventnor as an alternative to the change of trains at Sandown. A separate and independent route through to Ventnor could reduce rates and charges for the conveyance of passenger and goods traffic from Cowes and Newport to the 'English Madeira'. The C&N was certainly keen on the proposals but the IW(NJ)R was not and the IWR even less so. As an alternative therefore running powers to Ventnor over the IWR were again proposed.

As before, the S & C promoters were short of finances to underwrite the passage of a suitable Bill through parliament until Bohm again appeared on the scene with the necessary monetary assistance. The plans for the revised scheme were prepared by Robert Elliott Cooper, a civil engineer who was born in 1845 and brought up in Leeds and York, later to be knighted in 1919. His other Isle of Wight achievement was Victoria Pier at Cowes opened in 1902. Once completed, the plans were presented to the Private Bill Office in November 1886. Objections were lodged by both the IWR and IW(NJ)R companies and although the Bill passed the Lower House, an enquiry was required in the later stages of progress.

The hearing before the Lords Select Committee, under the chairmanship of Lord Belper, began on 9th May 1887. Rigg and Giles appeared as counsel in support of the Bill, Sutton acted as counsel for the IW(NJ)R and Balfour Browne QC for the IWR. The witnesses called included Henry James Damant, Clerk to the West Cowes Local Board; A.H. Estcourt, Deputy Governor of the Island and Clerk to the Commissioner of Highways; Henry Pinnock, Deputy Chairman of the Southampton and Isle of Wight Steam Packet Company; M. Morgan, one of the Highway Commissioners, a Guardian of the Poor and owner of a mill at Shanklin; Henry Ingram, a builder in Ventnor; R.E. Cooper, the engineer for the line; H.F. Tahourdin, Chairman of the Isle of Wight Railway; and Thomas Dolling Bolton, MP for North East Derbyshire and Chairman of the Newport Junction Company.

Evidence was given that there was no means of getting goods to the south and west of the Island except by cart over minor roads. When the Steamship *Cormorant*, laden with cotton, had become wrecked on the south coast, recovery of the cargo by cart had taken a month and cost £1,000. Several of the witnesses complained of the circuitous route to Ventnor via Sandown, high tariffs and connections with IWR trains at Sandown not made, resulting in great inconvenience in waiting there for onward trains. These claims were countered by the counsel for the IWR who demonstrated that there were seven trains daily each way from Newport to Sandown and thirteen on the line from Sandown to Ventnor, six of which offered two-minute connections out of trains from Newport.

It was clearly in the minds of the promoters that the line from Newport to Sandown, which at that time depended largely on local traffic, could, by extension to Ventnor, attract through traffic from the mainland to that tourist resort. It was admitted at the hearing that a route via Southampton and Cowes could hardly compete for London traffic with the IWR route via Ryde and thence to Portsmouth, but a significant amount of traffic from the Midlands and the West of England was (perhaps optimistically) expected.

Counsel for the IWR was able to make much play, at the promoters' expense, of the layout involving triangular junctions, at one point succeeding in getting one witness to agree that to work connecting trains on all the lines proposed by the Bill, the company would require five engines, a proposition which was clearly hopelessly uneconomic! Opponents of the Bill also pointed out that a through route via Cowes involved a sea passage of 11 miles, followed by a walk of 150 yards up a steep hill from the jetty to the railway station. Such a journey would never be able to compete with the IWR route from Portsmouth, which involved a sea crossing of four miles (or $2\frac{3}{4}$ miles from the pier at Stokes Bay) and then a cross-pier connection on to the train at Ryde.

Ingram's evidence, based on his experience as a builder, revealed an interesting insight into the existing facilities for handling freight traffic. Because of the high costs of routeing his goods over three different lines, he brought his materials in, not via West Cowes (which he said had better goods and warehouse accommodation and a deeper mooring for craft) but via St Helens. This was despite the fact that at St Helens goods could be offloaded only at high tide, and sometimes heavily laden ships had to lie offshore for a week to wait for a tide high enough to safely cross the bar (the alternative was to pay for lighterage to bring the goods to the quayside). Ingram purchased his bricks from the Medway area and the North of England and also brought in lime and timber. Ingram's evidence was somewhat undermined when he admitted that he had only had £36 worth of traffic handled by the IWR in the previous year, but the rates he quoted reveal something of why there was so much resentment amongst traders against the IWR and its 'monopoly' tariffs. The IW(NJ)R charged 3s. 1d per thousand to carry bricks the nine miles from Newport to Sandown. The IWR rates for the same load for the six miles from Sandown to Ventnor was 3s 9d.

As engineer for the line, Cooper must have expected the extensive questioning of his evidence. He was resident engineer for the Great Northern Railway line in Yorkshire (between Leeds, Bradford and Halifax) and in the eight years preceding the enquiry had been responsible for railways costing some £1 million. His evidence was highly optimistic. Although the Cowes & Newport, Newport Junction and Ryde & Newport lines had cost £22,410 per mile, he thought the S & C could be built for £6,000 per mile and could earn £25 per mile per week (the IWR, in its 'monopoly' position, achieved £58 gross earnings per mile per week, which was considered exceptionally high). The costs were summarised:

Railway No. 1, commencing at Godshill by a junction with the authorised S & C line, and terminating near Merstone [IW(NJ)R] – 2 miles 6 chains in length	£11,550 5s 6d
Railway No. 2, an eastern spur to connect with the S & C, facing towards Shanklin – 2 furlongs 5 chains in length	£4,330 14s 0d
Railway No. 3, a spur from the S & C line to the IWR – 2 furlongs 9 chains in length	£3,517 1s 0d

The Bill included running powers over the IWR to both Shanklin and Ventnor, and Cooper reminded the Committee that these powers were vital to the success of the project. If a working agreement with the IWR could be reached, the powers would not need to be exercised. Cooper saw no problems with line capacity on the IWR line, where the new junctions would provide two new block posts three miles apart. At that time there were fourteen trains per day in and out of Ventnor between 6.30 am and 9.45 pm. Goods traffic was already worked at night to increase line capacity during the daytime. The junctions with the IWR did not present any safety problems since the S & C line approached both on rising gradients (1 in 51 and 1 in 40). Cooper costed the junctions at £1,000 for the two, saying that he had installed one at Willoughby on the GNR, and others for £1,000, though he admitted that this did not include the cost of signalling, which at Willoughby (involving a level crossing) had been £600–700.

Cooper's evidence as to the possible income arising from the line did not stand up well to examination. The IW(NJ)R trains from Newport to Sandown cost 8d per train per mile and the IWR trains cost 2s $4\frac{1}{2}$d per mile to run. If the Ventnor traffic was siphoned off at Merstone, the IW(NJ)R trains would be increasingly uneconomic, and Cooper had no convincing answer as to how these services could continue to be worked.

Balfour Browne, as counsel for the IWR, made it clear that the IWR was objecting only to the running powers over the IWR included in the Bill, and would withdraw its opposition if the clause giving those powers to the S & C was dropped.

The evidence of the chairman of the IWR gave a lot of detail of how that company was then worked. The line was single except where the Ryde and Newport Railways ran parallel into Ryde. There were only three block sections – Ryde to Brading, Brading to Sandown, and Sandown to Ventnor. Over this line, with limited capacity, the company ran 22 trains in winter months and 26 in the summer. The station at Sandown was wholly owned by the IWR although the IW(NJ)R used the outside platform. The IW(NJ)R ran seven trains per day to Sandown, and every train had a connecting IWR service. The average journey time from Ventnor to Newport (including the change of train at Sandown) was 50 minutes. The interchange traffic at Sandown in 1886 had been £788 for passengers, £473 for coal, £169 for goods and £19 for parcels.

Tahourdin strongly objected to the running powers incorporated in the Bill. There was insufficient line capacity to handle the traffic, no facilities at Shanklin to cope with terminating trains, and no room at Ventnor to expand the station (situated in a cutting into the hillside) which already could scarcely handle the traffic of the IWR. The longest interval between trains on the Ventnor to Sandown section was 59 minutes, the shortest 13 minutes.

The evidence of Bolton, the chairman of the IW(NJ)R, was not supportive of the Bill. There had been no increase in the traffic from Cowes to Ventnor in recent years and he saw no realistic prospect that the new line would induce more travellers from the Midlands to enter the Island via Cowes. Many of the travellers were tourists who hardly objected to the 'longer' route via Sandown. The poor interchange from boat to train at Cowes was itself a sufficient incentive to dissuade passengers from defecting from the route via Ryde.

At the end of the enquiry the committee retired to consider the evidence. On returning, the Chairman, Lord Belper, announced that 'the committee was of the opinion the preamble of the Bill should be passed subject to the running powers to Ventnor and Shanklin being struck out.' For the S & C promoters the announcement was a disaster and the withdrawal of running powers effectively doomed the proposed railway to early demise. The IWR had succeeded in stopping the competitive venture entering Ventnor and in making the only destinations available a rural junction between Shanklin and Wroxall with no road access, or the small village of Chale. The Ventnor trade would still pass from the IW(NJ)R to the IWR at Sandown and leave very little traffic for the new line. Under these depressing conditions the Bill continued its passage.

The Shanklin and Chale Railway Act 1887 (50 and 51 Vic Cap clxiv) was passed on 8th August 1887 and granted the company powers to construct three additional branch lines and connections.

> Railway No 1, 1 mile 6 furlongs and 2 chains in length commencing in the parish of Godshill by a junction with the existing authorised railway at a point in field No 24, one chain west of the occupational roadway, 8 chains south of its junction with the public road from Sandford to Godshill and terminating in the parish of Arreton by a junction with the Isle of Wight (Newport Junction) Railway 12 chains east of the bridge carrying the road from Arreton to Little Budbridge over the railway.
>
> A triangular junction was to be formed by Railway No 2, 2 furlongs and 4 chains in length, wholly in the parish of Godshill, commencing at a junction with Railway No 1 7½ chains or thereabouts north of the southernmost corner of the field belonging to, or reputedly belonging to, M Spartelli, and terminating by a junction with the authorised Shanklin and Chale line at a point in a field belonging to F. Creeth, 3 chains north-east from the southernmost corner and a like distance measuring east from the westernmost corner of the same field.
>
> Railway No 3, 2 furlongs 9 chains in length wholly in the parish of Newchurch, commencing at a junction with the authorised Shanklin and Chale Railway at a point on the east side of the public road from Brading to Wroxall, 10 chains from the junction of that road from Sandford and terminating by a junction with the Isle of Wight Railway 15 chains north-east of the bridge carrying the road to Yard Farm over the railway.

The Act authorised the company to raise additional capital of £24,000 in £10 shares with borrowing powers of £8,000. Three years were allowed for the purchase of land and five years for the completion of works. Under the reference of the Act the company was not permitted to acquire land occupied wholly or partially by labouring classes.

The outlook was certainly bleak, with prospects of attracting shareholders even bleaker. The affairs of the company stagnated as the promoters lost the will for the fight. A significant change in island railway affairs had, however, been made on 1st July 1887 when the Cowes & Newport, Ryde & Newport and Isle of Wight (Newport Junction) Companies finally amalgamated to form the Isle of Wight Central Railway. This event, whilst not having an immediate effect on the S & C promoters, certainly offered hope to their ailing ideals. Once the new regime established its affairs, a close interest was taken in the dormant route which had parliamentary authority to build a railway into untapped country to the south of the island and certainly within striking distance of Ventnor. Thus at various times during the winter and spring of 1888 talks were held between S & C and IWCR officers to resurrect plans for the railway, possibly taking a different route. It was evident to both parties the IWR would never entertain running powers over their system, which would erode traffic receipts. Equally Chale as a terminus offered few attractions as a railhead for the local district when the hard economic facts were assessed. Having eliminated the differences in opinion over the junction with the Sandown to Newport line and agreed on Merstone, where a new station was to replace the existing single platform structure, the only outstanding problem was where to terminate the line. There was only one course of action. A revised route had to be adopted, terminating as near Ventnor as possible and taking a direct route south of Merstone, running via Godshill and Whitwell (following the route suggested in 1871) and this time tunnelling under the downland to emerge at St Lawrence. Cooper subsequently surveyed the route in the summer of 1888 and the necessary plans were then prepared for parliamentary approval.

The IWCR offered all support and agreed to work the new line as the promoters had no hope of ever operating their own concern. The Newport company could now at least offer token competition against the IWR for passenger and freight traffic from the mainland to Ventnor. It was also agreed that since the line no longer served Shanklin or Chale, its title would be amended to the Newport, Godshill and St Lawrence Railway, with an independent board of directors. The share issues authorised in the earlier Acts would be retained to form the basis of capital for the venture. Surprisingly, the IWR offered no objection to the forthcoming Bill as the days of the S & C drew to a close. Having established an east to west route after four fruitless years and two Acts of Parliament, the renamed company redirected its resources to building a line to run from north to south.

CHAPTER TWO

NEWPORT GODSHILL AND ST LAWRENCE RAILWAY

THE Bill authorising the abandonment of the old Shanklin and Chale group of lines and the re-routeing of the railway received the Royal Assent on 12th August 1889 as the Newport Godshill and St Lawrence Railway Act 1889 (52 and 53 Vic Cap cli). The statute authorised 'the building of a railway, 5 miles 5 furlongs 6 chains in length commencing in the Parish of Arreton by a junction with the Newport Junction Section of the Isle of Wight Central Railway at a point half a chain east of the Merstone Lane Level Crossing, near Merstone Station, and terminating on the East Side of the public road called St Lawrence Shute in the parish of St Lawrence in field No 14, $8\frac{1}{2}$ chains or thereabout north east of the north eastern corner of St Lawrence Church and 11 chains north-west of the junction of the public roads leading from Whitwell to St Lawrence and Ventnor to Freshwater'. Two years were allowed for the compulsory purchase of land and five years for the completion of the works. A single track railway was envisaged but sufficient land was to be purchased to enable the formation to accommodate double track.

Clause 16 of the statute empowered the company to abandon the works authorised in the Acts of 1885 and 1887 and change the title of the company to the Newport Godshill and St Lawrence Railway. The new company was to enter into a working agreement with the IWCR and plans for the railway were to be submitted to the IWCR for approval. Likewise construction works were to be completed in a workmanlike manner to the reasonable satisfaction of the IWC engineer. Under the powers of the Act the IWCR was responsible for constructing the junction at Merstone and to provide all facilities for accommodating traffic from the new line at Newport. The Act also authorised the payment of interest not exceeding 3 per cent on capital during construction.

The Newport Godshill and St Lawrence and IWC Railways were to be considered one railway in respect of fares and charges, whilst the IWC for their part were empowered to work and maintain the new railway after one year and 'run a reasonable proper and sufficient number of trains thereon' and 'afford connections with a reasonable number of trains on the Sandown–Newport line at Merstone'. The IWC was to retain 55 per cent of the gross receipts. The initial working agreement between the companies was to remain for 7 years and was subject to termination on the giving of 12 months notice by either party.

The chairman of the Newport Godshill and St Lawrence Railway was W. Bohm of 23 Old Jewry, London EC, with fellow directors Captain H. Mainwaring Dunstan of Queen Victoria Street, London EC, Henry Daniel Martin of Newport, Isle of Wight, T. Dolling Bolton of Temple Gardens, London EC, H. Magnus of Copthall Avenue, London EC, and Percy Mortimer of Overton, Hampshire. Martin, Bolton and Mortimer were also directors of the IWCR. The engineers of the new railway were Percy Dunstan and R. Elliott Cooper, both of Westminster. Immediately after the passing of the Act the land agent advised local landowners and tenants of the company's intention to purchase the land required for the railway, (using compulsory powers if necessary) as authorised by the statute.

The contract for the building of the new railway to St Lawrence was awarded to Messrs Westwood and Winley on 8th August 1891 but, because of objections to terminology and additional clauses, a second contract was signed on 15th January 1892.

The proposal to continue the line nearer to Ventnor was always the ultimate goal of both the Godshill railway promoters and the IWCR board. Having carried out preliminary surveys for the extension and received agreement on the working plans, the package for a line from St Lawrence to Ventnor was prepared for Parliamentary approval and passed to the Private Bill Office on the last day of November 1891. Unfortunately its passage was far from smooth and not unnaturally objections were raised by the IWR, as well as the Royal National Hospital for Consumption and Diseases of the Chest, and Captain Sewell (owner of Steephill Castle which was situated on the edge of Ventnor).

Once again the line's promoters found themselves embroiled in a hearing before a Select Committee of the House of Lords. The hearing, under the chairmanship of the Earl of Lauderdale, began on 28th March 1892. Messrs. Pember and Hans Hamilton appeared as counsel for the promoters, and Balfour Browne QC again represented the main objector, the Isle of Wight Railway. T.D. Bolton represented the IWCR (successor in this matter to the IW(NJ)R for which he had spoken at the 1887 hearing). Henry Sewell spoke for the Royal National Hospital for Consumption and Diseases of the Chest (and presumably also his own interests!). R.E. Cooper, engineer for the proposed railway, was first to give evidence, followed by T.D. Bolton as chairman of the IWCR; H. Simmons, manager of the IWCR; H.D. Martin, a civil engineer for 50 years and a long-term resident of the Island; T.R. Saunders, a surveyor who had lived in Ventnor for 20 years; W. Airy, a member of the Institute of Civil Engineers; and Sir Benjamin Baker, engineer for the Forth Bridge.

Cooper explained that the Bill proposed alterations to the level of the already authorised line to St Lawrence to enable the line to pass under St Lawrence Shute, and two new railways:

> Railway No. 1 – only 6 chains in length, to allow St Lawrence station to be more conveniently located as a through station.
> Railway No. 2 – 4 furlongs 8 chains in length. This was the railway to which objection was made.

The capital was to be £18,000 with borrowing powers for a further £6,000, which he considered ample. The new station to serve Ventnor would be on the same level as the town, whereas the IWR station was high above the town, nearly 300 feet above sea level. The undercliff area, along which the line was to be built, had 'for years and years' been laid out to roads and houses and there was no danger of further slippage. A low cutting would screen the railway from the Royal Hospital. Access to the new station would be both from an access road and from a footpath running by the side of the Steephill Castle Estate. The construction of the line would pose no threat to the stability of the structure of the hospital, but would bring 'a great saving on the cost of coal supplies to the hospital as cartage charges from the IWR station are heavy'.

Captain Sewell, who had tried to sell Steephill Castle the previous year but had found no bidders, might now find it easier to sell the property once it had easy access. The access road was to be 300 yards in length, at a gradient of 1 in 10. The passenger station on Railway No. 2 was also intended to handle light goods traffic only. The coal depot would be at the top of the slope at the end of Railway No. 1, and no heavy goods traffic would be worked into the passenger station, since road access to Railway No. 1 was easier.

The IWR, in an attempt to keep the new company out of Ventnor and maintain its monopoly, now offered running powers from Sandown to Ventnor, explaining that the introduction of electric train staff working had so increased line capacity that it was now able to offer this facility. How the additional traffic was to be accommodated at the two-platform station at Ventnor was not explained. The line to St Lawrence had not been objected to by the IWR since it had apparently not been regarded as a serious competitor; the extension towards Ventnor was quite a different matter.

The undercliff area had been formed, over a geological timespan, by slippage of the rock on an underlying strata of clay. There was much concern that the construction of the railway, and the vibration of the trains, would start a new era of movement of the whole undercliff, damaging the many properties built on it. Martin and Saunders were called as witnesses to try to allay these fears, though of course no-one could say just what the effects of building the railway would be. Saunders also voiced the long-felt grievances of the people of Ventnor against the IWR – there were no late night services (none after 8 pm) and the fares were high (4s 0d single from Ryde to Ventnor, which included 1s 0d toll for the pier railway). Airy appeared to offer evidence about the possible slippage of the undercliff, but admitted that his knowledge was confined to a walk along the proposed route because he had only been asked the previous week to give evidence. Pember, for the promoters, replied that there had been no movement of the strata for some years past, and that the formation had supported the old St Lawrence Church for over 100 years. Sir Benjamin Baker quoted instances of damage by subsidence the world over, but eventually admitted that building the railway would 'not bring the Hospital down'!

The committee withdrew for a short while and after deliberating the evidence the Chairman announced, much to the chagrin of the opponents, that by unanimous decision the Bill would be allowed to proceed.

The Bill for the extension to Ventnor was submitted to the board of the Isle of Wight Central Railway on 27th April 1892, and the directors were gratified to note that Clause 32 now included the provision that the guarantee payable to their company was increased to £2,000 per annum.

The Newport Godshill and St Lawrence Railway Act 1892 (55 and 56 Vic Cap CCXI), passed on 28th June 1892, authorised the company to construct the railway extension to Ventnor in two sections

> Railway No. 1, 1 furlong 6.50 chains wholly in the parish of St Lawrence commencing at the end on junction with the railway authorised in the Act of 1889 and terminating at the east fence of field No. 17, one hundred yards north west along the occupational road from the south west corner of Captain Fisher's stables.
>
> Railway No. 2, 4 furlongs 8 chains in length wholly in the parish of St Lawrence commencing at the termination point of Railway No. 1 and terminating near the western fence of Steephill Castle grounds in a field belonging to the Trustees of the Hon Evelyn Cornwallis Anderson Pelham and occupied by William Truslove at a point 9 chains from the north side of the public road leading from St Lawrence to Ventnor.

This Act also authorised alterations in the levels of the proposed railway between 5 miles 27 chains and the terminus in the parishes of Whitwell and St Lawrence, a diversion of the public road known as St Lawrence Shute, and an improvement in the bridle or occupational road, later known as Seven Sisters Road, between St Lawrence and Ventnor adjacent to the termination of the railway, to permit the use of the road as an approach to St Lawrence station.

Because of objections from the Hon Evelyn C.A. Pelham, Lord Cornwallis, the company was not permitted to provide a goods station or convey coal, minerals or heavy goods on railway No. 2, neither were they to erect buildings in field No. 12 or take more land than necessary for the construction of the Ventnor passenger station and adjacent carriage road leading from the St Lawrence–Ventnor public highway.

Three years were allowed for the purchase of land and five years for the completion of works. The Act also extended the five years allowed for the purchase of land and completion of works in the 1889 Act for a further two years and three years from 12th August 1891 respectively.

To complete these works the company was empowered to raise an additional £18,000 in £10 shares with borrowing powers for a further £6,000 when £9,000 shares issue had been raised.

Despite the success of gaining access powers to Ventnor, little actual work was being executed apart from the staking out of the proposed route of the railway. Local labour was, however, recruited from villages in the vicinity of the line and, with menfolk knowing that their earnings would be well above the going agricultural rate of pay, there was no shortage of volunteers.

Early in February 1893 the question of the intended junction with the IWCR at Merstone was raised. The subject was to become the focus for delicate discussion and negotiation, especially when it was realised the existing small station and layout was entirely inadequate for the interchange of traffic. On 21st February Bohm wrote to the Central seeking their views and on the following day the IWC Secretary was instructed to ask Simmons (the manager) to prepare plans of the land required for a new station together with estimates of costs, including the laying in of the physical junction. By 13th March the engineer provided estimates of land but no costs.

Evidently Simmons was unhappy with the further plans provided by the Godshill company for on 6th April he questioned the gradients shown on Cooper's diagrams. A week later a request was also made for specification of works. At an IWC board meeting these points were discussed together with the land requirement for the junction at Merstone.

The ceremony of the cutting of the first sod was performed at Merstone on Tuesday, 19th April 1893, by Miss Beatrice Martin, niece of Henry Martin. The *Isle of Wight County Press* reported that 'Merstone kept high holiday on Tuesday for on that day was taken the first step of elevating the pleasant hamlet to the position of junction'. The station was decorated with flags and bunting for the event. Miss Martin performed the ceremony using a small silver spade, the blade being engraved with the inscription 'Presented by Messrs Westwood and Winley to Miss Beatrice Kate Martin on the occasion of her cutting the first sod of the Newport Godshill and St Lawrence Railway, Merstone, April 19th 1893', and placed the earth into a ceremonial wheelbarrow made of mahogany. The barrow had a silver plate at the back with the name of the railway, date and Miss Martin's monogram. The spade and barrow were supplied by Mappin Brothers of London. Other directors and guests took their turn before the promoters and invited guests retired to enjoy a luncheon in the adjacent marquee whilst local schoolchildren were each presented with a bun. Beatrice Martin was subsequently presented with the ceremonial wheelbarrow and spade and these were kept for many years at the family home, Halberry House, Newport.

Simmons was growing impatient with the lethargic attitude of the Godshill company and in early May again complained to his directors of lack of information. The IWC board fully supported his case and on 17th May 1893 wrote to the Godshill company requesting the urgent provision of specification for the permanent way and works together with a gradient chart so that station sites could be agreed.

By 8th June 1893 Simmons was requesting further information including the detailed drawings of stations, station buildings and bridges. He also wanted to know whether the track was to be fang-bolted throughout and stipulated that creosoted sleepers were laid. The IWC engineer was also of the opinion that the slopes of the embankments and cuttings specified in the plans were too steep unless the formation was constructed of sand and gravel. Six days later the Secretary of the IWCR forwarded a letter to the NGSL board requesting information on the intended arrangement for Electric Block and Telegraph to be used by the company.

It was mid July before Cooper (engineer for the NGSL and by now consultant engineer to the IWCR) forwarded a tracing of the section of rail to the Central for approval, with the request for permission to order supplies. Henry Martin duly approved of the type of rail on 2nd August and consented to orders being placed. At this juncture the larger company also requested details of the positioning of fang bolt holes in the rails and although Simmons approved of the plans on 23rd August, he later rescinded the decision and agreed that the contractor utilise dog spikes instead of bolts to affix the rails to the sleepers. On 13th September 1893 the question of inspection of permanent way works was resolved when the Godshill board advised they had no objection to the IWC PW Inspector going over the new works and subsequently reporting any shortcomings to Simmons.

Negotiations on land purchase at Merstone were concluded in early October 1893 when Simmons advised that 1 acre, 2 rods and $1\frac{1}{2}$ perches of land had been acquired for the new station at a cost of £202-16s-0d. Preparation for the commencement of works on the new railway were proceeding apace and on 1st December Simmons requested final plans for the new station at Merstone. At the IWCR board meeting on 13th December the directors agreed to the plans being prepared, with the Godshill company bearing the full costs. At the same meeting a request from Cooper for an IWCR permanent way inspector to be employed full time on the new line during construction was flatly refused and an offer was made for 'one off' inspections only.

By early January 1894 the plans for the new Merstone station were completed but costings were held over pending the settlement of minor alterations. Tenders were, however, invited for the construction of a brick and timber signal box at Merstone to control the new junction layout. Three firms subsequently quoted, J.Ball & Son at £79, Barton Brothers £86 and T.Jenkins at £96-10s-0d. After due deliberation at their meeting on 28th February 1894, the IWC directors awarded the contract to J. Ball & Sons of Cowes. At the same meeting it was announced that the plans for Merstone station had been approved by the Godshill company board but no further action was agreed pending discussion between the engineers of the two companies.

The board of the Newport Godshill and St Lawrence Railway waited until 13th March 1894 to hold their inaugural meeting, at the office of Mr Bohm, 23 Old Jewry, London EC. George Reid was chairman of the meeting with E.G.Johnson and H.Magnus in attendance. The meeting considered the request of the engineer for a payment on account. As a result of the request the company secretary approached the contractor (who was subscribing heavily for shares) for payment of £500 to enable the railway to pay the engineer. The contractor was also required to pay the administration expenses and balance of account to Messrs Reid and Johnson in accordance with the contract.

During March one hundred and twenty £10 shares were transferred to Messrs Westwood and Winley as payment for completion of initial works, whilst the engineer suggested the publishing of notices for the compulsory purchase of land required for the extension railway between St Lawrence and Steephill.

A month later further drawings were forwarded to the IWCR for approval, including the cross-section of line at St Lawrence and the proposed retaining wall, the public road bridge at 3 miles 29 chains, the proposed station at Godshill and the bridge at 2 miles 7 chains. The IWC board duly agreed to the proposed structures but added a rider that the retaining wall at St Lawrence be constructed entirely of concrete to a thickness of 3 feet. This was later changed to Ventnor stone with concrete insert. Simmons reported that the Board of Trade had agreed to the plans for Merstone, Godshill and Whitwell stations. Authority was also finally given for tenders to be sought for the construction of Merstone station.

On 17th April 1894 the NGSLR board decided to alter the arrangement for payment of shares issued against certificates of completion of works presented by the contractor. Westwood and Winley were duly notified in writing of the proposed variation of the contract under which payment was to be subject to:

1. The engineer reporting the progress of the works as satisfactory.
2. The contractor to carry out the unperformed works under Clause 11 of the contract agreed on 8th August 1891 and Clause 7 of the contract signed and dated 15th January 1892 including the payment of £800 for administration expenses.
3. The contractor to pay to the company £500 on account of engineering as agreed in Clause 11 of the contract dated 8th August 1891.
4. When the £2 share is paid upon the balance of the unissued share capital, future certificates to be paid three-fifths in reduction of the liability remaining on partly paid up shares with the remaining two-fifths paid as debentures.
5. The contractor guaranteed 4 per cent interest on debentures from the time of issue until the railway opened to traffic.

Westwood and Winley duly considered the proposals but advised the board of certain reservations they had regarding the payments for future contracts. The NGSLR board reconvened on 1st May 1894 and resolved that no action would be taken until the engineer made a full report of the progress of works on the railway. The directors, however, agreed to authorise the payment of £8,000 to Westwood and Winley as the engineer had approved the standard of completed works.

Construction continued slowly and in June 1894 the contractors were paid a further £4,400 for completed works. The partners, wishing to ensure a continued workload, again requested possession of the site of St Lawrence station and the tunnel. The board, fearing delay in extending their railway to Steephill, were fully aware that the required land had not been acquired and requested the secretary to serve notice to the local landowners as a matter of urgency under the clauses contained in the 1892 Act. At the same extraordinary general meeting it was decided to appoint two additional directors to the board.

On 26th June 1894 H.Milkins was appointed as secretary of the NGSLR and his first duty was to report on the progress of obtaining the land for the track formation to Steephill from the Honourable E.C.A.Pelham and the trustees of the Right Honourable Viscount Oxenbridge. In accordance with the minute passed at the extraordinary general meeting, it was proposed the IWCR board members H.D.Martin and Captain Dunstan be elected directors. The appointments caused a split in the membership as the new entrants demanded the withdrawal of Westwood and Winley from the directorship.

On 29th June Westwood and Winley requested payment for further works completed, apportioned as £4,390 fully paid up £2 shares and £6,500 in debentures. As well as settling their account, the NGSLR board authorised the payment of £5,000 shares to the Isle of Wight Central Railway on terms of the agreed guarantee although no transfer was actually made.

During April and May the IWC approved plans for bridges on the new line at 3 miles 13 chains, 3 miles $43\frac{1}{2}$ chains and 5 miles 43 chains. Tenders were also received for the construction of Merstone station, J.Ball and Sons quoting £779, Barton Brothers £535 and T.Jenkins £913-17s-0d. On 27th June 1894 the board awarded the contract to Barton Brothers and duly requested the Godshill company to furnish £1,000 towards the impending alterations and improvements.

Beset by increasing monetary problems, Bohm wrote on 6th July 1894 asking the Central company to waive the right to £5,000 deferred shares of the Godshill Railway. The matter was raised at the board meeting on 11th July, and subsequently the IWC advised that, subject to the necessary powers, the directors were willing to concede any claim to the shares provided that the company deposited sufficient money to pay for all works on Merstone station and indemnified the Central from any claims for other works performed for the NGSLR. At the same meeting Barton Brothers advised of an error in their tender price for the Merstone contract. The firm were mistakenly under the impression that the IWCR authorities would deliver earth for infilling of embankments and formation of the yard free of charge. The secretary replied that the accepted price would be held but at the same time Simmons was to enquire of Barton the costs incurred in obtaining and transporting the earth. On learning the cost was a moderate £70, the IWC authorities reversed their decision and agreed to pay Barton for this additional cost.

On advice from Counsel, the surrender of the £5,000 was deferred but after further discussion on 25th July 1894 the IWC Board voiced their willingness to accept contract bonds on condition that the money was paid out of the first call on the Godshill Railway debentures.

Early in August the plans for Godshill station and a cattle creep at 4 miles 51 chains were approved, subject to a condition that the brick wall for the porters room and ladies waiting room would be substituted by matchboarding. The contract for the construction of both the station and the cattle creep was subsequently awarded to Barton Brothers and sent on 8th August.

The following month progress was hindered by the collapse of the retaining wall on the Ventnor side of St Lawrence tunnel. Simmons reported the matter to the IWCR board on 22nd September and two days later the item was mentioned at an IWCR board meeting. At the same meeting approval was given for the construction of a gatekeeper's cottage and footbridge at Dean Crossing (5 miles 26 chains), and for an occupation road bridge at 3 miles 61 chains. Approval of plans for another bridge at 4 miles 3 chains was given on 21st November 1894, and on the same day Barton Brothers requested £100 in respect of initial works completed at Merstone.

On 29th November 1894 the Secretary of the IWCR wrote to the Godshill company stating that it was his directors' opinion that because of the close bonds between the two companies, both financial and otherwise, a further two of their members should sit on the NGSLR board. To this end it was suggested that T.D.Bolton MP and Percy Mortimer be so elected. The matter was, however, deferred. Work on the railway continued despite the uncertainty in the boardroom and on 6th December Messrs Westwood and Winley were paid £28,800 for further completed works. At the same time the Honourable E.C.A.Pelham wrote claiming £16,000 compensation for land taken by the railway, whilst claims were also received for the repayment of money advanced to the Shanklin and Chale Railway to finance the Act of 1889.

Construction work continued steadily and on 21st January 1895 Cooper requested of the IWCR details of anticipated completion of works at Merstone. Later, during discussions on site, the question of replacing the level crossing at Dean with an overbridge was mooted. Martin subsequently enquired into costs of land purchase and construction of the bridge but on 15th March recommended against such action because of exorbitant costs. At the same time the IWCR proposed the provision of a subway for passengers to gain access to the south end of the station at Merstone to obviate the general public having to negotiate access either via a footbridge or from the level crossing. On 24th April 1895 the cost for the subway was estimated at £260 and Cooper was requested to prepare specifications.

On 25th January a letter had been received from the solicitors of the proposed Ashey and Horringford Junction Railway asking the NGSLR to call a special meeting to consider and approve the Bill then being presented to Parliament. With enough troubles of their own, the Godshill directors decided to defer any such decisions and notified the writers accordingly. A month later, however, a meeting was duly called but little enthusiasm was shown for the highly suspect proposals. It was rumoured that some of the Godshill directors had floated the nominally independent company to capture a share of the IWR Ventnor traffic by planning the line to Ryde. If authorised, the new line would have climbed southwestwards from a junction at Ashey on a 1 in 57 gradient piercing the gap between Ashey and Mersley Downs in a 220 yard long tunnel before falling at 1 in 55 to a junction at Horringford on the line from Sandown to Merstone. Direct access to the St Lawrence line would have been made possible only by a triangular junction at Merstone. No capital was ever raised and the scheme quickly fell into oblivion, being formally abandoned in 1898.

No untoward difficulties were experienced on the construction of St Lawrence Tunnel although the excavation took some eight months before the gangs from each end met at the initial break-through on 2nd February 1895. The semi-circular arch was of brick with Ventnor stone portals at each end. These contained a keystone bearing the date 1897, the ultimate completion date of this section of line.

The meeting of the Godshill company held on 4th March 1895 proved to be noisy and at times troublesome. A letter from Harry Magnus, addressed from his London home at Copthall House, EC, accused the board of the dangerous practice of agreeing to pay the contractors in future in partly paid up shares. He inferred there was now 'dissent and protest' within the ranks and advised that as a director of the company he was prepared to take legal action to prevent such action. The Chairman at the meeting, E.G. Johnson, supported the views expressed in the letter and openly stated that his fellow director Captain Dunstan should take no part in further discussions on the proposal, as he was in the employ of Westwood and Winley and was their representative on the board. Captain Dunstan vehemently denied the allegation and stated his only interest in the railway was as a director and not an employee of the contractors.

The proceedings ultimately quietened down to approve the agreement for the use of Merstone station. The secretary produced the agreement dated 13th May 1891 in which the IWCR gave up the right to 500 shares in the company on condition that the NGSLR paid £2,500 for the new station at Merstone. The chairman contested the agreement and objected to any alteration in the contract. Captain Dunstan argued that the contractors had paid considerable sums of money on the works and construction of the railway and he was of the opinion that they should have their debts settled before the promoters of the line.

After further arguments for and against the proposals for a change in the terms of the contract, the new agreement with Westwood and Winley was finally signed and a cheque was drawn for £2,500 to pay the IWCR a proportion of the costs for Merstone station.

Not all work on the construction of the railway met with everyone's approval for in March 1895 a Mr Gunner wrote on behalf of the High Commissioner complaining of the unsatisfactory state of the bridle road from Whitwell Church to Wroxall where the railway crossed the bridle track. The writer also pointed out that the course of the railway had for some distance deviated slightly from that authorised in Whitwell parish.

At the adjourned extraordinary general meeting held on 3rd March 1895 the Godshill directors announced they were creating £28,000 terminable debentures as authorised by the Shanklin and Chale Railway Acts of 1885 and 1887 and the Newport Godshill and St Lawrence Railway Act of 1889 with interest fixed at 4 per cent per annum. The debentures were to be issued when the railway opened to St Lawrence. Westwood and Winley would receive issues in accordance with the contract for construction of works in part payment on the engineer's certificates. As a result of the latter clause, debentures to the value of £15,600 were paid to the contractors on 4th April 1895.

On 22nd May 1895 a settlement of 4 guineas was paid to Winchester College for a small pocket of land at Merstone. At the same gathering the IWCR directors finally approved of the plans for the station at Whitwell subject to the construction of a subway in place of a footbridge to connect the up and down platforms, minor alterations to the parcels office and the provision of iron railings instead of wooden fencing along the back of the platforms. In the event neither the subway, footbridge nor iron railings were provided.

Progress continued at a steady rate until May 1895 when some of the contractor's labourers employed at Whitwell walked out on strike. Their grievance was that whereas labourers at all other sites received 5d per hour, the rate of pay at Whitwell was $4\frac{1}{2}$d per hour. The matter was never resolved, for in an area of relatively high unemployment new men were soon employed at the going rate and the offenders left to seek work elsewhere.

On 19th June Messrs J.Ball and Son tendered for the subway at Merstone at £389. Compared with the engineer's estimate the sum was considered exorbitant and advertisements were subsequently placed in three local newspapers during the second week of July. Evidently few replies were received and of these H.J.Street quoted the lowest price at £362-9s-6d. At a meeting on 7th August the IWC directors decided this charge was still too high and requested R. Elliot Cooper to execute the work.

On 5th July 1895 A.Harbottle Estcourt wrote to the Board of Trade, on behalf of the Isle of Wight Rural District Council complaining of the proposed footpath crossing bisecting the railway south of Whitwell. The footpath connected various farms and smallholdings with Whitwell village and school and was considered dangerous for children. The letter was passed to the Godshill company for comment and on 10th August Cooper replied that the crossing was not dangerous and on checking discovered only nine children used the path to and from the village school. An alternative access to the village was possible using Nettlecombe Lane which passed under the railway by Whitwell station.

Despite the many payments made (or perhaps because these 'payments' were mostly in paid up shares in the railway which bore no immediate benefit), Westwood and Winley were in dire financial straits and on 27th June 1895 the NGSLR directors were concerned to receive a letter from Messrs Woodham, Kirby and Mundy & Co advising that they had been appointed as receivers to the contractor. The letter requested a full statement of the present financial state between the two parties.

Within a week Mr Kirby as Receiver advised the railway company that all works performed by the contractor were to cease forthwith. This came just when advantage could be taken of the good weather and long daylight hours. The engineer was duly advised and asked for positive action to be taken to minimise the delay. Arrangements were made for an inspection of the railway and on 31st July 1895 Mr Liddell, representing the Receiver, visited the Isle of Wight to walk the course of the line with Mr Hall, the resident engineer. On 8th August the engineer reported from 8 The Sanctuary, Westminster, London SW1, the results of the walk which included a close inspection of all bridges.

The inspection committee found that the railway was completed except for station buildings and goods yards for a distance of 3 miles 3 chains from Merstone. On this section some remedial work was also required on three of the bridges. From the 2 miles 3 chains mark to Whitwell most of the embankments and cuttings were joined together with a deep cutting on the approach to the site of Whitwell station. Beyond Whitwell, bridges and culverts were unfinished but the formation was partially completed to the mouth of the tunnel under the Downs. The inspection revealed that most of the tunnel had been cut and at two points near each entrance the diameter of the full bore completed. Evidently the tunnel work had been carried out on a piecemeal basis for on investigation and questioning the contractor's men it was discovered that much work had been executed by hand using timber struts to hold up the roof. The foreman advised that 'this was a dangerous practice which might lead to an accident and duly trusted that when workings resumed they would be using the proper plant and equipment'. With correct equipment to hand and the absence of any problems with water seeping through the workings, it was hoped to complete the tunnel within six months. The investigating committee found little progress in construction of the railway beyond the tunnel. Work had ceased as land was required from the Trustees of Mr Pelham's estate at St Lawrence. The Committee was advised that if possession was not taken quickly it would be impossible to proceed. There was also no suitable site to dump material removed from the south end of the tunnel.

The inspection committee was advised that the railway was planned to a site nearer Steephill Castle as the station site at St Lawrence was completely unsuitable as a terminus for any length of time. It was thought while the railway stopped short of its ultimate goal at Ventnor, intending passengers would continue to use the Isle of Wight Railway route to the town.

Returning to the works already completed, it was considered the main problems were the drainage of the cutting between 2 miles 40 chains and 3 miles from Merstone and repairs to two bridges especially that spanning the bridleway to Bridgecourt. It was also pointed out that the IWCR required the NGSLR to purchase larger quantities of new permanent way materials than the Godshill company thought necessary. The IWCR considered the materials would be damaged by the contractor using them for preliminary works, after which they would be unfit for use. Hence it was established that permanent way material for use on the line had been unjustifiably used for other purposes. It was established that the IWCR had used new material supplied for the NGSLR in lieu of secondhand material to make repairs to their own line. The investigator summed up by advising that the contract for the construction of the railway was already a year behind schedule, much to the disappointment and indeed disapproval of the shareholders who expected better things.

When the matter was placed before the Godshill board, Captain Dunstan reported that Mr Myales had been appointed as agent to take charge of the remedial works and, having been supplied with the necessary funds, was carrying out the repairs to the first three miles of line from Merstone. He had also arranged the tenders for sub-contractors to build the station buildings and platforms and completion of the tunnel boring at St Lawrence. At the same meeting a letter dated 5th July 1895 from the Railway Department of the Board of Trade enclosed a petition from the Rural District Council of the Isle of Wight requesting the provision of a subway connecting the platforms at Whitwell in place of the foot crossing. The poor financial status of the company, however, precluded the provision of the subway. One of the last claims registered by the defunct contractor was a request for reduction of charges for conveyance of ash. It was alleged the IWC had failed to provide wagon loads and had consistently delayed material in transit. The IWC authorities, however, refused to entertain the claims for demurrage and further claims for a reduction in charges for turning the contractor's locomotive to prevent tyre and flange wear.

At the end of September 1895 C.J.Westwood dissolved his partnership with Winley and subsequently on 4th October the contract for the construction of the line was transferred entirely to Westwood after the shares and interest had been transferred between the former partners. In the same month both the Godshill company and Westwood were summoned by the Isle of Wight Rural District Council for obstruction of the public road at St Lawrence. The NGSLR Secretary duly requested their solicitor, Mr Pittis, to appear before the magistrates to explain the remedial steps being taken by both parties to remove and clear the debris.

By 4th November C.J.Westwood & Co. recommenced the task of building the line. Two days later Woodham Kirby and Mundy's report on the terms of receivership of the contractors was the subject of a paper to the directors of the IWCR.

Because of the difficulty in obtaining the land at Steephill, the NGSLR board resolved on 11th November 1895 to make application to Parliament for a bill to extend the railway through the grounds of the Steephill Castle Estate and to this end the engineer and solicitor were requested to liaise and arrange for the parliamentary agents to deposit the necessary notice in time for the next parliamentary session. So confident were the directors that four days later they agreed the draft contract for the construction with C.J. Westwood, the approval being subject to the contract being valued at £22,000 so as to provide the company with reserve cash of £2,000.

The secretary later reported that the plans and reference books had been deposited in the Parliamentary Private Bill Office and with the Clerk of the Peace for the Isle of Wight at Newport and Parish Councils by 9th December 1895.

The Isle of Wight Rural District Council again complained to the Board of Trade on 4th January 1896 of the unsatisfactory road near the proposed St Lawrence station. The road known as St Lawrence Shute had been diverted to cross the railway on a 1 in 8 gradient at right-angles followed by two sharp turns on and off the bridge. It was considered the curves were so sharp 'that a heavy dray waggon drawn by horses could not negotiate the turn'.

On 29th January 1896 a letter was received from the Clerk to the Isle of Wight County Council requesting the provision of workmen's trains (with resultant cheaper fares) on the new railway when opened, but despite return correspondence from the Godshill Railway Company no further communication was received from the IWCC on the subject. The following month correspondence was entered into with the IWCR after the engineer and contractor had found a quantity of defective bricks in a consignment obtained from the larger railway. As a result of the complaint a sample of bricks was to be made available to the engineer for inspection from every new consignment received.

On 11th February 1896 Mr Blake of Merstone wrote claiming compensation of £60 in respect of the loss of one of his colts which had died after getting entangled in the lineside fencing.

The Godshill company replied disclaiming responsibility stating that the fencing was not new and had been erected for over two years.

After two months of negotiations with the Isle of Wight County Council, the NGSLR finally obtained permission to divert the public road which crossed the proposed railway at St Lawrence.

At the board meeting on 23rd April 1896 the Godshill directors received the welcome news from the contractor that the line was expected to be available for opening within a short time. A month later C.J.Westwood and his former partner, F.C.Winley, again requested the company to accept £15,600 of debentures for cancellation, reissuing in return like debentures to C.J.Westwood only.

Early in the new year Cooper had approached Simmons to arrange a site meeting at the St Lawrence terminus to survey the area where the Godshill company proposed to raise the formation of the line 5 feet for a distance of 220 yards. The meeting was subsequently held during the first week of February, and on 26th of the month the IWCR board approved of the alterations in gradient. At the same gathering the question of drainage of Merstone subway was reviewed. Simmons later suggested the purchase of a 2 hp oil engine to pump excess water from the subway to a tank where the supply could be used for replenishing the locomotives working the Sandown–Newport or Ventnor line services. By May 1896 eight quotations for the oil pumping engine were received ranging in price from £155 to £240. At the IWCR board meeting on 20th May the decision to purchase was deferred when Cooper advised that an oil pumping engine had been offered for sale by the Lancashire Derbyshire and East Coast Railway at a cost of £94.

In May 1896 the IWCR agreed to the National Telephone Co erecting telegraph poles along the route of the railway from Merstone to Ventnor at a wayleave charge of 1/- per mile per annum providing the railway telegraph was permitted to use the same pole route. On 28th May Cooper approached the IWC proposing the installation of a siding adjacent to the public road leading from Whitwell to Ventnor adjacent to Dean level crossing. Simmons, after discussions with his colleagues, was unhappy with the idea and proposed an additional siding connecting off the proposed siding at St Lawrence station so as not to provide an additional connection from the main single line. Neither was in fact built.

At the IWC board meeting on 17th June 1896 the directors minuted the company was willing to increase their guarantee by £200 per annum once the NGSL line was opened for traffic to Ventnor. At the same meeting Simmons voiced dissent to the agreement arranged with the National Telephone Company and thought 1/9d per pole might produce better returns.

Dissatisfied with their previous negotiations, the National Telephone Company sought further meetings with both railway companies and on 29th June 1896 the Godshill Board considered a joint letter from the Telephone Company and IWCR requesting permission for a telephone pole route alongside the railway from Merstone to Ventnor. The new approach brought results for on 1st September it was resolved to allow a single wire to be erected between the two points. The Godshill secretary subsequently wrote to the Telephone Company granting permission to erect the line with the proviso that the NGSLR have free use of all telephone and telegraph services.

In June 1896, on advice from counsel, the terms agreed with the IWC for working the Godshill Railway were extended from 7 to 21 years, the other terms remaining unchanged.

Because of the continued delay in agreeing to the issue of new debentures, the Godshill company requested the contractor to pay over £650 on 10th July to enable the engineer's and solicitor's fees to be settled for the year ending December 1895.

The Bill for the extension of the railway at Steephill received the Royal Assent on 2nd July 1896 as the Newport Godshill and St Lawrence Railway Act 1896 (59 and 60 Vic Cap x lvii) and empowered the company to build a line 2 furlongs 8.60 chains in length commencing in the parish of Godshill at the termination of the authorised line of the 1892 Act and terminating in the grounds of Steephill Castle at a point 75 yards east of the north-east corner of the Steephill Estate stable building and on the west side of the road leading to the Ventnor station of the Isle of Wight Railway, from the public road between St Lawrence and Ventnor. The Act also permitted alterations in the St Lawrence parish and a 150 yard deviation of the public road leading to St Lawrence Shute. Clause 5 repealed the restriction on the building of a goods shed and working of goods traffic to Ventnor mentioned in the Act of 1892.

Three years were allowed for the purchase of the additional two acres of land required for the extension, and five years for the completion of works. Previous periods for purchasing land were again extended, to two years from 28th June 1896. The company was allowed to raise an additional £18,000 capital in £10 ordinary or preference shares and to borrow up to a further £6,000 after £9,000 shares had been issued.

The illicit practices of some of the contractor's men finally came to light in August 1896 when the agent was fined £35 by the local magistrate for depositing 500 lbs of gelignite in an outside lavatory at Godshill which was being used in lieu of a proper licensed explosives store.

At the general shareholders meeting held on 31st August 1896 the gathering agreed to each share being divided to preferential half shares and deferred half shares to the following values:

11,605 deferred half shares	£58,025
11,605 preferred half shares	£58,025
395 undivided shares at £10	£3,950
	£120,000

The Contractor advised the NGSL board by letter dated 22nd September 1896 that unless otherwise instructed it was his intention to proceed with the construction of the railway through the grounds of Steephill Castle as authorised under the Act of Parliament. Despite the lack of new debentures and shortage of finance, the board readily agreed to the proposal and the contractor's men began the new works in mid-October.

Plans for the new station at Ventnor had been forwarded to Newport on 8th September 1896 but Charles Leonard Conacher, the new general manager of the IWC, was unhappy with some of the proposals and requested a meeting. The IWC chairman also complained to Cooper about the water at Merstone subway and wished these improvements to take priority. A site meeting was subsequently arranged and at the IWCR board meeting on 18th November Cooper reported by letter that the provision of inclined platforms instead of steps on the approach to the Ventnor station was unworkable. He agreed, however, to the platforms being 12 feet wide and for a canopy fronting on to the station building affording protection to the platform. The NGSL engineer also suggested the installation of iron sheeting over the subway at Merstone, but again his suggestion was frowned upon as it was considered the iron sheeting would fail to keep out the rain. The subway was never used by passengers and ultimately became a reservoir for the ready supply of water for locomotives.

During a subsequent inspection of the new line Conacher requested accommodation for the St Lawrence station master and his family and instructed that a bedroom and kitchen be added to the plans for the new station.

As the railway approached completion between Merstone and St Lawrence, various outside bodies took an increasing interest in the new line. The contractor reported on 2nd October 1896 that he had been approached regarding the carriage of coal and the letting of land adjacent to Whitwell station as a coal ground and distribution point for the village and surrounding area. The NGSLR board were obviously at a loss for an answer and sought the guidance of the IWCR, not only for the conveyance charges per ton per mile but also on guidance as to what rent to charge for coal grounds at their stations.

Because of the proposed extension of the railway from St Lawrence to Steephill it was necessary to amend the working agreement with the IWCR. Unable to come to amicable agreement, the proposal was sent for arbitration to the Railway Commissioners.

Construction work progressed satisfactorily but by 21st October 1896 Westwood was delayed from commencing work on the bridge at 5 miles 17 chains near St Lawrence as the engineer had not finished the necessary drawings of the structure. As well as requesting the bridge drawings, Westwood requested a copy of No. 3 contract for the extension of the railway to Ventnor with the relevant drawings and cross-sections.

In the same month the IWCR replied regarding the cost of conveyance of coal, suggesting a rate of 3d per ton per mile. No details were offered regarding the size and rentage of coal ground at the NGSLR stations and this was left to local agreement.

Complaints were received regarding the contractor's performance at Dean Crossing, where the public highway was again obstructed at regular intervals for some weeks in the autumn of 1896. The board immediately requested Westwood to complete all the necessary works as a matter of urgency to obviate further problems. The complaints continued to be made into November when A.Harbottle Estcourt wrote strongly on behalf of the IW Rural District Council.

Contract No. 3, authorised by the Act of 1896, was put to the Godshill board of directors for their approval on 21st October 1896 but, because of certain incompleteness, a committee formed of E.G.Johnson and Captain Dunstan was appointed to settle the outstanding terms.

On 12th November 1896, with permanent way works almost completed, the Godshill board awarded the contract for the installation of Block Telegraph and Signalling to Messrs Saxby and Farmer. At the same juncture the IW Rural District Council requested the railway company to resurface the public road at Noddy Hill.

The differences between the IWCR and Godshill company were highlighted when Cooper wrote on 14th November 1896 that Westwood & Co. proposed to erect a corrugated iron cottage for the crossing keeper's accommodation at Dean Crossing. Alarmed at such a cheap and shoddy proposal, the IWC replied that the contractor was to build a brick cottage similar to those on the Lancashire, Derbyshire and East Coast Railway.

The full cost of Merstone station totalled £1,523 but the question of the subway was as yet unresolved. Dissatisfied with previous proposals, Cooper was advised by the IWC board on 16th December to prepare plans for an iron footbridge to connect the platforms to the roadway. At the same time agreement was reached over the subject of the steps to the approach to Ventnor station which were to be 'as wide as possible'. Having expended a considerable amount of time and money on the Godshill line, the IWC directors also finally proposed to extend the agreement between the two companies from 7 to 21 years.

At the Godshill directors meeting held on 25th January 1897 the secretary read a letter sent to the Board of Trade by Mr A.Harbottle Estcourt, acting in his official capacity as clerk to the IWRDC, regarding the bridge over the railway adjacent to the site of St Lawrence station. The highway at this point had run diagonally over the route of the railway on a steep grade of 1 in 8. During the construction of the bridge the highway had been diverted to cross the railway at right-angles, with two steep turns both on and off the bridge with another turn immediately below the bridge. Mr Estcourt's objections were that the bends created in the siting of the new road were too severe for horse-drawn waggons to negotiate. The directors were informed that the deposited plans of 1892 showed the middle of the bridge as 20 feet wide but the 10th section of the NGSLR Act (52 and 53 Chapter CC1) showed a sharp corner on a steep gradient which was dangerous for heavy traffic and would cause accidents. Because of the anomaly the secretary was instructed to write to R.Elliot Cooper inviting him to the next board meeting.

Cooper replied on 12th January 1897 advising that what Estcourt had stated was perfectly correct. The road known as St Lawrence Shute, nominally a public road, was really an old pack road and bridle path leading from Whitwell to St Lawrence. Although it was possible to take vehicles up and down the track, it was a matter of great difficulty to negotiate the steep gradient and acute curves, especially in wet weather. The existing road or track was $10\frac{1}{2}$ feet wide, and at the point where the diversion was to be made the gradient was 1 in 8. With the approach over the bridge the gradient was eased to 1 in 10 although the remainder of the road descending from the summit of the Down varied from 1 in 8 to 1 in 4, the greater length being at the latter. Cooper therefore thought Estcourt's suggestion that the alterations in the road were highly dangerous was absurd, as the gradient had been eased. The road had never been built for heavy traffic but it was not impossible for light traffic to use it. The engineer concluded that the bridge and approaches were constructed strictly in accordance with the Act of Parliament.

Whilst advising on the problems of the bridge at St Lawrence, Cooper also reminded the directors he had received no intimation of the change in debentures, neither had he received 'a single sixpence'. He thus advised that if there were any default in construction and the company declined to meet its obligations he wished to be absolved from all liabilities. The directors advised the engineer that the additional debentures were issued without permission at the company's discretion but matters including the out-of-pocket expenses would be settled amicably.

The contractor advised during late January the purchase of the Steephill Castle Estate was progressing and it was subsequently agreed by the board that the first 800 four per cent debentures would be issued to Mr Percy Mortimer who was negotiating purchase of the estate with his brother Charles.

Early in February 1897 the IWCR advised that they agreed to the reduction in working charges on the understanding that a subsidiary agreement be entered into whereby the bonds held by the company would be extended to two years.

As the railway neared completion, Cooper requested from the IWCR details of additional requirements, if any, for signalling and telecommunications. On 20th January 1897 he was advised to provide block signalling telegraph throughout the line. The block sections were to be from Merstone to Whitwell and Whitwell to St Lawrence. The telephone was to be provided at all four stations. The final specifications for St Lawrence station were also agreed. These included a platform of sufficient length to accommodate trains of 8 to 10 coaches, lavatories for both sexes, and two living rooms for the station master and his family. The track layout was to include a spur road at the Ventnor end of the station (in addition to a run-round loop) to enable coaching stock to be stabled and as much siding accommodation for goods and coal traffic as the restricted siding layout would permit.

The final months of construction work were not devoid of accidents for on Thursday, 14th January 1897, an incident occurred on Whitwell New Road to a young man named Lewis of Whitwell employed as a carter by the railway contractor. Lewis was driving a cart loaded with drain pipes from Ventnor IWR station to the works site when, on passing the Ventnor steam roller, the horse was frightened, shied and bolted. Lewis was thrown from the driving seat under the wheels of the cart which passed over his leg. He was subsequently detained in the Royal Isle of Wight Infirmary with fractures. Another incident on Tuesday, 23rd February, involved William Harley, a labourer living at Whitwell. Working near the cliff face, he fell 60 feet over the edge, but fortunately received only a severe shaking.

On 24th February the plans for the signalling arrangements at St Lawrence were approved whilst the IWC supplied a list of furnishings required for stations and signal boxes. The Godshill board originally thought the IWC should provide the equipment but later agreed to finance the furnishings and the provision of clocks out of their meagre funds. Further estimates for drainage work at Merstone reduced to £100 the cost of clearance of water from the subway, but before letting the contract the IWC requested the estimates for cost of a new water tank.

In January 1897 H.D.Martin resigned his post as director of the NGSLR because of ill health and differences within the board. He immediately claimed the repayment of £4,400 debentures, a claim which the company could ill afford.

Further complaint was made regarding St Lawrence Shute when A.J.Morton Bell, Her Majesty's Coroner for Gloucestershire, wrote to the Board of Trade from Stroud on 12th March 1897 on behalf of residents and owners of property in the vicinity of the station. His argument favoured the resiting of the station as the narrow strip of land reserved for the structure should be part of the public road with a high fence and wall protecting the road from the railway. Cooper in response replied the gradient was improved to 1 in 10 from 1 in 8 but that the station could not be resited.

On 10th April 1897 Percy M.Dunstan, secretary of the NGSL Railway, wrote from 8 The Sanctuary, Westminster, to the Board of Trade advising that the first section of railway would be ready for inspection in six weeks. At a meeting on 26th April Cooper advised that he had received correspondence regarding the opening of the line. At this same meeting a letter from the directors of the Ebbw Vale Steel Company was read requesting that deferred shares be deposited with them in lieu of cash as payment for steel used on bridges.

A letter dated 13th May 1897 from the Rural District Council to the Board of Trade, signed by Estcourt complained of the dangerous diversion of the Whitwell to Ventnor road at Dean Level Crossing where the highway was laid to incorporate a dangerous corner and that St Rhadegund's footpath near the southern entrance of the tunnel was considered to be in need of protection because of the close proximity of the railway. On receipt, the Board of Trade forwarded a copy to the Godshill company for comments. Cooper duly replied on 26th May stating the road approach could be improved by the purchase of a strip of land. The crossing was laid out in accordance with plans agreed by Act of Parliament and an additional clause added by the Board of Trade, to which the local authority had not objected. The engineer advised that since the letter was received, St Rhadegund's footpath had been fenced alongside the railway.

A further accident occurred on Monday, 14th June 1897, when an unnamed navvy fell 40 feet down the cutting face at the north end of St Lawrence tunnel. The man was knocked unconscious by the fall but had recovered sufficiently to resume work the next day.

Early in May 1897 the question of rolling stock and working of the new line was considered. With the opening proposed for 1st July, Conacher was rather belatedly preparing the timetable for trains and on 16th June reported to the IWC directors on the train service from Merstone to St Lawrence and the connecting horse omnibus service thence to Ventnor. Conacher and Cooper were also investigating the water supply for locomotives at Merstone but the suggested schemes proved excessively costly so a decision was deferred. Water was to be taken from a temporary supply at Dean Crossing.

In late June 1897 a further enquiry was made by an island coal merchant requesting the provision of sidings and coal grounds at the various stations on the line but, because of local agreements, the NGSLR sought the IWC views before granting permission. The outcome of this and the earlier enquiry was the establishment of a standard rent for coal grounds in the goods yards at £3 per annum and the letting of the sites was subsequently advertised in the *Isle of Wight County Press* and other newspapers.

At the beginning of June Cooper sent the necessary plans and civil engineering details to the Board of Trade, and by 7th July Percy M.Dunstan had made second application for official inspection of the line. The impending inspection brought forth a succession of complaints against the new railway. On 3rd July the Ventnor town clerk reiterated the dangers of St Lawrence Shute whilst on the 7th John Petchley, clerk to Whitwell Parish Council, asked the Board of Trade not to sanction the opening of the line until the problems associated with Dean Level Crossing and St Lawrence Shute were resolved. The following day the Rural District Council raised the question of level crossings in the Whitwell parish. This was followed a week later by another broad epistle from the Isle of Wight County Council.

Another letter from the IWCC complained that no remedial work had been carried out to the road at Noddy Hill. When asked for an explanation for the delay, Westwood advised that his men had commenced work the same week as the IWCC complained.

In July, T.D. Bolton, H.D. Martin and Percy Mortimer were re-appointed to represent the IWC on the Godshill railway board. The draft of the working arrangement for the St Lawrence–Ventnor omnibus service was signed with F. Baker of 22 Pier Street, Ventnor. At the IWC board meeting on the 14th the company solicitor was advised to take proceedings against Westwood and Company if outstanding accounts remained unpaid on 21st July. It was also agreed to appoint an independent engineer to inspect the NGSL Railway, and Conacher subsequently approached the engineer of the North British Railway to do this. The directors also asked for work on the sinking of a well to supply water for locomotive purposes to be given immediate urgent priority.

The Board of Trade inspection of the line was made by Lieutenant Colonel G.W. Addison on 17th July 1897. The inspector noted that the section of line being offered for examination between Merstone and St Lawrence was 5 miles 55 chains in length with the width of formation varying between 16 and 18 feet. Fencing was of iron wire with the top strand of barbed wire. The steepest gradient on the new line was 1 in 55 for over half a mile while the sharpest curve was of 12 chains radius, although Addison remarked that the curves on the line were easy. He noted the railway was generally either in cutting or on embankment, the former having depths of up to 25, 29 and 39 feet whilst the largest embankments were up to 22 feet, 23 feet and 25 feet high. On the St Lawrence side of the tunnel the inspector remarked 'a very extensive slip occurred recently of the cliff which almost overhangs the railway and this part needs a very careful watch especially after rain or frost'. The cutting between 2 miles 45 chains and 3 miles was also to be continually examined for slippage although it was noted the 'banks at the Merstone end made some years ago appear to be standing well'.

In his report the inspector then turned his attention to bridges and culverts. Of the four overbridges on the line, two were of steel lattice girder and were used as footpath rights of way, whilst the remaining two carried roads over the railway. These were of 15 feet span with brick arches and concrete masonry abutments. At the time of inspection the girders of the footbridge at 4 miles 59 chains were not in position. The twelve underbridges also received attention and Addison found two had brick arch tops on concrete abutments, the span in each case being 12 feet, whilst the remainder had steel superstructure on concrete abutments (except one constructed of masonry) with spans varying from 8 feet to 25 feet. The longer spans were found to have plate main girders and trough floors whilst the shorter spans had trough floors only. All structures gave moderate deflection under test with the exception of the trough floor bridge at 2 miles 37 chains and the inspector remarked 'this bridge should be examined in order to ascertain the measurements of deflection and it will be necessary to test again later on'. There were also cracks in the abutments of the bridge at 1 mile 72 chains which were apparently reported as 'old' and needing attention. The one culvert, constructed of brick, was 6 feet in diameter.

Addison spent some time on the inspection of the tunnel which was reported as 620 yards in length with refuges for platelayers at one chain intervals. The inspector noted that only 90 yards of the tunnel was provided with 18 inch lining and considerably more than half only 9 inch thick lining, the latter being considered only a skin to prevent falls of loose earth. Addison concluded 'the responsibility for dispensing with the lining of full thickness cannot rest with the engineer – it is impossible to say whether the 9 inch lining will be sufficient – not having seen the construction work in progress'.

Addison had inspected the new Merstone Junction station in 1895 but he remarked on the subway leading to the island platform still being a source of trouble through flooding in wet weather. If further remedial measures were unsuccessful, a footbridge was to be constructed. At Godshill the inspector noted that a single platform had been built with associated buildings providing accommodation for both sexes. There was a siding with points facing trains proceeding to Merstone. The points were worked from a lever locked and unlocked by a key attached to the train staff. Godshill was not a block station but protection was provided by home and distant signals for each direction worked from a four-lever frame on the platform. Addison noted the station was not a staff station. Whitwell was reported as being a staff station with a passing loop and station buildings with 'sufficient accommodation' for both sexes on the down platform and a small waiting shelter on the up side. The sidings were entered by facing points in the down loop line and all points and signals were worked from the 10-lever frame in the signal box 'all in use and correctly interlocked'.

St Lawrence was reported as the present terminus of the line with the single platform provided with station buildings 'incomplete at the time of inspection but which should afford sufficient accommodation'. A 5-lever ground frame worked signals and points to enable engines to run round their trains for the return journey, 'arrangements which are temporary pending completion of the line'. The inspector detailed 15 level crossings on the railway, one being across a public road where gates and a lodge were provided at 4 miles 58 chains. Dean Crossing had been the subject of correspondence between the local authority and Board of Trade. Addison noted the crossing was made in accordance with the conditions laid down by the Act of 1889 and 'sided with the railway company', reporting that it 'therefore rests with the road authorities to prove contradiction if they require the company to alleviate. The crossing is certainly far from satisfactory as a coach road for which I understand it has been lately improved elsewhere.' He concluded 'the contractor is willing to cut off one bad corner if the necessary land is placed at his disposal and it is hoped the local authority will arrange accommodation'. Of the two footpath level crossings objected to by the local authority, that at 4 miles 20 chains was shown as a bridle road on plans but was in fact only a footpath. The objectors required a footbridge on the basis of its status on the plans, but Addison refused to endorse the request, finding the crossing no more dangerous than any other crossing on the railway. The second footpath known as St Rhadegund's path at 5 miles 26 chains was considered rather close to the exit of the tunnel, and protective fencing and a bell to give warning of the approach of trains was required.

Lieutenant Colonel Addison required the following remedial work to be executed.

1. Occupational crossing gates to be hung to only open outwards from the line.
2. Additional fencing between $\frac{3}{4}$ and 1 mile posts.
3. At Godshill move the safety points of the siding nearer to the main line. Gauge tie also to be provided.
4. Provide handrails at the St Lawerence end of the bridge at 2 miles 7 chains and on the bridge at 3 miles 43 chains.
5. At Whitwell improve the sighting of No 10 distant signal or provide a repeater. Rearrange the siding and cover the signal wire.
6. At Dean Crossing place a bell in the block circuit to ring in the caretaker's lodge so as to give warning of the departure of trains on either side. 'It will be necessary for me to reinspect the arrangements when the footbridge is erected as the view of the crossing may then be interfered with'.
7. More ballast at several places especially in the tunnel.
8. At St Rhadegund's footpath provide an electric bell to be set in motion by the engine passing over a treadle in the tunnel at least 300 yards from the crossing, the bell to continue to ring until the engine passes over a second treadle just past the crossing.

Because of the steep gradients on the line, especially between Whitwell and St Lawrence, the speed of trains was to be restricted to moderate limits and the 'Isle of Wight Central Railway should be asked to state what they propose to do in the matter. It will also be necessary to state the mode of working.' The inspector also stipulated that no shunting was to be allowed on the main line at Whitwell without the locomotive being at the lower end of the train. Concluding his report, Lieutenant Colonel Addison recommended the line be opened for passenger traffic subject to the completion of remedial work with the least possible delay.

On the same day as the inspection Conacher also invited the press to sample the delights of the new line. Evidently the special train conveyed both the inspecting party and reporters, for after departing from Newport a halt was made at Merstone where Charles Westwood, the contractor, Mr Wynter, the contractor's engineer, and Mr Knights, assistant engineer, joined the train. After inspecting the junction, the party were conveyed by the special, stopping at all stations, bridges, Dean Crossing and the tunnel to enable Colonel Addison to make his inspection. After arrival at St Lawrence guests attended a party at Elm Dene as guests of Mr and Mrs C.Westwood before returning to Newport by the special train which completed the journey from St Lawrence in under 14 minutes for the 9 miles 35 chains journey. Most of those who travelled were impressed by the scenery, but the reporter from the *Daily Telegraph*, who had earlier visited the line, was less than enthusiastic for he tersely commented in the issue dated 2nd June 1900 'for the traveller to the English Madeira, this could be taken at best as a pious fraud and less charitably as a joke in poor taste'. On the factual side, reporters were advised that all the latest improvements were incorporated on the new railway, including electric block telegraph and telephonic communications between stations.

In statements to the press the total population served by the railway was rather optimistically quoted as 40,000, and it was the opinion of the directors that the opening of the line would encourage the building in the Undercliff and certainly half a mile of the extension to Ventnor was said to be already completed. It was not expected that the new line would attract London traffic to Ventnor as that was adequately covered by the IWR route – the chief aim was to attract passengers from the Midland and South Western Counties via Southampton and Cowes. Finally, the gathering was informed that nine trains would run each way with through coaches to Cowes and Newport by the 12 noon and 5.17 pm from Newport. When the line reached completion, St Lawrence was to become the Ventnor goods station with only passenger trains travelling beyond to the new Ventnor passenger station. The promoters (and to a lesser extent opponents of the line) presented heavily biased versions of the 'facts' and in some cases downright and blatant fabrications aimed at furthering their own objectives.

The formal opening of the new railway took place on Monday, 19th July 1897 when guests travelled down from London in a special carriage attached to the 9.15 am ex-Waterloo. After crossing Spithead, the party arrived at Ryde Pier Head station shortly before 1.00 pm where they joined a special train for the run to St Lawrence. The train was hauled by IWCR 4–4–0T No. 6, gaily decorated overall and carrying a headboard bidding 'Success to the Newport, Godshill and St Lawrence Railway' and crewed by Driver J.Pierce and Fireman F.Young. On arrival at Newport local dignitaries joined the mainland contingent in the decorated saloon carriages for the run to St Lawrence. Approaching the temporary terminus, the engine exploded detonators and entered the station, decorated overall with flags and bunting, to the cheers of those on the platform, punctually to time at 1.40 pm. After the guests alighted, the train shunted back up the line towards the tunnel as the crowd congregated at the west end of the platform for the official opening ceremony. Escorted by Messrs Westwood, Wynter and Knights, Mrs P.Mortimer, wife of the NGSL director, was handed a brand new specially made spanner decorated with red, white and blue ribbons which she inserted over the head of the last bolt and proceeded to tighten this in the fishplate. Mrs. Mortimer gracefully performed the deed to the cheers of the onlookers and announced she had 'great pleasure in declaring the Newport Godshill and St Lawrence Railway open'. The ceremony of the proving of the joint was then enacted as No. 6 and her train slowly ran into the station, again to the cheers of the guests, after which the whole company retired to Elm Dene for lunch in a spacious marquee erected in the grounds for the event. After the usual junketings, the gathering returned to the station for the return journey to Newport and Ryde.

The public opening of the line was on Tuesday, 20th July when 'many residents and others made journeys'. To ease the problems of connecting Ventnor with St Lawrence station, the IWCR had made arrangements with F.Baker junior of 22 Pier Street, Ventnor, to run a conveyance to and from St Lawrence station in connection with each train and, according to reports, 24 passengers were conveyed on the first day of operation at a fare of 6d in each direction.

IWCR Black Hawthorn 4–4–0T No. 6 with the special opening train at Newport on 19th July 1897. The personnel standing by the train are J. Seymour (Locomotive Superintendent), C. L. Conacher (Manager IWCR), J. Pierce (driver), S. Lovett (clerk), W. Matthews (guard), W. Bell (carriage examiner) and, in the cab of the locomotive, F. Young (fireman).

CHAPTER THREE
EXTENSION TO VENTNOR

ON 26th July 1897 the report of Lieutenant Colonel Addison, the BOT inspector, was discussed by the Godshill board and the relevant section relating to the working of the line passed to the IWCR authorities. The contractor was also given details of the remedial works on the formation requested by the Colonel. The IWCR, in response to the items raised by the inspector, advised three days later that nothing would be discussed until their board meeting scheduled for 4th August.

It was also suggested a permanent way inspector be appointed to take over routine maintenance of the track from the contractor. To this end Cooper, the engineer, was requested to recommend a suitable man and also advise on salary. After due consultation Mr Williams was offered the post but unfortunately declined, and Messrs Conacher and Cooper were requested to reconsider the matter.

The new railway was soon to host a visit by royalty for on 31st July 1897 Princess Henry of Battenberg (Beatrice, youngest daughter of Queen Victoria and Governor of the Isle of Wight 1896–1944) travelled over the line from Merstone to St Lawrence. The contractor had received notification five days previously and Mr Bohm, the chairman, travelled in the train with the Princess, who later opened a new wing at Ventnor Hospital.

In response to Addison's report and subsequent letter of 24th July from the BOT, the IWC secretary was requested at the board meeting on 4th August to reply on the various points raised during the inspection. Speeds on the falling gradients between Whitwell and St Lawrence were to be restricted, with drivers and guards instructed that trains were to enter St Lawrence station capable of being stopped by using the hand brake only. In addition drivers were instructed to shut off steam 1,000 yards on the approach to the station. The BOT was advised that the line was to be worked by the Train Staff and Ticket in conjunction with Absolute Block. The company also gave the undertaking that no shunting would be permitted on the main line at Whitwell unless the engine was at the lower (Merstone) end of the train.

Also on 4th August the Godshill company consulted the IWCR regarding the advertising of coal yards at stations, and after agreement over the wording, advertisements were place in local newspapers. Within two weeks two replies were received from Messrs Frazer & White, and Mr Odell.

As no monies had been received from Westwood by the beginning of August, the Godshill company advised the contractor that if £50 was paid within the week, the balance of the debt could be paid over an extended period to ease his position.

At the Godshill board meeting held on 19th August 1897 a letter was received from the secretary of the IWCR regarding the working of the line and the items raised by the BOT inspector. It was pointed out to the NGSLR that no mention was made in the original correspondence as to the method of shunting freight trains on falling gradients at Whitwell but the IWCR had taken steps to prevent runaway movements. Whitwell again came in for criticism in September when the IW County Council requested the widening of Nettlecombe Lane which passed beneath the railway south of the station.

The NGSLR were forced to decline any assistance for such a scheme as there were no funds at their disposal.

By the end of August, Westwood had failed to pay his debts or indeed any money over to the IWCR. Subsequently a writ was served on the contractor, but the directors agreed no further action until Conacher had personally negotiated with Westwood as to his future actions.

With the opening of the railway the directors expected a steady upsurge of traffic but, despite the publicity surrounding the journey by HRH Princess Beatrice and the initial interest by local people, traffic receipts were poor. Ever optimistic, the Godshill board and IWC railway officers thought business would pick up once the Ventnor extension was opened. Arrangements were made for road conveyances to meet all trains at Whitwell for Niton and Blackgang in addition to the St Lawrence to Ventnor omnibus, but potential users of the line were discouraged by the fare structure, for charges to St Lawrence were similar to those charged by the Isle of Wight Railway to Ventnor. The added burden for passengers on the new route of the 6d fare for conveyance by road between St Lawrence and Ventnor town centre nullified the attractions of the line.

At the August meeting of shareholders the IWR chairman, Horace Tahourdin, poured scorn on the new venture, 'the Isle of Wight is already well endowed with enough railways. It is true the new line passes through some very pretty scenery but it serves few people and I think the shareholders will have to wait a very long time before they receive any return on their investment'. How right he was!

When footplate staff working the line complained of rough riding, the IWCR authorities questioned the quality of ballasting and formation of track. Remedial work was quickly put into effect and by 22nd September 1897 the contractor reported that all the outstanding requirements of the BOT had been completed except the 'top up' ballasting and the footbridge at Dean Crossing. Percy Dunstan duly advised the BOT of the position.

By now the Godshill company was in serious financial difficulties and on 22nd September it was resolved that no permanent way inspector would be appointed until the company could afford to pay his wages. To ease the monetary problems the IWCR paid over £100 as the NGSLR proportion of initial receipts. This enabled the directors to pay off some of the outstanding expenses but even then there was still insufficient available to pay the fees of the solicitor.

The need to economise in every way resulted in the NGSL directors taking a much more belligerent attitude against complainants. On 29th September 1897 when their old opponent Mr Estcourt wrote asking for the company to make alterations to the road at Dean Crossing he received the short terse answer that 'as the public would benefit most from such alterations the public should bear the cost'.

As some newspaper traffic for the villages and Ventnor had been routed over their system, the NGSLR directors issued free passes for the use of W.H.Smith and Sons employees when travelling with newspapers on the line.

At the end of September Lieutenant Colonel Addison intimated that he wished to inspect the railway for the second time. The Godshill board on receipt of the letter notified the contractor that they expected all deficiencies to be made good in readiness for the visit.

On 20th October 1897 Cooper and Knight advised their choice for the post of permanent way inspector. The names mentioned and considered suitable were those of T.Connell and J.Osborne although the appointments were to be held in abeyance until the necessary finances were available to pay the wages.

Tenders invited by the IWCR for the provision of water supply at Merstone resulted in the following offers:

Ransome and Rapier	£155
Alagran & Sons	£120
Muntz & Co	£147 10s
J Meader	£111 11s

Meader was duly awarded the contract on 21st October 1897.

Early in October 1897 a Mr Beckers applied to the Godshill company for a coal storage site at each station yard and the application was subsequently passed to the IWCR for attention.

The opening of the railway to traffic attracted considerable interest from commercial companies wishing to provide a service at the stations, each hoping to reap somewhat meagre financial rewards. One such company, the London and Provincial Automatic Machine Company wrote requesting permission to locate sweet and other vending machines on the platforms at Merstone and Ventnor. In replying to the company the NGSLR secretary, granting permission for the installations at the junction station, pointed out the firm was a little premature in requesting a site at Ventnor but until the line was opened machines could be sited at St Lawrence. The site rental was fixed at £2 per machine per annum.

It was resolved at the NGSLR meeting held on 20th October 1897 to award the secretary an annual salary of £100. Four days later it was learned that Westwood, the contractor, had dismissed all his men from the line and ceased to maintain the railway, an action completely in breach of his contract, under which he was obliged to maintain the works for 12 months from the date of opening to traffic.

On 30th October P.M.Dunstan advised the IWC board the contractor had ceased work on the railway and argued that to save precious time the IWC company should complete the construction, charging the Godshill company for work performed. The IWC authorities were, however, not keen to enter into the dispute of the ailing company and its defunct contractor.

Following this action the Godshill company sought legal redress and on 13th November the board served 21 days notice of termination of contract on Westwood. As the Board of Trade inspector was to reinspect the formation of the permanent way on 18th November, the contractor was firmly requested to re-engage men and complete the ballasting of the line as required by his contract. No reply was received and after a further appeal from the Godshill board, on 16th November the Central agreed to complete the ballasting programme.

The IWCR directors meeting on 17th November was a lively affair with several important issues on the agenda. Merstone occupied a good percentage of the discussion. South Arreton Parish Council requested the provision of a new footpath in place of one closed and diverted by the Godshill railway near the station, and the land agent and engineer were requested to investigate. On the credit side a good water supply was now available for locomotives, and authority given for storage tanks to be supplied. Conacher was of the opinion that as the new railway was now open to traffic, the Godshill company should bear half the costs of working the junction station. Finally the question of the danger from the overhanging cliffs at St Lawrence was raised when Conacher was asked to report on the provisions made by both companies to protect the line from rock falls.

Lieutenant Colonel Addison duly reinspected the Godshill railway on 18th November 1897 and found that some of the remedial work was completed but that a few occupation crossing gates still opened towards the railway. The inspector noted the several items to which little or no attention had been given. 'Little has been done to improve the arrangements at Whitwell. The line leading to the sidings is so close to the parapet of the underbridge that there is danger during shunting or other movements.' On measuring the reverse curves, the passenger line leading to the down platform was found to be only 8 chains radius although nothing was shown on the table of curves or gradients furnished to the BOT for the inspection of the line. Addison stipulated the fitting of check rails whilst the curves remained in use and, as an added precaution, all trains were to enter the station at low speed. 'I strongly recommend the company make alterations to get rid of the bad curves on the facing road which must be serious trouble when working the line.' Turning to the bridge at 2 miles 37 chains, the Lieutenant Colonel found nothing had been done to ascertain if there was a defect in construction to account for the deflection, when tested, and this required immediate attention. He also required cement 'tell tales' to be placed across the abutments of the bridge at 1 mile 72 chains to check for further settlement. The temporary water tank for locomotive supplies located near Dean Crossing was also to be moved back from the line and lowered as Addison considered the tank interfered with the driver's view of the gates from the engine of a down train.

Concluding, the Lieutenant Colonel regretted the line compared unfavourably with the condition four months previously. Additional ballast was required at several places and sleepers required packing and lifting. It was, however, noted the contractor, who should have maintained the line for twelve months, had withdrawn his men at short notice and the railway had subsequently 'not received the amount of attention which every new line requires'. As a postscript Addison mentioned that the Merstone subway appeared sound but with the absence of wet weather it was impossible to say whether steps had been taken to remedy defects.

Rumours abounded that the line was in danger of being closed. To save the situation the IWCR was requested to carry out the completion of works and on 1st December agreed provided that they could initially utilize the ballast already owned by the NGSL Railway.

Troubles on the new railway became accentuated as the year drew to a close. Westwood went into receivership on his own petition, and with most of his remuneration in paid up shares which were worthless, he admitted substantial net liabilities. His only locomotive *Godshill* was the subject of a seizure order and was consigned to Mr A.Wood for delivery to Newport. The movement was made in November but as late as 15th December correspondence on the subject was still being

Merstone Junction station from the south-east, showing the original tunnel access to the platform and the unmetalled Merstone Lane crossing the line in the foreground. To the left is the newly installed No. 1 siding alongside the Ventnor Town line. The Sandown line is on the right with No. 2 siding alongside. When this picture was taken, the signal box had yet to receive the 'sentry-box' verandah at the top of the stairs.

COLLECTION R. SILSBURY

received by the IWC at their Newport offices. On the same day the rental payable by the Godshill company for use of Merstone station was fixed at £100 per annum.

Three days before Christmas 1897 complaints were received regarding the diversion of St Rhadegund's footpath which came off the Downs at St Lawrence. The engineer was requested to visit the line early in the New Year to investigate the problem. On the last day of December 1897 the IWCR received £450 as their proportion of working receipts for the period ending 30th September.

The New Year initially brought few problems and the railway had settled down to provide a useful service to the local community. Early in February South Arreton Parish Council again wrote requesting the diversion of the footpath which crossed the railway near Merstone station. After investigation the Godshill company replied they could not effect any diversion but promised to raise the subject with the IWCR.

After the initial impounding *Godshill* returned to work the branch passenger service but availability left much to be desired. On 19th January 1898 Conacher reported to his board that the breakdown of locomotive *Godshill* was causing concern and therefore, to avoid delaying the forward thrust to Ventnor, the IWC company had hired the locomotive *Sandown* from the Isle of Wight Railway to work the passenger service, thus releasing *Godshill* and other locomotives for contractor's works.

Train services were disrupted in the third week of February 1898 when cattle belonging to Mr Lawes wandered on to the railway near Merstone. The cattle had evidently broken the fence to gain access and Lawes was held responsible. On 28th February the company duly notified the farmer that unless repairs were completed promptly proceedings would be instituted to obtain the finance for the necessary work.

At a meeting on the same day Conacher suggested the fencing off and subsequent sale of surplus land on the west of the railway in an endeavour to raise additional capital. It was hoped the local farmers would readily agree to purchase.

The rigours of winter weather also caused the road surface to disintegrate on Dean Crossing and the bridge on the approach to St Lawrence station. As the railway was responsible for the maintenance of the road surface, the usual spate of complaints were received until repairs were executed.

At a meeting of the IWCR board held on 23rd February 1898 it was resolved that under the power and authority vested in the IWCR by the Act of 1890 and agreement of 13th May 1891 between the IWCR and NGSLR, three directors would be appointed to sit on the Godshill company's board to safeguard IWCR interests. To this end Thomas Bolton, Henry Martin and Percy Mortimer were nominated directors of the NGSLR until 28th February 1899 or until removed from office by the IWCR. Henry Martin died in September 1898.

Pickfords, the local agents for the railways, commenced handling Ventnor traffic via St Lawrence with Mr Baker as carrier involved, but complained of lack of facilities at the temporary terminus. Failure to agree to the carrier's wishes would have meant the Isle of Wight Railway retaining the monopoly of the railborne goods traffic to Ventnor. Determined not to allow this to happen, the IWCR agreed to build a small transit shed at St Lawrence to allow Pickfords to store items locked under cover until the railway was extended.

On 1st March 1898 Cooper reported to the BOT that ballasting was completed. In accordance with the inspector's edict he tested the bridge at 2 miles 37 chains but could find no fault with the floorplate. The average deflection of the plate by the movement of the heaviest locomotive used on the test was $\frac{3}{32}$ inch at centre with 'no permanent "set". The ballast was also opened out and the asphalt joints found 'perfectly secure'. At Whitwell the curves had been checked and an engine could run round its train 'without difficulty' although he optimistically added 'at up to say 30 mph'. As an added precaution, all trains stopped at the station. The diversion of the footpath at Whitwell was also completed at a cost to the local authority.

On 6th April 1898 a weighing machine was purchased for use at St Lawrence station. Ten days later Colonel Addison reinspected the line. During his visit he noted the arrangements at Whitwell station were improved with check rails fitted to the 8 chain radius curves, and that the speed of trains was restricted to 10 mph on the approach to the station. The tests carried out on the troughing floor of the bridge at 2 miles 37 chains by Cooper were considered sufficient to dispel any doubts. Of the bridge at 1 mile 72 chains Addison remarked 'No further signs of opening mischief as regards the abutments, but the tell-tale arrangements adopted are not satisfactory. One wing wall in the lower side of the bridge appears to be bulging slightly'. Because of a fresh crack the Lieutenant Colonel required the bridge to be carefully watched 'as settlement is highly probable in wet weather'. He concluded his report by noting that large quantities of ballast had been brought to the line and 'when properly in place the condition of the line will be satisfactory'.

Following the inspection the Godshill railway secretary confirmed on 24th April that speed on the approach to Whitwell would be restricted to 10 mph whilst a continued watch would be maintained on the bridge at 1 mile 72 chains.

The outstanding liabilities left by C.J.Westwood came to light in May 1898 when Saxby and Farmer Ltd, the signalling manufacturers, wrote to the Godshill company requesting settlement of payment for the provision of signalling equipment and interlocking of signals and points on the line. The NGSLR directors were adamant they would not settle the debt as Westwood had awarded the contract.

The construction of the transit shed for Pickfords at St Lawrence authorised by the IWCR was completed by early June, but complaints were quickly made by loading staff who advised that parcels and packages being unloaded from railway wagon to shed or from shed to carrier's waggon were spoiled during wet weather. To avoid unnecessary claims Conacher requested an awning be erected above the doors of the transit shed.

In spite of the completion of compulsory purchase of land for the extension to Steephill, certain landowners continued to defy the railway and refused to release land. To resolve the problem the NGSLR board decided on 5th June to set up a working party in an effort to resolve the matter.

By 30th June 1898 the Godshill company had expended £118,331 on works and expenses but unfortunately only £89,640 of the authorised £120,000 share capital and £27,100 of the £40,000 4 per cent debentures had been sold, leaving a deficit of £15,450.

Mr W.A.Parnell, Westwood's Trustee, wrote on 21st July 1898 regarding material and especially the contractor's locomotive *Godshill*. The matter was raised at the IWC board meeting on 3rd August when the secretary was requested to inform Parnell that the IWCR had not removed any material belonging to Westwood from the railway. *Godshill* had been utilized by the IWC for various shunting duties for $45\frac{1}{52}$ days and Westwood's account credited £45 10s 0d at the rate of £1 per day for hire. Westwood, however, owed the IWCR company £194 2s 11d for keeping the engine at Newport awaiting disposal instructions for the owner or owners.

In July a letter was received from the telegraph company claiming payment for material used on the line. Once again it was found that Westwood had arranged the contract and therefore the company was not liable. On 29th July 1898 the Godshill directors forwarded the claim on to the receiver, absolving themselves from all liability.

By August the NGSLR working party had almost settled matters regarding the extension to Steephill and arranged to purchase not exceeding 6 acres of land from the Steephill Estate at a cost of £5,000, terms as originally negotiated by the engineer. Since Henry Sewell did not wish to live next to the railway, the property was subsequently purchased by Charles Mortimer, brother of the chairman of NGSLR, who in turn resold further required land to the railway company.

After some hard bargaining with Westwood, Mr Parnell wrote on 21st September 1898 suggesting that as settlement for failure to complete the contract, Westwood would forfeit 1,545 £10 shares. The money so recovered and the plans for works at the time of the recovery order would then be used by the new contractor. After considerable discussion, the Godshill board approved of these terms and on 2nd February the deferred shares were transferred to Westwood's trustees, Parnell and King.

In the early autumn South Arreton Parish Council were again concerned with the closure of a footpath which bisected the railway near Merstone station. After various site meetings the IWC authorities agreed to provide land for a new footpath provided the parish council executed all the work at their own expense. This required the provision of post and rail fencing and the planting of quick growing hedges between the railway company's land and the new path. The IWC also required the existing gate leading to the station yard to be removed and the provision of a new approach road. The council agreed the proposals and the directors ratified the agreement on 2nd November 1898.

The subject of Ventnor station was the main topic for discussion between the Godshill company and the IWCR in the early months of the new year. On 25th January 1899 the Central board approved of plans for the new station and listed their own additional items:

1. Ticket barriers to be erected at the entrance to both platforms.
2. Station Master to be provided with an office by screening off a portion of the clerk's office.
3. Booking Office to have protection against draughts.
4. Long spring plungers to be provided at the buffer stops to prevent the risk of damage to vehicles overrunning while descending the falling gradient.
5. In the Goods Shed, a small chicken box to be provided and the loading stage and the craneage to be double the proposed capacity (having regard to the foundations) since the proposed craneage capacity of 30 cwt was not sufficient for expected traffic.

6. Station Master's house to be provided. If the Godshill company cannot finance the building of the structure, the IWC to charge house rent.

On 8th January arrangements were made to provide a 2 ton crane but a fortnight later this was rescinded and the 30 cwt craneage capacity was agreed.

The plans for the new station were again subject to revision in April when the following was approved by IWC board:

1. Platforms to be continued behind the buffer stops to avoid the provision of a footbridge across the line to connect the platforms.
2. Provision of steps from the north side platform to the approach roadway.
3. Goods shed to be constructed as on the provisional plan with accommodation for four wagons.
4. Water Crane, Engine Inspection Pit, Carriage Dock and Loading Dock omitted from the new plans.
5. Station buildings platform to be 15 feet wide and loop platform to be 12 feet wide.
6. Truck weighbridge to be supplied.
7. Costs required for the provision for a living room for the Station Master in the Station buildings.

Cooper submitted revised plans for Ventnor station in October and on 2nd November Conacher made arrangements to meet the Godshill company engineer to obviate possible delays in placing the contract.

By early November the negotiations over the land purchase from the Steephill Castle Estate were completed and the necessary agreements signed and sealed. The lack of access to Ventnor was a constant source of worry to the directors of both companies as traffic to St Lawrence and thence by road to the town was (on most trains) minimal. Passengers from Cowes and Newport still preferred to travel by IWCR to Sandown and thence IWR to Ventnor. The poor traffic returns even filtered down to the London and Provincial Automatic Machine Company who asked for a reduction in the rental charged for their machines, a request which the NGSLR board conceded until the line was opened for traffic to Ventnor.

On 2nd February 1899 Godshill Parish Council wrote asking for the footpath to Bagwich to be diverted where it crossed the railway. The letter was passed to the engineer for comments but no action was taken.

In accordance with the resolution passed on 28th February 1898 the IWCR directors on the NGSLR board were changed with effect from 25th February 1899 when Thomas Dolling Bolton, John Winterbotham Botten and Percy Mortimer were appointed.

On 17th March 1899 the Godshill company issued £1,700 debentures and £10,500 shares to the new contractor, Mr J.T.Firbank, as settlement for £12,200 the contractor had paid for the purchase of land from the Steephill Estate. The deeds of conveyance were subsequently transferred on 14th April. The purchase enabled the contractor to proceed with the works towards the new Ventnor terminus. As a preliminary the engineer advised and subsequently sought approval from the I.W. County Council for alterations of approach to the station and goods yard. By 3rd May application had been made by Cooper and Pickfords for the erection of a goods shed at the proposed Ventnor terminal.

Having obtained the Steephill Castle land, the directors were ever optimistic and suggested an extension to a central terminus near the Royal Hotel, Ventnor. Financial difficulties precluded anything other than proposals and no Parliamentary proceedings were instituted.

Correspondence was received in May 1899 from Messrs Roberts and Chubb representing the British Electric Co Ltd. The directors of the company considered a plan to purchase the line and operate it by electric traction using lightweight multiple units. Had the scheme succeeded, the idea might have changed the whole structure of rail traction and indeed transport on the Isle of Wight. Unfortunately no record exists of the NGSLR directors' reply; no further action was taken and the scheme fell into oblivion.

By 17th May 1899 Cooper's response on the outstanding items at Ventnor station was considered by the IWC directors.

2. Flight of steps to be provided as required.
4. Engine pit to be provided away from the running road, with Cooper suggesting the spur end of the South platform road. The water crane to be sited in the 6 foot between lines at the top points (Merstone end of station). Carriage and Loading Docks to be placed where originally agreed whilst the Cattle Pens were to be sited at the end of the back siding.
5. A clear space without pillars 12 feet wide is now acceptable but provision still to be made to cover the north side platform.
6. If the truck weighbridge is not provided a cart weighbridge to be installed.
7. If the Station Master's house is not provided the NGSL company agree to pay rental.

Further interest was shown by local coal merchants wishing to establish coal grounds at Ventnor and all applications were passed to the IWCR for attention. At the end of June, Pickfords had evidently satisfied the railway company of the need for an independent goods shed or lock-up and rental terms were later agreed at £2 per annum.

The new contractor, J.T.Firbank, pressed on with the works at the Ventnor extension using plant left behind by Westwood, and at the end of July Cooper requested final details of the Godshill directors' requirements for Ventnor station building and accommodation for the station master. The directors replied that because of monetary difficulties only £5,400 was available for works and the contractor would have to restrict the works within this budget. The limits imposed meant that Ventnor, the most important station on the line, would receive a far less imposing station than St Lawrence, Whitwell and Godshill despite the many promises. Doubtless the directors would have liked buildings on both platforms but had to accept the fact there was only enough finance for buildings on one.

Anxious to join the London and Provincial Automatic Machine Company on stations, the Pictorial Post Card Company made application to erect one of their machines on the new Ventnor station and offered the railway company a rental of £1 10s per annum. This was not considered sufficient and by 29th August the Post Card Company accepted the NGSLR request for £2 per annum.

At their meeting on 6th September 1899 the Godshill board agreed to the contents of a letter received from Mr Parnell acting as trustee over the bankruptcy of Charles John Westwood, in which he accepted the surrender of 1,545 £2 shares in forfeit of failure to complete contract.

After investigating the monetary restrictions on the building of Ventnor station, Cooper reported in November that the construction costs would exceed the contractor's estimated price because of the station master's house. The NGSLR direc-

IWCR Beyer Peacock 2–4–0T No. 5 passing Ventnor Town distant signal with a Ventnor Town to Merstone train in 1900, seen after the opening of the extension beyond St. Lawrence.
L & GRP, CTY. DAVID & CHARLES

tors, not wishing to pay rent allowance of the station master, agreed to the purchase of £350 Lloyds Bonds to cover some of the costs. Cooper also advised the installation of electric lighting but the company was adamant that gas be adopted as it was cheaper.

As the century came to an end, traffic returns were declining and it was evident that the terminating of the line at St Lawrence was the chief factor dissuading prospective travellers from using the railway. The directors held lengthy discussions on ways of attracting trade until the railway could be opened through to Ventnor but little action was taken.

Early in the new year Messrs Martin (unconnected with H.D.Martin) advised that they were willing to advance £250 towards the cost of coal stores and £550 for the station master's house at Ventnor, receiving in return Lloyds Bonds to the value of £800.

On 26th February 1900 Conacher advised the IWC board of proposals necessary to alter the facing points and signalling to allow for trains running through Whitwell. Two days later the board advised Conacher that as traffic receipts did not warrant additional expenditure, no alterations were necessary as all trains could stop at Whitwell. It was also agreed at the same meeting that when the extension to Ventnor was opened it would no longer be necessary to operate St Lawrence as a block station and as such the temporary signalling facilities could be removed. Despite this response regarding the alterations at Whitwell, plans of the south end of the station layout were presented to the IWC board on 28th March 1900. As a result of deliberations, the secretary wrote to the Godshill company asking if they were willing to pay the cost of retention of the siding at the station as well as bearing the expenses of providing a loading dock at an estimated cost of £58. Unfortunately the NGSLR had no funds available and as the IWC was in no position to compel the company to provide assets deemed by Conacher necessary for traffic requirements, the IWC was forced to fund the improvements out of its own coffers.

On 23rd March 1900 E. Whitehead, clerk to South Arreton Parish Council, wrote to the BOT regarding the dangerous situation of the footpath which crossed the St Lawrence line just south of Merstone Junction. The matter was passed to Colonel Von Donop who was to inspect the railway within a month and it was suggested that George Coombes, chairman of the South Arreton Parish Council, attend the inspection to explain the case for diversion. Before visiting the line Von Donop ascertained that the footpath in question enabled pedestrians to leave from Merstone station and gain access to another road without making a long detour. Users had a clear view of the railway towards Merstone but the cutting obstructed the view of trains approaching from the Ventnor direction. Although all trains stopped at Merstone and speed over the crossing was minimal, there were undoubtedly certain dangers. The IWCR had offered to give necessary land for making a new footpath on the opposite side of the Sandown line from Merstone station provided the council maintained the route and erected the necessary fencing. The Council was prepared to abide by their side of the bargain but objected to the route of the path through the former Merstone station goods yard. Thus the matter rested pending the inspector's visit.

The first passenger train to pass over the Ventnor extension ran on Wednesday, 18th April 1900, conveying officials of the London & South Western Railway and other interested parties for a private visit to the line. The excursion was arranged by Charles Conacher to enable the officials to sample the new route to Ventnor. Travelling from Southampton to Cowes, the party, including Sam Fay, LSWR Superintendent of the Line, Mr Frazer, LSWR Superintendent at Portsmouth, and J.J.Burnett, Secretary of the Southampton and Isle of Wight Steam Packet Company, joined the special train formed of a saloon coach hauled by 0–6–0 'Terrier' Tank No 9 for the visit to the line. After departure from Cowes the train stopped briefly at Merstone where the new station and facilities were inspected. Further stops were made at Godshill and Whitwell stations for similar examination before the special pulled into St Lawrence to allow Mr Swan, the contractor's agent, to join the train. During the journey it was optimistically announced the new route to Ventnor would become the main line with the Merstone to Sandown section relegated to the status of a branch line. On arrival at the incomplete Ventnor terminus the train pulled into the platform to allow the officials to visit the building and inspect the offices and other facilities. All present expressed admiration of the standard of amenities provided for both passenger and goods traffic at the five stations, before the party joined the train for the return journey to Cowes. Pausing momentarily at St Lawrence to allow Mr Swan to alight and for the driver to collect the single line staff, the train then ran the 13 miles 62 chains to Cowes in 30 minutes.

On the same day Conacher unveiled the new train imported to the island especially for the Cowes to Ventnor service, providing seating accommodation for 200 passengers. The train, formed of five coaches of 'uniform' appearance, was transferred from Southampton by barge and offloaded at Medham. The local press took the opportunity to inspect the new coaches together with new 'Terrier' tank locomotive No 10 and were then given a sample ride from Newport to Cowes and back.

Work progressed towards completion of the line to Ventnor and on 3rd May 1900 the local directors advised the contractor of their modified requirement for the terminal station which included, at Conacher's request, the provision of a refreshment room. This was no doubt considered a necessity because the IWR possessed a similar asset at their Ventnor station. At the same meeting a request for an additional siding at St Lawrence was declined as the opening of the extension was imminent and it was considered traffic would decline as Ventnor attracted traffic away from the temporary terminus. Saxby and Farmer received the contract for signalling work on the extension but were not paid until work was completed.

With the impending opening of the Ventnor extension the proposed train service requirements were discussed within the IWCR and proposals sent to the Godshill board for information. At the same juncture the IWC board approached Mr Williamson, assistant engineer of the Cambrian Railway, to carry out an independent inspection of the extension. The inspection was completed by mid-May with Williamson receiving a fee of 5 guineas for his services. All work was considered of necessary quality except for the siding at St Lawrence which required expenditure of £30 to bring it up to Board of Trade standards. As the IWC required the siding for future traffic purposes, authority was given on 23rd May 1900 for work to be carried out. At the same meeting the through fare structure from Waterloo negotiated with the London & South Western Railway and the revised Ventnor line timetable were discussed.

IWCR Beyer Peacock 2–4–0T No. 5, with steam shut off, drifting down the gradient towards Ventnor Town with a branch train in 1900.

Colonel Von Donop carried out the official inspection for the Board of Trade of the Ventnor extension on 21st May 1900. He noted the extension was 1 mile 39 chains in length with falling gradients of 1 in 55 for the first 11 chains from St Lawrence and 1 in 58 for a distance thereon for 55 chains. The sharpest curves on the section of line were short lengths of 15 and 18 chains radius, whilst the longest embankment of 32 chains was 33 feet high. The deepest cutting, 26 feet in depth, was 31 chains in length. Von Donop advised that subject to the completion of minor remedial work and making good deficiencies including repairs to the approach roadway to Ventnor station, the erection of nameboards and provision of names on the station gas lamps at the terminus, and minor work at the bridge at 6 miles 69 chains, the line could open for traffic. An important requirement was that all trains approaching Ventnor were to be halted at the home signal before being permitted to enter the platform, on account of the falling gradient.

On the afternoon of Thursday, 31st May 1900, Charles Conacher invited the local press representatives, including a lady reporter, to visit the new section of line. The extension was opened to Ventnor Town on Friday, 1st June 1900, a day of heavy and continuous rain. Once again local dignitaries were invited to travel on the line at the invitation of both railway companies before attending a celebratory dinner at the Royal Hotel, Ventnor. Mainland visitors travelling via Southampton and Cowes arrived at Ventnor just before 2 pm.

After the meal W.Bohm, chairman of the Godshill company, proposed the toast to 'The Queen' after which T.D.Bolton MP, chairman of the IWCR, replied. Dr Robertson, chairman of Ventnor District Council, then wished 'Success to the New Railway' and advised the gathering that Ventnor District Council, in order to show what possibilities the new line had to offer, had contracted to have their gravel conveyed via the route.

Bohm then recalled the delay in completion of the final terminus and voiced the gratitude of the NGSLR to Percy Mortimer and his brother Charles for purchasing the whole of the Steephill Estate, before disposing of the land required for the station at a reasonable rate to the railway company. 'It was because of this gesture the station is on the present site.' After the meal the guests left Ventnor Town by the 4.10 pm train.

With little realistic hope of infiltrating the near monopoly of the IWR route to Ventnor from London, publicity was geared to offering a service to passengers approaching the island via Southampton and Cowes, thence direct to Ventnor via Newport. The association of certain directors with the Midland and South Western Junction Railway ensured positive efforts were made to attract the potential traffic flow from the North and West Midlands via Cheltenham, and thence over the MSWJ which had running powers to Southampton. The 'English Madeira' at Ventnor was within easy reach.

CHAPTER FOUR

ISLE OF WIGHT CENTRAL TAKEOVER

TO attract attention to the new extension Conacher sought and received approval for the erection of a new notice board on the platform at Merstone Junction: 'JUNCTION WITH THE NEW AND DIRECT LINE TO VENTNOR TOWN. QUICKEST AND SHORTEST ROUTE FROM COWES AND NEWPORT.'

Following the opening of the extension on 1st June 1900 the IWC was rather concerned at the inspector's stipulation that all trains were required to stop at Ventnor Town home signal before entering the station. The matter was raised on 20th June when the secretary was also asked to approach the Godshill company to ascertain whether an order had been placed for the provision of steps up the station embankment approach from the main road to ease access to the terminus.

In August 1900 a rate of 1/9d per ton was agreed as the IWC proportion of through coal rates to Ventnor Town, the whole of the charge being passed on to traders. It was also reported to the board that an average of four coaches was provided on passenger train services to Ventnor Town, which was considered adequate for the amount of traffic.

Despite improvements at the terminus, complaints from the travelling public and local authority led the IWC and NGSL companies on 26th September 1900 to contribute £5 each for lighting the approach road to Ventnor station. On 19th December it was also agreed the IWC company would provide direction plates in the town extolling the virtues of Ventnor Town station and its train services.

During the construction of the approach road to Ventnor Town station a certain amount of expenditure was involved laying access from Castle Road. With IW County Council permission, the paving had been repositioned and a direction sign erected. Because of minor damage caused, the IWCR agreed to pay for any liability with the proviso that the local company paid a further £5 towards the cost of compensation.

By the end of September 1900 the station works were completed and application was duly made for a licence to sell intoxicating liqueur in the refreshment room.

In October 1900 Ventnor Urban District Council made representations concerning the poor service provided on the new line by the IWCR. The matter was raised at the board meeting on the 24th when the directors (after consultation with Conacher) decided that the service would remain unchanged for the time being and duly advised the council of their decision.

Meanwhile in London the lease of the office of the Godshill company expired at the end of 1900 and the Chairman advised the board on 10th October that he would find an office at a rental of less than £100 a year and also the services of a secretary. As a temporary measure Edward Victor Maetzker was appointed to the post although later he became permanent secretary. Eight days later the directors were stunned when Captain Dunstan announced he wished to resign from the board. His resignation was received 'with regret' and Leonard Mortimer was appointed to the vacant position.

In November Messrs Wooldridge advised there was an error in the wording of the licence for the refreshment room. This was later rectified and the company then considered the letting of the premises for day-to-day operation. At the same juncture the London and Provincial Automatic Vending Machine Company rental came up for renewal. The machine company offered £8 per annum for their three machines but the NGSLR authorities thought this too small a price and finally obtained £10 per annum.

On 4th January 1901 Von Donop completed the re-inspection of the Ventnor extension and found that all out-

Ex-Cowes & Newport Railway IWCR 2-2-2WT No. 2 entering Merstone with a Sandown–Newport train in 1900. Together with No. 1, this engine worked the Ventnor Town services on occasions.

A1 Class 0–6–0T IWCR No. 10 approaching Ventnor Town station in 1900 with a train of 4-wheel stock. The lightly laid track, and large covers over the economical facing point lock mechanisms, show up clearly in this view.

An early view of the new Merstone Junction station c.1900 with IWCR 'Terrier' No. 9 standing in the up platform with a Sandown to Newport train. No. 1 siding had not been installed at this time and the down platform up direction starter was adjacent to the signal box and not on the platform. No. 9 was used to haul a special train conveying officials of the LSWR and other interested parties to Ventnor Town on 18th April 1900.

standing items had received the necessary attention and recommended final sanction for the line to be brought into use.

The new year found the NGSL Railway Company in continued financial difficulties, so that when in February both Conacher of the IWCR and Cooper the engineer advised on the provision of stop blocks for Ventnor station and goods yards, the directors were adamant they were to be obtained for the cheapest price possible. Conacher was still far from happy with the facilities on the line. On 25th February 1901 he advised the IWC board of the desirability of erecting cattle pens at Ventnor Town and at the same time submitting a list of outstanding requirements necessary on the Ventnor extension:

1. Reduce the width of coal stage to suit rolling stock.
2. Paint water tanks dark red and repair to prevent leakage.
3. Make up approach to cattle dock to reduce present levels.
4. Provide cattle pens and also stop blocks to all sidings.
5. Fix hand rail opposite booking office windows to assist ingress and egress of passengers.
6. Paint station road fencing.
7. Complete station road lighting.
8. Make up platform to original level where sunk.
9. Support platform embankment by stone wall.
10. Drain and put approach road to Goods Yard into thorough repair.
    Station furnishings – provide a complete set of fire irons and coal scuttles for all fireplaces.

Needless to say, the IWC directors were concerned at such shortcomings and arranged for the report to be sent to the Godshill company for action.

The remedial work at Ventnor commenced at the end of March 1901 when the tender of G.Childs was accepted for the repairs to the approach road with prices of £80 for repairs to the roadway and £17 for pitched drainage channel.

Mr Bohm, chairman of the NGSLR board, died on 19th March, and at the board meeting on 27th March Percy Mortimer was elected to the vacant position. At the same meeting the IWCR requested early completion of the outstanding works at Ventnor station and goods yard by the contractor.

The tender for the accommodation works at Ventnor station was also advertised in March 1901 and on 15th May the contract was awarded. The NGSLR board objected to the excessive requirements of the IWCR at Ventnor with the inference that the Central wished to have equal facilities as the IWR had at their Ventnor terminal. It was subsequently arranged after heated discussion that the IWCR would finance these schemes and at a later date debit the sum from the Godshill Railway proportion of receipts.

On 22nd May 1901 the seal of the working agreement between the IWCR and NGSLR was sent to the Board of Trade with the addendum that the line was to be worked by Train Staff and Ticket method of working combined with Absolute Block. Merstone Whitwell and Ventnor were to be staff stations.

Unfortunately, the contractors had made little progress at Ventnor and the original list sent by the IWC to the Godshill board for remedial action was superseded in May by a much longer and revised list which highlighted many of the shortcomings of the original contractor.

Old List
1. Pelham Woods Spoil Heap. Level top and make good slopes.
2. Trueloves Occupational Level Crossing. Fix penalty board.

3. Fix Buffer Stops at all sidings. Ventnor Town station.
4. Stools for point rods Ventnor Station. Ballast up.
5. Extend platform coping at Ventnor Station to Board of Trade requirements if at any time required.
6. Provide cattle pens.
7. West platform provide shelter and lighting.

New List
1. Provide fixed ground crane with movable jib to lift 5 tons similar to that provided by the IWR for furniture, van bodies, casting machinery.
2. Provide 10 ton weighbridge, as recently fixed at Newport, to ascertain weight and compute charges for traffic.
3. Reduce width of coal stage to clear rolling stock.
4. Paint water tanks and prevent leakage.
5. Approach to horse and carriage dock, reduce present levels.
6. Raise Station Road fencing where sunk.
7. Reconstruct platform with gravel where necessary and make up where sunk.
8. Support platform embankment by stone wall.
9. Turf or sow grass on embankment opposite platforms.
10. Drain Station Road and remetal where necessary.
11. Complete Station Road fencing to enclose area let to Pickfords and Co.
12. Increase width of bay to Goods Shed to accommodate increased traffic, not anticipated at time plans submitted.
13. Make up 6 feet space between main line and coal siding to proper level also between coal and goods sidings to facilitate shunting operations.

It was also agreed the Godshill company would pay £8 11s 9d towards direction plates at Ventnor.

On 24th July the certificate of working for the portion of line from St Lawrence to Ventnor as required by the Board of Trade was signed and sealed by the Godshill board. At the directors meeting which was called essentially for this purpose it was also agreed to open an account for the NGSLR with the London City and Midland Bank, Lombard's branch.

The services of a secretary for the Godshill company were finalised on 18th September 1901 when G.Fletcher Jones offered the use of his office in the City at 12 Old Jewry Chambers and his services as secretary at a cost of 52 guineas per annum, with six months notice of termination by either party.

In the autumn the IWCR and NGSLR authorities reached agreement for extending the platform in the goods shed at Ventnor 12 feet at each end with a width of 6 feet. By 25th September the staging was completed at a cost of £4 9s 0d. Two months later the IWC required £38 9s 0d for further repairs to the approach road to Ventnor station but the demand was ignored by the Godshill company.

During a visit to the IWC system on 15th September 1901, the Inspecting Officer had commented on the requirements for a light to illuminate the crossing gates at Merstone. The matter was raised with the IWC board at their meeting on 18th December when it was thought the light from the signalbox provided enough illumination. To comply with the Board of Trade requirement it was agreed the gates would be independently illuminated by two oil lamps in addition to the mandatory red warning lamps.

The New Year brought no respite for either the IWCR or NGSLR boards. Following the many complaints received about the branch service it was agreed on 8th January 1902 that Conacher would draft a new timetable to include through trains from both Ventnor Town and Sandown to Newport and Cowes in an effort to popularise the route and appease local travellers.

Despite the refusal of the NGSLR to respond to the further request for repairs to Ventnor station approach, the IWC invited tenders for the work on 5th February 1902. By the 26th the contract was awarded to Henry Ingram of Ventnor who tendered at £73 against £82 quoted by G.Childs.

The provision of water supply to Merstone was a constant problem to the IWCR for often there were inadequate quantities available to replenish fully the locomotive working the Ventnor Town services. In an attempt to resolve the situation, authority was given on 24th February 1902 for the well to be sunk a further 2 or 3 feet deeper. The work ultimately involved excavation to a depth of a further 5 feet and the well was available at its new depth from December.

Another item raised in February 1902 was the rate chargeable to the Godshill company for the conveyance of coal from Medina Wharf to Ventnor Town. Unfortunately, no agreement was reached by November of the same year and as a result a contract for conveyance of fuel to the Ventnor Gas Company was lost. The Gas Works was at Wheelers Bay, remote from the IWR station and further still from Ventnor Town. Coal was shipped by sea direct to the gasworks and evidently the railway company was attempting to take over the conveyance of fuel.

The railway now settled to an uneventful period serving the sparse population of South Wight. In March 1902 the surplus land not required by the Godshill company was assigned to Mr Mortimer. The refreshment room at Ventnor station was let to a Mr Moss in May 1902 for £20 per annum, the tenant paying for cost of gas and other outgoings. When Moss asked for sleeping accommodation to be provided adjacent to the refreshment room, his application was politely declined.

The Godshill company's finances were still in a precarious state and when in January 1903 debentures came up for cash redemption the holders were refused additional debentures in lieu of cash and offered extension of their debenture holdings for a period of 3 to 5 years. On 25th February, however, the board agreed to the issue of £40,000 debenture stock to be made available to all holders of the existing 4 per cent debentures in lieu of debenture bonds.

At the end of March 1903 the Secretary of the Godshill company was requested to visit the Isle of Wight and arrange a meeting with the manager of Ventnor Gas Works and IWCR representatives to ascertain terms for the conveyance of coal traffic.

Mr Baker, the agent employed by the IWCR/NGSLR for parcels delivery service at Ventnor, tendered his resignation in March 1903. A successor was soon found and on 1st April Mr Russell was engaged initially on 3 months trial at a rate of 7/6d per week, the Godshill company agreeing to pay half of this sum as their portion.

The NGSLR never produced its own timetable, details always being included in the tables produced by the IWCR. The latter were initially produced without charge to the smaller company but by 1903 losses were being made and Conacher requested a contribution towards the production costs. The Godshill directors, aware that they had to date received an advantageous deal, agreed on 3rd June to making a contribution towards any loss incurred providing payment did not exceed £10 per annum.

The completion of the railway had left the embankments and cuttings as a scar on the landscape and complaints were received from various landowners including Steephill Castle Estate who made a claim for damages. In order to appease the complainants, £10 was made available by NGSL directors for the landscaping and planting of shrubs in the vicinity of Steephill to obliterate the bare whiteness of the chalky strata.

The exposed situation of Merstone station, sited within an amphitheatre of hills to the north and south-east, meant that, with the prevailing south-westerly wind blowing for much of the year, passengers waiting for or interchanging trains were subjected to frequent discomfort from blowing dust or driving rain. To obviate the problem the IWCR chairman authorised on 22nd July 1903 the planting of a line of Scots fir trees to provide a windbreak.

Planning for the winter 1903 timetable commenced in July but serious reservations were voiced at the continuance of a through service from Cowes or Newport to Ventnor Town as receipts were far less remunerative than on other lines. After consideration the IWCR board at their meeting on 26th August 1903 decided to make all services run direct to Sandown for six months from 1st October 1903 leaving the Ventnor Town line operating as a self-contained branch from Merstone. Immediate objections were made and a month later the Godshill company secretary asked Conacher 'if through coaches to both Sandown and Ventnor could be worked by all trains'.

The 1903 winter service was subsequently introduced without the through Ventnor carriages being included. Ventnor District Council and A.H.Read of Niton complained vehemently but Conacher was unmoved and replied to the effect that 'the working was only a trial and subject to review within six months'.

By the autumn of 1903 the IWCR permanent way required renewal and repair at various places. At the time the NGSL company was storing 20 tons of steel rails in the goods yard at Ventnor Town. To save purchasing new equipment, the Newport company offered to purchase the redundant rails. Initially the asking price was £5 per ton but the Central was only willing to pay £4. After due bargaining, the rails were purchased for the lower price in December with associated fish plates, point rodding and fang bolts priced at £5 10s 0d per ton. The financial settlement was made by the IWCR taking a reduced portion of receipts.

At the end of September 1903 the IWC proposed amendments and alterations to the working agreement with the NGSLR. Not all of the NGSLR directors were happy with the proposed arrangements and at a heated meeting held on 2nd December two directors voiced complete opposition to the scheme.

In the meantime the tenant of Ventnor Refreshment Rooms had given notice of termination of lease and the vacant possession was duly advertised. In late November the Portsmouth Brewery Co wrote offering to take over the lease of the room and terms were later agreed at £18 per annum.

With the impending summer service both the Godshill company and Ventnor District Council were concerned with the service offered by the IWCR and in particular lack of through trains or coaches. Despite protestations in May and

Beyer Peacock 2–4–0T No. 5 at Ventnor Town in the early 1900s with a train of three ex IW(NJ)R 4-wheel coaches. The leading vehicle is first/second composite IWCR No. 30 followed by second/third composite IWCR No. 28 and two-compartment brake third No. 29. The vehicles, originally built by the Bristol Carriage and Wagon Company, were subsequently rebuilt as vans.

June 1904 Conacher advised that the Cowes–Newport–Sandown service was to be retained for a full twelve months with connections for Ventnor being made at Merstone.

By September 1904 negotiations were concluded with the Anglo-American Oil Company for the establishment of a small terminal in the goods yard at Ventnor. The company subsequently set up a depot for the distribution of oil and paraffin for which the NGSLR received an annual rent of £10.

When the IWCR found that the cost of the publication of their timetable showed a loss of £29 12s 5d the NGSLR was requested to pay a proportion of the deficit, equal to a third (£9 17s 6d), on 23rd November 1904. Equally in the new year the Godshill company requested the IWCR for half of the cost of placing an advertisement in the London and South Western Railway official guide to which the Newport company agreed a sum of £2 15s 0d out of a total of £5 10s 0d.

The threat of competition from the internal combustion engine came in April 1905 with the introduction of a motor bus service operated by the Isle of Wight Express Motor Syndicate Ltd. As a result the whole question of the future of the railways was raised and as a defensive stand against competition it was agreed on 28th June 1905 that fares from Newport to Ventnor IWR via Sandown would be no less than via Merstone or Godshill. Earlier the secretary of the NGSL had again questioned the method of working the line and was advised that only during July, August and September would a through Cowes to Ventnor Town service be reinstated (passengers for Sandown changing at Merstone).

In late August 1905 a Mr Heal suffered fatal injuries on the railway when he was hit by the branch train and at the inquest on 4th September a verdict of accidental death was recorded. Mrs Heal wrote on 23rd September saying she had no interest in suing the company and accordingly a payment of £5 was paid to the widow.

At the end of the summer season trains again ran direct from Newport to Sandown with Ventnor passengers changing at Merstone. In November 1905 Ventnor District Council complained not only of the withdrawal of the through facilities but also the reduction of train services to Ventnor Town.

Few improvements were made to the infrastructure during 1905 as the Godshill finances remained at a low ebb. The position had become critical by December when the balance in the bank was a mere £145.

The facilities at Ventnor again came under scrutiny in April 1906 when the rental for the goods shed was raised and arrangements made for the Refreshment Room to be repaired after Portsmouth Brewery Co had made several complaints.

As early as 1904 the IWCR were contemplating employing a steam railcar on the Merstone–Ventnor Town services because of the poor patronage and low receipts. After several forays to the mainland to view vehicles on the LSWR and Rother Valley Railway, tenders were sought on 23rd November for a vehicle capable of conveying 50 passengers. The contract for the railcar was subsequently placed with Hurst Nelson and Company of Motherwell who subcontracted the locomotive portion to R & W Hawthorn & Co. and supplied at a combined cost of £1,450. Delivery was promised for June 1906 but because of delays the new machine arrived on the island on 4th October being landed at St Helens Quay. Numbered 1 in the IWC fleet, preliminary trials were run on the branch the following day.

Conacher reported to the IWCR board on 13th August 1906 that the new railcar was to work the service between Merstone and Ventnor. The new vehicle was found adequate for the lightly trafficked line but unfortunately was withdrawn temporarily from traffic in mid-October with the engine axle bearing overheating. The railcar subsequently took up regular working on 2nd November 1906.

On 18th March 1907 the IWCR approached the BOT applying for permission to construct a short siding to serve a small quarry half a mile from Ventnor Town station. The siding was to be under the control of the staff at the station and the points secured by Annetts Key attached to the Train Staff. The letter advised that the main line was straight where the siding intended to diverge with a 1 in 65 falling gradient towards Ventnor. The company undertook to shunt the siding with the engine at the lower end of the gradient at all times. As a rider the authorities advised that the siding was required to facilitate the delivery of road stone for maintenance of the public highways on the Island and general delivery of quarry stone. The letter was passed to Major Pringle who sanctioned construction on 22nd March.

In June 1907 the sandpit at Whitwell cutting was reportedly 'worked out' and in order to obtain continuing supplies the IWC negotiated with F.A.Joyce for the leasing of the sandpit near Godshill station at an annual rent of £12. Before negotiations were concluded, however, Conacher reported that more sand had been found at Whitwell. As a result of the new findings the negotiations over the Godshill site were concluded.

By 19th August 1907 the Ventnor Quarry siding was ready for inspection and although Colonel Druitt was delegated to inspect, it was Colonel P.G.Von Donop who attended the new works on 20th September 1907. The inspector duly noted that the new siding connection faced up trains and that points were locked and unlocked by a key on the Train Staff. On being assured again that the siding would be shunted with the locomotive at the lower end of the train, Von Donop sanctioned the opening of the siding to traffic.

Drainage problems continued to persist in the subway at Merstone station. Reporting on the egress of water, Conacher suggested further work to improve the situation. Although sanction was given on 3rd July 1907 it was not until 20th December that the IWC board authorised Mr Tomkins to carry out the remedial work at a cost of £20 19s 5d.

On 24th August 1908 Conacher reported that station master F.Newland of Freshwater had in the course of his duties neglected to collect outstanding monies owing to the company from traders in the district, resulting in the loss of £21 9s 8d. In reprimanding Newland, Conacher proposed to send the errant station master to Whitwell on probation at a salary of £1 2s 6d per week with a further reduction of 2/6d per week until the arrears were settled. Mr Urry, the Whitwell station master, was subsequently appointed to Freshwater at a salary of £1 8s 0d per week and the transfer was effected in the autumn of the same year.

From 28th February 1907 the following IWC directors were appointed to the board of the Godshill Company: Thomas Dolling Bolton MP, Percy Mortimer JP and Colonel John Henry Chenevix Harrison RE. Major John George Gibson was also elected for the years 1908–1910 inclusive.

From the opening of the Ventnor extension, goods facilities at the terminus had been restricted by the lack of a fixed

Ventnor Town distant signal is 'off' for the 10.00 a.m. Cowes to Ventnor Town train hauled by 2-4-0T No. 8 approaching the terminus on 11th June 1910.
LCGB/ KEN NUNN COLLECTION

craneage facility for lifting bulky materials into and out of wagons. The IWCR authorities had often complained that traffic was being lost to the IWR or carriers' waggons because of the lack of equipment but their pleas had fallen on deaf ears. The Godshill company finally relented and tenders were subsequently invited. The full co-operation of the IWCR was sought and the various replies received were forwarded for approval. Conacher advised on 4th September 1907 the acceptance of F.Bradley's tender for the provision of a 5 ton capacity fixed crane. The crane was subsequently installed during the summer of 1908 and Bradley's account paid on 30th September, needless to say by the IWCR.

During September 1908 a review of annual rental payments received by the Godshill company revealed the following: –

		£	s	d
Sweetmeat Automatic Co	Rent of machines at stations	15	0	0
Pickfords	Goods Depot, Ventnor	2	0	0
A.Butt	Shed, Whitwell	2	10	0
G.Childs	Garden Ground, Ventnor	3	0	0
Anglo American Oil Co	Depot at Ventnor	10	0	0
Portsmouth Brewery Co	Refreshment Room, Ventnor	18	0	0
W.H.Smith	Bookstalls	Variable rates		

Flooding in the vicinity of the railway at Whitwell during the autumn of 1908 caused slight undermining of Nettlecombe Lane bridge. Conacher spent some time negotiating with the Godshill company on the apportionment of costs for repairs. On 22nd December 1909 the NGSLR directors finally agreed to pay £20 as half of the repair bill.

In March 1910 the insurance of station buildings on the branch was increased to a premium coverage for £4,150. In the same month £12 was paid to the IWCR after their engineer had made further repairs to the brickwork and plating at Nettlecombe Lane bridge. The IWCR was also requested to contribute costs when it was decided to renew the advertisement for the route in the LSWR Railway Guide.

The troubles besetting the NGSLR company came to a head in July 1910 when two debenture holders commenced proceedings against the railway for failing to repay £900. Mr Percy Mortimer, the chairman, had also started proceedings against the company and served notice of the appointment of a receiver on 7th July. Harry Magnus, a founder director, attempted to avert the inevitable by purchasing some of Mortimer's stock but to no avail.

As a result of Mortimer's action against the Godshill company heard in the Court of Chancery on 22nd July 1910, the company was declared bankrupt and a receiver appointed.

On 8th August 1910 Miss Emily Lamb Tuckerman, driving one of the few motor cars then on the Island, collided with the level crossing gates at Merstone. Miss Tuckerman, with other occupants of the vehicle, was injured and the car damaged. Ten days later the IWC board was advised that further investigations were being made into the incident but in the meantime the railway company had made a claim for damage done to the crossing gate, alleging the driver had failed to have proper control and stop the car.

After the opening of the railway to traffic there were many incidents of animals straying on the line usually as a result of gates being left open. In March 1911, however, defective fencing between Whitwell and Dean Crossing allowed a mare owned by Mr Beaden of Whitwell to trespass on to the track. Unfortunately the animal was killed by a passing train. Accepting negligence, the IWC settled Beaden's claim by offering the farmer a free pass for one year between Newport and Ventnor Town in recompense.

At their meeting held on 26th April 1911 the IWCR directors agreed to the closing of their London office at 11 Ironmonger Lane on and from 1st October 1911. Two months later a new working agreement covering the three years from 1st July 1911 to 30th June 1914 was signed by officials of the NGSLR and the IWCR with no alteration in terms.

Ex-NER 0-4-4T No. 2 approaching Ventnor Town with the 11.45 a.m. Cowes to Ventnor Town on 11th June 1910. This tank engine was considered too heavy for the light permanent way on the branch but on occasions worked the services.
LCGB/KEN NUNN COLLECTION

By now the IWC was in full command of the line and consultations between the two companies became less frequent. One factor which was raised in correspondence in May 1911 was a complaint from the secretary of the NGSLR regarding the larger company removing without due notification sand and ballast from the cutting north of Whitwell station. It was thought that the monetary value of the sand should have been placed in the empty coffers of the local company.

In April 1911 father and son Harry and Russell Willmott secured control of the IWCR, the former, as chairman, appointing the latter as manager. Finding their company in dire straits, they commenced a programme of economies. Conacher in the meantime left to take up the management of the Cambrian Railways, though he was to remain at Oswestry only a matter of months.

As a result of this situation, on 16th August 1911 the IWCR duly advised the Godshill company of the termination of the working agreement on and from August 1912 and proposed a reduced train service in the interim because of continued poor traffic receipts.

The programme also sought to improve assets and in September 1911 approval was given for works at Merstone station including sundry items on the station and to the water supply for £5, installation of acetylene platform lighting replacing oil for £15, and additional asphalting of the platform at £3.

On 5th October 1911 station master George Healey requested an extension on the station house of St Lawrence but, because of its financial position, the Godshill company was unable to comply with the request. The identity of the NGSLR was gradually being overlooked and many people disregarded its actual existence and wrote direct to the IWC as operators of the railway. One such instance occurred when the Water Company placed one of their main pipes under the railway at Dean Crossing with full consent of the IWCR. Only later was it realised that the local company had not been consulted.

On 5th October 1911 the IWCR confirmed its intention to terminate the existing working agreement on 16th August 1912. At the same time it advised details of the revised service to be provided to Ventnor. The local company officials were distressed at the planned reduction, restricting operation between Merstone and Ventnor and the withdrawal of through services. Far from happy with the IWC reply that the service provided had been under-utilised and that traffic receipts were falling, on 9th November the NGSLR board asked for a breakdown of train and traffic returns.

On 8th November 1911 the NGSL advised the IWC that because of financial difficulties it was impossible to obtain the sanction of the court on the proposed agreement by the 14th. As a result of this default the existing working agreement was extended for a period of three weeks.

A broken rail on the Ventnor branch near Merstone on 2nd December 1911 almost caused the derailment of a train. Fortunately the engine and coaches passed over the defective track at slow speed and no damage was sustained. The offending rail was removed and on later inspection was found to have been manufactured in 1893 by the Ebbw Vale Steel Company with original weight of 67 lbs per yard. At the time of breakage the rail weight was $64\frac{1}{2}$ lbs per yard. The remaining track on the Ventnor line was inspected but no further faults were found. On 7th December authority was given for the provision of a new oil engine and pump for the water supply at Merstone at a cost of £56 (£6 above estimates provided the previous June).

The revised working agreement with the Godshill company was approved by the proprietors of the IWCR on 7th December 1911 at a meeting held in the Great Eastern Hotel, Liverpool Street.

Because of increasing agricultural traffic in the area, an additional siding at Merstone was authorised in January 1912 at a cost of £160 (later increased to £180).

By the end of January 1912 the affairs of the Godshill company were in total disarray. A letter from Mr G.Fletcher-Jones, the Godshill solicitor, intimated that dissenting debenture holders had filed an affidavit against the company questioning the expenditure and working expenses together with figures for receipts. Percy Mortimer, chairman of the Godshill company, had in turn made an affidavit in reply and the whole issue was referred to the Master in Chancery for hearing on 29th January. Within a fortnight the Godshill solicitor informed the IWCR directors that the Receiver advised that the Master in Chancery had agreed to make the necessary order for the confirmation of the proposition subject to a new agreement:

1. Existing indebtedness by the Godshill company to the IWCR cancelled.
2. Any difference between earning and guaranteed income under the new agreement should be debited to the IWCR.
3. Percentage payment to the NGSLR under the new agreement to be 38 per cent and not 35 per cent.
4. Maximum guarantee payable to be £2,000 instead of £500.

After consultation with the chairman and directors, the IWCR solicitor replied that his company could not in any way entertain the suggested alterations to the agreement and unless the proprietors agreed the proposal it was the intention of the IWCR to cease working the Godshill company's line from August 1912.

At about 7 am on 6th March 1912 a large portion of the chalk cliff opposite St Lawrence station fell across the track, completely blocking the line. The train service was suspended until 12 noon the following day as IWC engineering personnel cleared the debris. In the intervening period a horse bus conveyed passengers from Whitwell via St Lawrence to Ventnor. The continuing wet weather, however, caused a further fall of chalk on the night of the 7th. Once again engineering staff cleared the track by the following day and then set about consolidating the embankment. To avoid the risk from further falls during this remedial work a shuttle service ran between Ventnor Town and St Lawrence where passengers walked past the site of the fall to join another train which shuttled between St Lawrence and Merstone Junction. Through services were finally reinstated on 15th March 1912. The cost of the remedial work was £50 and the IWCR requested a £25 payment from the Godshill company as their portion of costs.

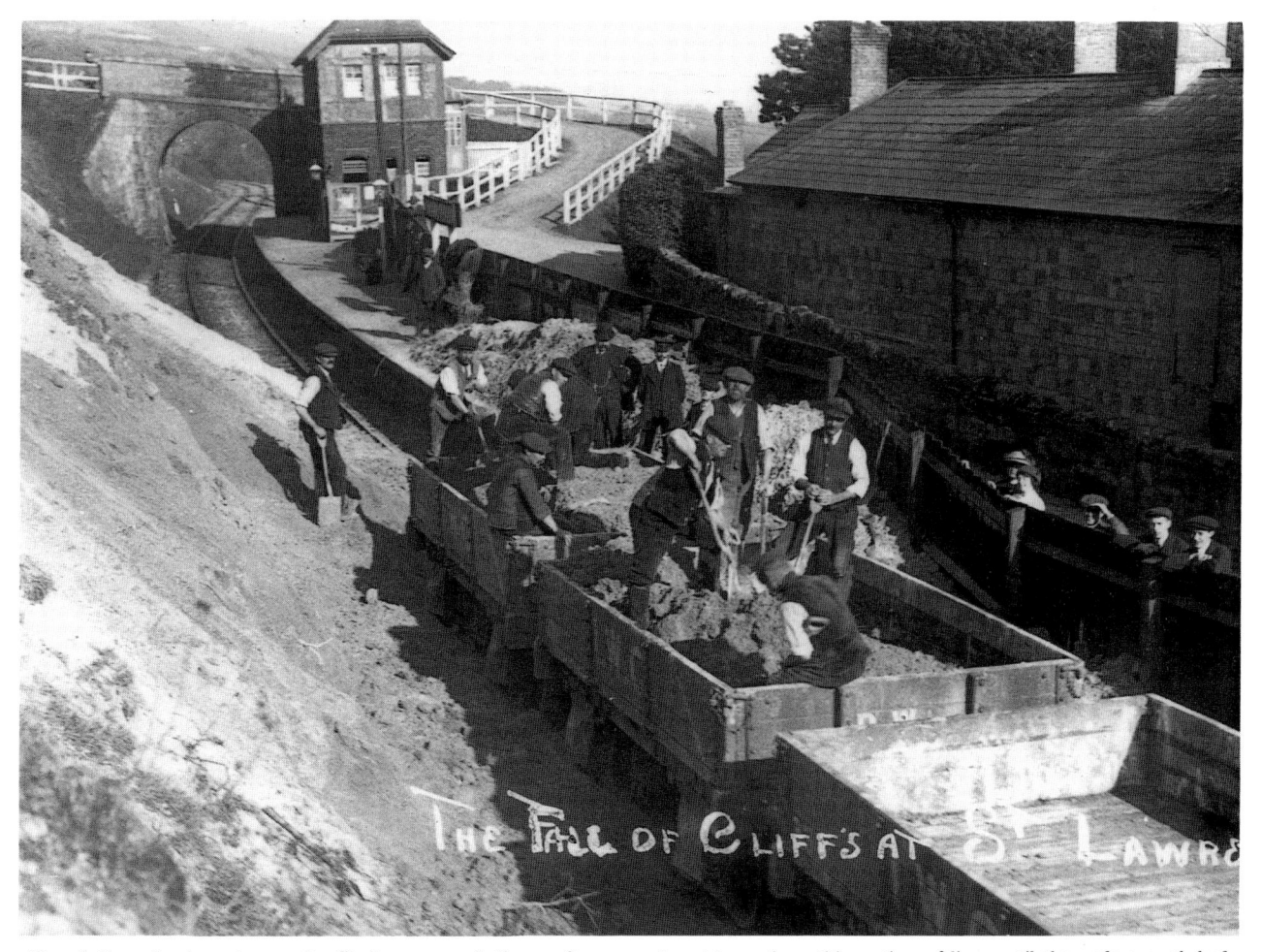

The chalk embankment opposite St. Lawrence platform often caused problems along this section of line; until the undergrowth had fully grown, cliff falls were common, especially after wet weather. In August 1912 a cliff fall opposite the station caused closure of the line for a day and permanent way staff who are clearing the line are watched by local residents. The short siding serving the small goods yard can be seen just beyond the overbridge.

In June 1912 Russell Willmott, the IWCR General Manager, made a detailed inspection of the Ventnor line and on 27th advised the Godshill board that the railway was to be brought up to good condition within three months, with such works lasting not less than 3 years without undue wear and tear. On 27th June the IWCR secretary advised his directors that the Railway Commissioners had refused to approve the new working agreement as there was no special clause in the IWC or NGSLR Acts generally authorising the working agreement between the two companies. The existing agreement authorised by the Godshill company's Act of 1889 was therefore to be terminated as arranged on 16th August 1912. Local Press reports even rumoured the line would close and the *Isle of Wight County Press* on 3rd August 'hoped steps could be taken to prevent the line having to be closed'.

Early in July the Godshill secretary approached the IWC with a request for the larger company to pay the balance of the guaranteed £250 for the half year ending 31st December 1911. In addition a request was made for the IWC to pay the £1,000 government duty for the half-year ending 6th December 1911. Under the old agreement, payment for the latter was not due until August, hence the request. After much negotiation the IWC board agreed to making a payment of £700 only.

On 21st May 1912 a new working agreement was tentatively made with the IWCR but was later declined. A second attempt was made in June but this again reached stalemate. Finally, on 18th July 1912, agreement was reached on the following terms: The Newport Godshill and St Lawrence Railway was to be worked and maintained for two years ending 1st July 1914 with the Isle of Wight Central Company taking 65 per cent of receipts. In return the Central Railway was to give an undertaking to work the line on satisfactory terms to the Godshill company. If such a service were provided the NGSLR would return £500 out of the guaranteed £1,500 receipts for the years 1911-12 whilst the IWCR would also forfeit the right to have any representatives on the local railway board. In the event of a refusal to the terms by the IWCR, the Receiver would apply for permission to approach the Railway Commissioners to adjudicate on terms between the two companies. The Receiver would also have power to apply to the Courts for liberty to use any NGSLR money available after paying the 3 per cent debentures, as authorised by Act of Parliament, and after obtaining alternative powers of the company to work the line. The IWCR refused to accept such proposals and on 30th July 1912 G.Fletcher Jones, the NGSLR solicitor, sought the opinion of counsel as to the legal construction of certain clauses of the working agreement of 27th December 1888.

The dissension over the terms of the working agreement resulted in the decision by Harry Willmott, the IWC chairman, to continue negotiations whilst his company in the meantime worked the line to the best advantage. Such negotiations continued throughout the late summer with operations extending beyond the critical 16th August 1912. At the eleventh hour, on 15th August 1912, the IWCR and NGSLR finally reached agreement as to the future working of the Ventnor line.

1. IWCR to have continuing running powers over the Godshill railway until February 1913.
2. The IWCR to pay a proportion of receipts to the Godshill company for year ending 30th June 1912, £1,500 and no more, and also pay £1,500 for the period July 1912 to February 1913.
3. If the amounts were less than £1,500, no more than 35 per cent of the gross receipts to be paid and the difference to be retained as a discharge of or to be added to the debt due from the Godshill company.
4. Two IWC directors to be appointed to the Godshill company board for the period of operation.

The agreement was ratified on 9th October 1912.

At 7.30 pm on 26th August 1912 heavy rain caused a further fall of the cliff opposite St Lawrence station. The line was blocked until 3 pm the following day with passengers being conveyed by bus between St Lawrence and Ventnor.

By 13th November 1912 the two companies, following further negotiations, reached the inevitable agreement for the IWCR to purchase the Merstone-Ventnor line, offering £36,000 in IWCR 4 per cent debentures at face value with a proviso for reasonable compensation to be paid to the NGSLR secretary. The takeover was subject to Parliamentary approval and the added approval of the Godshill shareholders, and to the debenture holders' withdrawal of action in the Court of Chancery. The interest on debenture stock exchange was agreed at £1,440 against the old guarantee of £2,000 and new guarantee of £1,500 per annum. Seventy-five per cent of the debenture holders of the IWCR and Godshill company were to approve of the takeover. The terms of the Bill were to be subsequently submitted to a meeting of Ordinary, Preference and Deferred shareholders of the Godshill company and agreed. The final schedule for the bill was signed by Percy Mortimer and P.N.Gilbert, directors, and Edward V.Maetzker, secretary of the NGSLR, and on behalf of the IWC by H.Willmott and Sidney Herbert, directors, and Russell Willmott who had become secretary in addition to his other functions.

One of the final acts of the NGSLR board was to herald an action which indirectly led to the closure of the railway 39 years later. On 6th December 1912 the Anglo American Oil Company was granted permission to set up a Motor Spirit (Petrol) Store next to their premises in Ventnor goods yard to service motor cars in the area.

The Bill for the takeover was subsequently deposited with the parliamentary agent on Tuesday, 17th December. The Bill received unopposed readings by the Lower House and was approved by the IWCR proprietors on 31st January 1913 at a Wharncliffe meeting, as well as by Godshill shareholders.

In the later stages a petition against the Bill was made by two Godshill company debenture holders, Lieutenant L.D.Fisher and Captain B.D.Fisher, on the grounds that the IWC debentures did not fully cover the value of the Godshill company debentures. Despite their minor opposition, the Bill passed all stages and by June was waiting Royal Assent. The railway had cost £250,000 to build and had never made an operating profit. Under the terms of the act the proprietors were to receive a meagre £36,000 in IWCR 4 per cent debenture stock.

In the preliminary information appertaining to the Bill, it was revealed that up to 30th June 1912 the IWCR contributed £8,059 6s 6d in excess of the proportion of gross receipts payable under guarantee to keep the Godshill company solvent. None of this sum had been repaid although under article 10 of the agreement of 1888 the IWC was only liable for an annual payment of £1,500.

At the end of June 1913 the Portsmouth United Brewing Company surrendered the tenancy of the refreshment room at

Ventnor Town station for which they paid rent of £5 per annum. With the impending amalgamation, the IWCR agreed to take over and operate the refreshment room.

On 28th July 1913 the IWC directors agreed to pay £200 to the secretary of the Godshill company including £105 for costs incurred in the winding up of the former line. A cheque for £120 was also paid to P.N.Gilbert for his negotiations between the two companies.

The Isle of Wight Central Railway (Godshill Transfer) Act of 1913 (3 & 4 George 5 Cap xiii) received the Royal Assent on 4th July 1913 and authorised the total transfer of the Ventnor Town branch to the larger company. In consideration of the transfer, the IWCR authorities were to pay £36,000 in Debenture C stock from 1st July 1913 paying interest at the rate of 4 per cent per annum. The apportionment was £75 IWC debentures for each £100 NGSLR debenture stock, £75 IWC debenture stock for each £100 Godshill debenture bonds and £5 IWC debentures for each £20 preferred Godshill half share of £5 each. The Secretary of the Godshill company was to be paid £200 as compensation for loss of office. The IWCR formally assumed control of the line on and from 1st October 1913.

The IWC general manager reported at a meeting of shareholders on 12th February 1914 that the Newport, Godshill and St Lawrence Railway had no rolling stock of its own and on acquisition the company had purchased no new stock. In the past the IWC used their own stock to operate the services but now that the company had taken over the line on a permanent basis it was imperative that new stock be acquired, initially 3 or 4 new coaches. The request was however turned down when the auditor agreed that subject to Clause 32 of the Godshill Transfer Act, cost of maintenance only could be attributed; if new stock were acquired it was chargeable to the IWC Capital account. As a result of this decision, the 1914 capital allocation included, the renewal of eight wagons Nos. 25, 55, 97, 122, 124, 125, 191 and 194 together with five carriages Nos. 1, 5, 15, 41 and 42, whilst the cost of the new firebox for locomotive No. 8 was also salvaged from the Godshill takeover.

The outbreak of World War One on 4th August 1914 found the IWCR (with other British railway companies) under Goverment control. Train services continued to run to pre-war timetables and goods traffic flourished as increased produce was despatched to make up for loss of imported food. Local railwaymen soon answered the call to arms and the IWC, finding a shortage of manpower, was forced to recruit women on a temporary basis although, as far as is known, none were employed on the Ventnor Town branch.

The IWC operation of the branch suffered from torrential rain which fell from 4 pm on 9th December 1914 until 5 pm the following day. The resultant torrent caused a bank slip near Roud, although fortunately no train was trapped south of the site. Remedial work was soon arranged and between 60 and 70 wagons of ballast were required to make good the slippage. The IWC authorities showed great credit in such prompt repairs, for the Ventnor Town line was reopened in time for the passage of the 10.20 am ex Newport train on 11th December. The torrential rain also caused bank slips between Shide and Blackwater, and Horringford and Sandown Waterworks siding, although these were less severe than the incident at Roud.

In July 1916 Percy Mortimer, the former chairman of the NGSLR and owner of Ventnor Stone Quarries (located alongside the railway near Ventnor Town station), offered to sell the quarry to the IWCR for £450. The offer was turned down but in August 1916 Mortimer advised he was willing to accept the sum of £250 for the freehold of approximately $2\frac{3}{4}$ acres. The matter was put to the directors on 9th August. The secretary reported that the company had provided a siding some 225 feet in length connecting with 165 yards of tramway type track which facilitated loading of the stone. The plant at the quarry consisted of a stone crusher, 3 tipping wagons, a grindstone, two huts and some timber with an ascertainable value of £100. The stone extracted from the quarry when crushed was suitable for railway purposes and in fact the IWCR was paying 3/6d per ton for shingle suitable for ballasting permanent way. The new offer was considered a bargain and was readily accepted by the IWCR board.

Heavy and continuous rain during November and December 1917 culminated in a further fall of rock on to the railway near St Lawrence station on New Year's Day 1918. The line was blocked to traffic but was cleared in time for the passage of the 1.50 pm passenger train ex Newport.

In June 1918 the Government control of the railway and withdrawal of finances led to a realisation that arrears of maintenance and renewal of works were mounting. A final damning condemnation of the former Godshill line came five and a half years after the takeover at the IWCR annual general meeting held on 20th February 1919. The meeting voted a generous remuneration of £3,000 to Russell Willmott as a reward for his effective and economic management of the railway which resulted in a viable undertaking. The 1913 takeover of the NGSLR was especially mentioned on account of the large saving it had produced. Percy Mortimer, the former chairman, was aggrieved and insulted by this latter statement and contended the line only lost money because of the very poor service provided by the Central company. He suggested that if the railway had been run as he intended, it would have been profitable. Willmott in reply rebuffed the challenge and somewhat truthfully said as far as he was concerned it was 'a worthless railway'.

A wave of serious industrial disputes brought havoc to the railways in the post-war years and from 26th September to 5th October 1919 there was a general railway strike when the Ventnor Town branch was closed. This event, coupled with the Coal Strike in 1921 and the General Strike of 1926 when services were again withdrawn, started the decline in railway freight traffic when farmers and growers realised for the first time that goods could effectively be sent by road instead of rail (using in some cases old army vehicles).

Thus, with the internal combustion engine showing its competitive powers against the railway companies, and rural bus services commencing operation in many parts of Britain, the time was ripe for the grouping of many small companies into four larger units. The necessary powers were sought and the Railways Act of 1921 effectively numbered the days of the old Isle of Wight Central Railway.

The epitome of the Ventnor West branch train in the early years of the Southern Railway before push/pull working was introduced. 'Terrier' W11 (later named Newport) is approaching Ventnor West with a train of six 4-wheel coaches.
COLLECTION R. SILSBURY

CHAPTER FIVE
SOUTHERN RAILWAY

ON the grouping of the railways from 1st January 1923, the Island railways (with the exception of the Freshwater, Yarmouth and Newport), together with the former joint railways ferry services, came under the control of the Southern Railway. The Southampton and Isle of Wight Shipping Co remained independent but offered through booking facilities. The new ownership initially brought few changes to the branch but from 1st June 1923 Ventnor Town station was more appropriately renamed Ventnor West, as the station, although on town level, was over half a mile from the centre of the community. The company also added informative appendages to the nameboards advising passengers that Ventnor West was 168 feet above sea level and the former IWR terminus 294 feet above sea level. By high summer the financial arguments over takeover of the FYNR were finally resolved and the line was absorbed into the Southern Railway on 1st August 1923.

In the same year the first serious threat to the monopoly the railway enjoyed came when Dodson Brothers Ltd increased their fleet of buses to a total of eighteen vehicles. Dodson and Campbell Ltd had established bus operations on the Island in 1921 with a fleet of three solid-tyred Daimler 'Y' type AEC 29-seater vehicles, DL2446, DL2447 and DL2448. The buses, in red and blue livery bearing the fleet name 'Vectis', gradually entered service on every important road on the island. Offering almost a door-to-door service, the buses made inroads into the passenger receipts of the railway. A Newport–Godshill–Shanklin bus service commenced on 1st June 1922 to be followed later by a Carisbrooke to Niton via Newport and Godshill service which was then extended to Ventnor. In October 1923 competition grew with the commencement of a service from Newport to Ventnor via Chale, Blackgang, Niton and St Lawrence.

In an endeavour to arrest the loss of passenger traffic from the branch and to counteract the competition, the Southern Railway authorities sought ways of reducing operating costs and improving the service. The Ventnor West line with its meagre returns was a prime candidate for push and pull operation and in 1924 two ex London Chatham and Dover Railway two-coach 4-wheel permanently coupled sets, Nos 483 and 484, were shipped to the Island. There were, however, no locomotives equipped with push-pull equipment until O2 class 0-4-4Ts No. W23 and W24 were transferred to the Island in 1925. The sets were therefore rostered to work on the Freshwater line until suitable locomotives were equipped.

The line was not without accident or incidents and suffered its fair share of problems. At 2.40 pm on 27th October 1924 a light engine, running from Newport to Merstone to take up working the Ventnor West branch, became derailed near Blackwater down distant signal. Heavy rain during the previous few days saturated the peaty subsoil in the vicinity, with the result that the permanent way became unstable and the leading pair of wheels of the locomotive came off the track. Fortunately, the locomotive crew were uninjured and the fireman was able to report the incident promptly. As a result of the derailment, the 2.47 pm Newport to Sandown train terminated at Shide before returning to Newport, from where the locomotive was used to take a fitter to the accident. Eight trains were subsequently cancelled before the normal working was resumed with the 5.47 pm Newport to Sandown train.

Services were again delayed by a landslip near the north end of St Lawrence tunnel on 2nd January 1925. Sixty hours of continuous heavy rain later in the month culminated in the flooding of the railway at Shide and in three places between Merstone and Sandown in the early hours of 27th January 1925 after the Rivers Medina and Eastern Yar both burst their banks. Initially both the Newport to Ventnor West and Merstone to Sandown services were suspended but the line at Shide was available for the passage of the 12.47 pm Newport to Ventnor West service. Thereafter a full service was maintained between Newport and Merstone and Merstone to Ventnor West but the line between the junction and Sandown was blocked until the following day. A seven-day rail strike later in the year contributed to a further decline in traffic.

In 1926 push/pull train working commenced after four 'Terrier' tank locomotives were fitted with the necessary control equipment.

Services on the branch were badly affected by the General Strike in early May 1926. Union members withdrew their labour in support of the miners, train services could not be guaranteed and for several days services were suspended. Fortunately wiser counsels prevailed and railwaymen returned to work within days but the impact of the continuing miners strike meant that coal stocks available to the railway company were low. The SR authorities decided on the only course of action available and reduced train services to conserve supplies of coal. During these problematic times the Vectis bus company operated extra journeys.

At 9.0 am on 3rd July 1926 the porter at Whitwell station discovered a packing case on fire on the down platform. The case (containing lamps) was completely destroyed and, before the flames could be extinguished with buckets of water, the window frame to the staff room and the canopy roof were scorched. The fire was attributed to sparks from the engine of the 8.28 am ex Ventnor West train, as it started away from the station, igniting straw in the packing case.

On 10th November 1926 the 8.50 am Merstone to Ventnor West goods was shunting the siding at St Lawrence at 9.6 am when two wagons were derailed at the points leading from the main single line to the siding. The breakdown vans were summoned from Newport and arrived at 10.15 am. After necessary jacking and packing, the wagons were rerailed and the line cleared by 12.01 pm with two trains cancelled. At the subsequent enquiry it was concluded that the weight of the engine on the heel of the switch of the catch point had caused the tip of the switch to rise and derail the wagons. It was also noted that the sleepers were in poor condition but, as the siding had not been used for the previous six months, little inspection had been made of the permanent way.

At 1.55 pm on 22nd June 1927, during a movement of empty wagons from the Up siding to the Sandown loop line at Merstone, the eleventh vehicle from the engine became derailed at the catch points in the siding, resulting in an obstruction of the loop line. The Newport breakdown gang was requested to attend to the blockage and reached Merstone at 2.40 pm. The offending wagon was quickly rerailed and

IWCR No. 8, built by Beyer Peacock & Co. in 1898, waiting to depart from Ventnor West in early SR days, working bunker-first to Merstone and displaying the wrong head-code. No. 8 was finally withdrawn in November 1929.
REAL PHOTOGRAPHS

normal working resumed at 4.15 pm. The derailment was caused by one of the flanges of the wheel of the vehicle (which was being taken for scrap) being 'sharp edged'. During the obstruction all trains used the Ventnor loop line at Merstone, causing inconvenience to passengers interchanging to and from branch services.

Whilst the majority of the former IWCR system was relaid with bullhead track supported in chairs over the period 1912 to 1917, the former NGSLR line still retained flat-bottom track spiked directly to the sleepers. After taking stock of their island assets, the new management soon decided that energy and capital should first be spent on the main Ryde–Ventnor line where traffic was most lucrative. Next for consideration came the Ryde–Newport–Cowes line with its heavy freight flows and residential passenger traffic. Despite serious discussions both at Waterloo and Newport to find ways of generating traffic on the Merstone–Ventnor line, little could be achieved. As the IWCR had previously experienced, the SR found the branch was losing money and was proving a financial burden to the rest of the Island system. As a result of their findings, the new management instituted a further series of economies which transformed the line into a 'basic railway'.

Station staff at Godshill and St Lawrence were withdrawn with stations reduced in status to halts, leaving Whitwell manned by one porter/signalman. In 1926 the loop at Whitwell was secured out of use, the signal box closed and points to the goods yard transferred to a ground frame locked and unlocked (as were those at Godshill and St Lawrence) by an Annetts Key attached to the train staff. The crossing loop, little utilized since installation, was an expensive luxury the new company did not need and could ill afford to upkeep. At Ventnor West the signal box was switched out except when trains required to shunt the sidings in the goods yard or when the push-pull set was not used on the passenger train. As a result of the rationalisation, the branch was reduced to the 'one engine in steam' method of working operated by push-and-pull train using the ex LCDR sets 483 and 484 hauled by Terrier tank locomotives. In 1928 the SR commenced the relaying of permanent way, replacing the flat-bottom track with bull-head rail.

After the rationalisation programme the branch continued as a sleepy backwater of the Island railway system, surviving the bout of branch line closures which were effected in the late 1920s and early 1930s by the Southern Railway and other systems. Certainly former Island railwaymen thought the branch would follow the fate of the Basingstoke and Alton line or Bishops Waltham branch but unconfirmed reports suggest the line survived because holiday traffic in summer months bolstered the flagging receipts. The branch was certainly popular with travellers for its scenic quality (said to be the best on the Island). The other factor was that in the event of problems on the former IWR route causing lengthy blockage, the Ventnor West branch was an alternative route.

Under powers granted to the main line railway companies by the Railway (Road Transport) Act of 1928 enabling them to operate road passenger vehicles, the Southern acquired a fifty-one per cent interest in the Vectis Omnibus Company in August 1929 with the other forty-nine per cent retained by Dodson Brothers. The new alliance was renamed the Southern Vectis Omnibus Company and operated thirty-six vehicles, retaining the red and blue livery. In that year the company was operating a Newport to Ventnor service via Rookley, Godshill, Whitwell, Niton and St Lawrence in direct competition with the branch.

A Southern Railway directors special train visited the branch in the spring of 1931 when the chairman, Brigadier General The Hon Everard Baring, Sir Herbert Walker, general manager, and other directors toured the Island system and inspected the new installations at Medina Wharf. After staying overnight at Ventnor, the party travelled in the special train consisting of four-wheel saloon and four-wheel two-coach push-and-pull set from Ventnor West to Newport, Cowes, Medina Wharf and Freshwater.

The 'Terrier' tanks became the standard branch engine on introduction of push-pull services but from the early 1930s Sunday services which operated to Cowes or Freshwater were diagrammed for O2 class engines, which necessitated the opening of Ventnor West signal box for the locomotive to run round the train.

After eleven years in the bus operating business and with a fleet increasing from three to sixty, Dodson Brothers relinquished their shareholding in Southern Vectis in 1932, selling out to Messrs Tilling and British Automobile Traction Ltd. The Southern Railway, through holding the controlling interest, diffused the road competition against the Island railway and services were reformed into an integrated system providing connecting services to places on the Island not served by rail. At the same time the livery of the buses was changed from red and blue to the familiar green and cream, and joint rail/road bookings were introduced. By 1933 SVOC Route 9 was running from Newport to Ventnor via Godshill and Whitwell parallel to the railway.

Because of continuing ailing finances on the branch and in an endeavour to effect further savings, the Southern Railway authorities decided to operate the Merstone–Ventnor back shift passenger services without a guard during the winter months commencing in October 1934. The initial arrangements involved a Junior Parcels porter working early turn in Newport parcels office one week and late turn on the branch on the alternate week. The duties of the post on the branch included the issue and collection of tickets at Godshill and St Lawrence, and also at Whitwell and Ventnor West if no staff were in attendance, booking, loading and unloading of parcels including livestock and cleaning the train at each end of the line. After the last trip to Merstone the coaching stock was berthed in the siding and the porter then travelled in the cab of the light engine back to Newport station before booking off duty.

During the summer months working using two shift of guards continued. Of the many guards who worked the branch, several were involved in incidents. George Francis, in attempting a quick shunt into No 1 siding at Merstone, isolated the brakes on the coaching stock from the engine after discovering a brake pipe on the seat of a carriage. The driver on 'Terrier' tank No 11 was aghast to find on applying the Westinghouse brake that no retardation was taking place. To everyone's chagrin the coaches collided with wagons loaded with ashes standing hard against the buffer stops, severely damaging the end wagons and covering Merstone station and surrounding area liberally with a blanket of ash dust. In another incident at the junction Guard Bill Dibden gave Driver Hollands on No 11 the 'right away' without ascertaining if the points were set and the signals cleared. Hollands was as much to blame for what subsequently occurred. He had been oiling up the 'Terrier', and on hearing the whistle and seeing the green flag he leapt on the footplate, opened the regulator without checking the signals. The engine was derailed 'all wheels'.

Heavy rain during October 1937 caused a landslide at the vulnerable south end of St Lawrence Tunnel, closing the branch to traffic until civil engineering staff could clear the line.

Despite the distant rumblings of closure, throughout the 1930s the Southern did much to advertise the attractions of the line to the travelling holidaymakers, and ran trains hourly over the branch throughout most of the day and twice each way on Sundays during the summer timetable. In 1938 three former London Brighton and South Coast bogie coaches were transferred from the mainland to replace the four-wheeled coaches. Services were then generally run with one coach in the winter months and two coaches during the summer, all vehicles forming set 503 and allocated to Newport.

Just prior to the outbreak of World War Two, the SR, like the other major railway companies, came under the control of the Railway Executive Committee. Local bus services were

A1X 0–6–0T No. W13 Carisbrooke *by the coaling stage at Merstone, sandwiched between ex-LCDR push/pull sets 483 (behind bunker) and 484, on 13th September 1937. Vehicles shown are Brake Third 4111, Composite 6368 and Composite 6369.*   S. W. BAKER

drastically reduced and some removed from the road by petrol rationing. There were indeed plans to eliminate rail services on the Ventnor West branch but after reviewing the use of the route as an alternative to the Ryde–Ventnor line, the service was retained, although now reduced to four trains in each direction weekdays only.

In order to reduce risks during air raids at night when station lamps were dimmed, staff utilized shielded hand lamps to attend to train and shunting duties. As a precaution against enemy attack, the station nameboards were covered or removed and stored under lock and key in lamp rooms and signal boxes. On the outbreak of hostilities the Southern authorities decided to shunt rolling stock from the branch stations into St Lawrence Tunnel at night to prevent damage. The procedure was soon abandoned as shunting took a considerable amount of time after the passage of the last train at night and before the first train in the morning. Tank traps were also placed across the line at the south end of St Lawrence Tunnel but were considered ineffective and quickly redundant.

The agricultural nature of freight handled at Godshill and Whitwell and to a lesser extent at Ventnor West was of importance as the need for the provisions of home-grown food increased. The traffic despatched from goods yards was in greater quantities than had been experienced since the line opened to traffic. The colossal growth in the carriage of sugar beet in the war years occasionally necessitated the running of special goods trains in the 'lifting season'.

During hostilities the branch experienced a few narrow escapes. On 14th November 1940 at 11.45 pm a delayed action bomb fell on an earth bank just under a quarter of a mile from Ventnor West station and 90 feet from the Whitwell Road. As a result, the line was closed to trains between St Lawrence and the terminus, and Ventnor West station closed. The branch remained closed for almost two days until services resumed with the passage of the 5.8 pm Newport to Ventnor West train after the military authorities stated the line was safe.

The resumption of services was short-lived, however, for the following night another delayed action bomb fell near St Lawrence Tunnel. The line was immediately closed to traffic as a precaution. Before traffic resumed, a further bomb exploded in the same area and the line remained closed during the morning before reopening with the passage of the 1.08 pm Newport to Ventnor West service.

On 25th November 1940 another bomb fell in soft ground 400 yards from Ventnor West station. The bomb failed to explode and was defused by the Bomb Disposal Unit. Trains were again terminated at St Lawrence for the emergency period.

During an air raid on Ventnor on 17th January 1943 the signal box and station buildings at Ventnor West received superficial blast and shrapnel damage. Further damage was caused on 26th April 1944, and on 15th July of that year a V1 flying bomb exploded in the air half a mile from Ventnor West station, again causing superficial damage.

The Isle of Wight was in the front line throughout World War Two and, after the 'phoney war' period, restrictions were placed on casual visitors to the Island. From 1940 until 1944 there were no enhanced summer train services and surplus rolling stock was given a coat of protective grey paint and stabled in various sidings including Merstone, Whitwell and Ventnor West.

In the autumn of 1945 the branch was used by a film company making a travel documentary called a 'Chip Off the Old Rock'. To take scenic shots a flat truck (fitted out to carry a camera and camera crew) was propelled by an engine hauling a single saloon coach. The intention was to get a panoramic view of the Undercliff and sea as the train emerged from St Lawrence Tunnel. Unfortunately, when organising the event, someone had overlooked the fact that the civil engineering staff were working at the south end of the tunnel and had placed detonators on the line for protection. The thunderous explosion as the wheels passed over the detonators within the confined space and blackness of the single bore so startled the continuity girl who was sitting on a deckchair on the leading vehicle that she nearly suffered heart failure.

During one unfortunate incident at Merstone, 'Terrier' tank No 11 was left by the driver 'in gear' and with the handbrake off. The locomotive had a leaking regulator gland, enabling a small amount of steam to leak to the cylinders. This combination of circumstances resulted in the unattended No 11 slowly moving away from the platform with the branch train. The signalman fortunately noticed the train moving and managed to open the gates before the engine collided with the woodwork. Before the driver could be summoned the locomotive with its two-coach train had stalled on the curve.

After the war the railways resumed peace-time activities with run-down rolling stock and a considerable backlog of maintenance. Questions were raised in Parliament regarding the deteriorating services offered by SR and the poor condition of the rolling stock. After the General Election of July 1945 the Labour Party committed itself to the nationalisation of the railways and the days of the Southern Railway were thus numbered. The Transport Bill received the Royal Assent on 6th August 1947.

The Isle of Wight was renowned for its fine and sunny weather but occasionally during the winter months the Island experienced considerable snowstorms. 1947 was notoriously bad throughout Britain and early in the year driver Harold Lacey and his fireman were stranded in a blizzard between Merstone and Godshill and spent several hours isolated with the 'Terrier' tank and its train in the snowdrift. Driver Ted Joyce and fireman Ken West were sent with O2 W26 *Whitwell* to rescue the train with the help of local permanent way staff. After extracting the 'Terrier' tank and its coach, W26 hauled the branch train to Merstone. As the snow had eased, it was decided to try to get a train to Ventnor West using W26 and the one coach. At several points en route the snow was over the rails and filling the cuttings, but, by rushing the minor drifts, Ted Joyce managed to get the train to the terminus and then return to Merstone and Newport.

One of the last arrangements the Southern Railway authorities made before nationalisation was to transfer ex-LBSCR Class E4 0-6-2 T No 2510 to the Island for trials. During initial tests the locomotive ran on all lines with Walter Gear as nominated driver. A motive power inspector accompanied the trip over the Ventnor West branch and the run was uneventful until the engine reached Dean Crossing where the gates were closed across the railway. Unfortunately, the staff at Newport had advised all staff that the branch was to be opened especially on Sunday for the test run – except the woman crossing keeper. After some delay the good lady was found attending morning service at St Mary and St Rhadegund's Church, Whitwell.

CHAPTER SIX

THE ROUTE DESCRIBED

Interior of ex-LCDR push/pull Brake Third at Merstone on 24th August 1936. H. F. WHEELLER

INITIALLY the direction of travel on the line was designated down to Ventnor and up to Merstone but the IWCR later reversed these designations and the SR retained the notation of 'up' to Ventnor and 'down' to Merstone. In this account the later (up to Ventnor) terminology is used. Mileage was measured from zero at Cowes.

Merstone station, at 8 miles 17 chains from Cowes and 5 miles 16 chains from Sandown, was the junction for the Ventnor West branch. The construction of the new railway necessitated the abandonment of the old Isle of Wight (Newport Junction) station east of the level crossing and construction of a new station completed in 1895 on the opposite side of the crossing.

The island platform at Merstone Junction station (renamed Merstone from 1st October 1911) was 301 ft in length with booking office, waiting rooms and staff rooms contained within the single building, fronted by a canopy over each platform face. The bargeboard and end canopies supported a beautiful display of climbing roses in summer months. The track layout consisted of up and down loop lines, the down or western line used by Ventnor West branch trains being 385 ft in length from the branch points to the entry points to No. 1 siding. The siding was entered by points facing trains proceeding down the loop line which led to a 360 ft headshunt at the Newport end of the station. An engineers siding (380 ft long) ran back from the headshunt alongside and parallel to the down loop. Adjacent to this siding was a row of pine trees planted in 1903 by the IWCR to form a windbreak to protect the station and waiting passengers at the exposed location. If the down platform was required for a Sandown to Newport train to cross a Newport to Sandown working, the Ventnor West branch train was shunted into the siding until the down train had passed.

On the opposite side of the island platform was the up loop line and the parallel No. 2 siding (380 ft long) entered by trailing points for up trains. This siding, when not used for the storage of spare coaching stock, was utilized as the coal siding by local fuel merchants, and for their convenience a gate in the south end boundary fence gave access to a trackway from Merstone Lane.

At the south end of the station, the up and down loop lines were crossed on the level by Merstone Lane, the minor road leading from Arreton and Merstone village to Rookley. The gates were the only double line barriers on the Isle of Wight and the only gates operated mechanically from a signal box.

Merstone station, facing Sandown from the up home signal, showing the 380ft No. 2 siding, up platform road, down platform road, the 380ft No. 1 siding, and in the foreground the 360ft holding siding with locomotive inspection pit. The pine trees at the back of No. 1 sidings were planted by the IWCR in 1903.
COLLECTION
A. BLACKBURN

Merstone station from the Newport end, looking across No. 1 siding with ex-LBSC push/pull set No. 503 alongside the down platform. The other coaching vehicles occupying No. 2 siding in the background include ex-LBSC saloon recently ex shops and ex-SECR full third, possibly in unlined crimson.
COLLECTION
R. A. SILSBURY

Merstone station, facing Newport. The No. 1 siding headshunt on the left was used by Ventnor West trains during stand-over periods. The high ground to the right is St. George's Down.
J. H. MOSS

Facing Newport in 1949 with an engineers train on No. 1 siding. The signals are the down starters from the down and up platform roads. J. H. MOSS

The 301ft island platform at Merstone, viewed from the signal box, looking towards Newport. Through trains to Ventnor West from Cowes, Newport or Freshwater could only gain access to the branch from the down side platform.
J. H. MOSS

Merstone station, this time facing south-east, with Merstone Lane level crossing gates closed across the line. The water storage tanks were fed from the flooded underground passage. The churns are evidence of a healthy milk traffic even in 1950. St. Martin's Down is in the far distance.
J. H. MOSS

Merstone station on 24th August 1936 with Class 'O2' 0—4—4T No. 30 Shorwell waiting to depart with a train to Sandown. In the opposite platform is a Sandown to Newport train. The Saxby & Farmer signal was soon replaced by a standard SR rail-built upper quadrant (seen on page 43). The original access way from the subway tunnel (see page 19) had been boarded over to make a walkway from Merstone Lane.
H. F. WHEELER

Merstone station, facing Newport, in the late 1920s with an engineering train being shunted over the level crossing.

The Sandown–Cowes train, held at Merstone home signal while the Ventnor West branch train, formed of push/pull set 503 and 'O2' No. 35, swings round the curve towards the level crossing at Merstone station on 28th June 1950.
PAMLIN PRINTS

'O2' 0–4–4T No. 20 Shanklin in early BR malachite livery, pulling into Merstone with a Sandown to Cowes train in 1949. In the foreground is the sloping path access to the station which replaced the underground tunnel because of consistent flooding.
J. H. MOSS

MERSTONE 1924 Track Plan

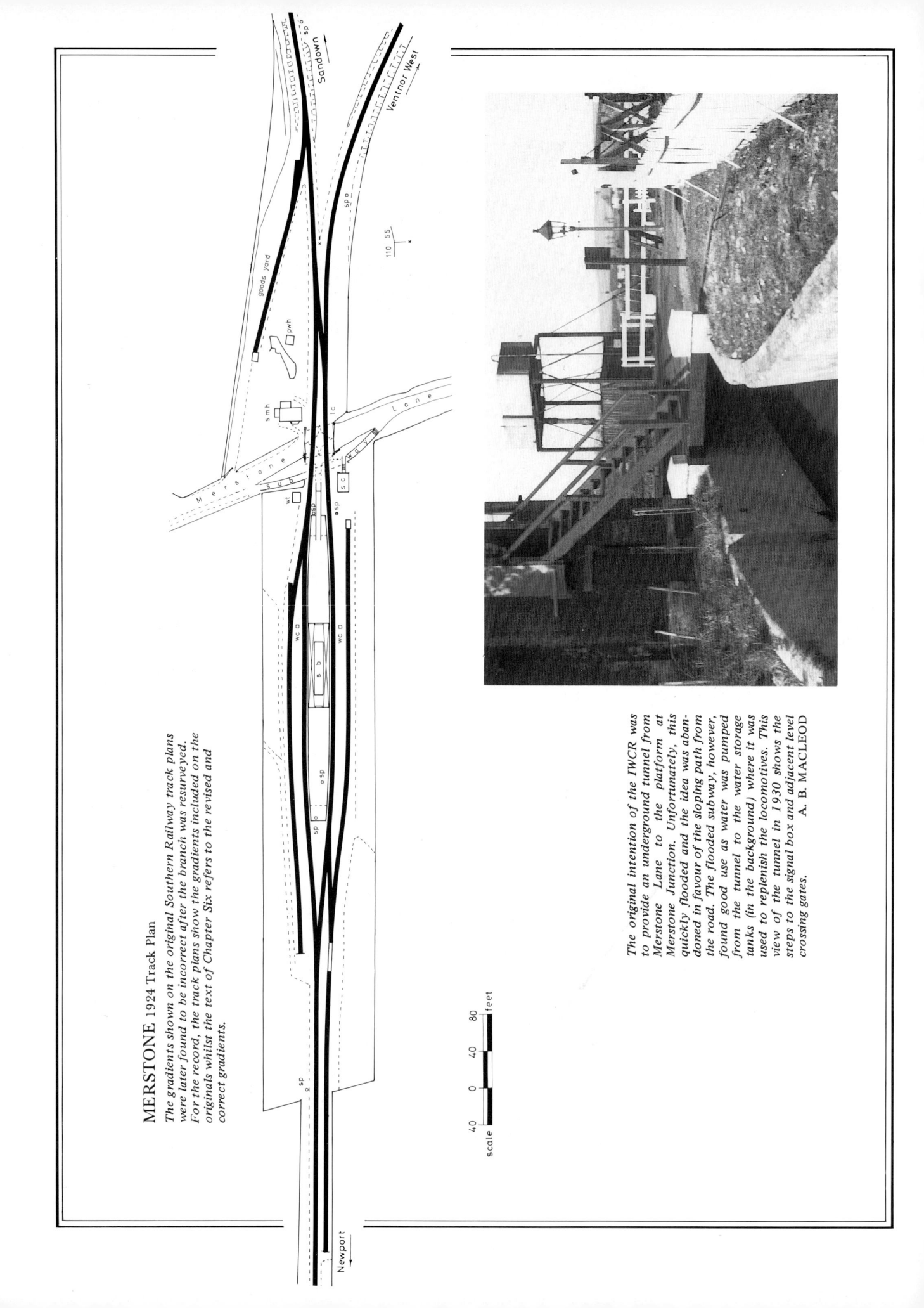

The gradients shown on the original Southern Railway track plans were later found to be incorrect after the branch was resurveyed. For the record, the track plans show the gradients included on the originals whilst the text of Chapter Six refers to the revised and correct gradients.

The original intention of the IWCR was to provide an underground tunnel from Merstone Lane to the platform at Merstone Junction. Unfortunately, this quickly flooded and the idea was abandoned in favour of the sloping path from the road. The flooded subway, however, found good use as water was pumped from the tunnel to the water storage tanks (in the background) where it was used to replenish the locomotives. This view of the tunnel in 1930 shows the steps to the signal box and adjacent level crossing gates.
A. B. MACLEOD

Merstone station from the south-east, looking across the level crossing in 1951. The gates were the only ones operated on the island from a wheel within the signal box.
COLLECTION R. A. SILSBURY

Entrance to the station was initially planned as an underground tunnel (IWCR No. 37, SR No. 16) passing under the down line but, because of consistent flooding, a path was installed from the roadway to the platform. The flooded subway later became the source of water supply for the replenishment of engines, the water being pumped from the subway to a lineside tank.

The level crossing gates, signals and points were operated from the adjacent signal box located on the down side of the down loop line adjacent to the crossing. The signal box was equipped with a frame for 28 levers and possessed an enclosed porch at the top of the stairs. Beyond the crossing and served by trailing points from the up Sandown line was the original goods siding, 200 ft in length, which saw little use in later years other than for the storage of coaching stock or loading sugar beet in season.

Away from Merstone the Ventnor West branch curved away from the Sandown line on a 12 chain radius right-hand curve,

The interior of Merstone signal box showing the 28-lever frame and the wheel to operate the level crossing gates. The key token instrument at the far end of the box was for the section to Newport. On the block shelf above the lever frame was the bell for the KT instrument and (nearer to the camera) the Preece's block instrument for the section to Sandown, with its associated switch handle by which the indication on the block instrument was altered.
E. GAMLIN

Merstone station facing Newport in 1929 with the lines to Ventnor West (left foreground) and Sandown (right foreground).

Facing south-east from Merstone signal box in 1950. To the left is the original site of Merstone station and behind that the goods yard siding. The line to Sandown can be seen in the centre of the picture, curving away to Little Budbridge and Redway Bank whilst the Ventnor West line heads away on a 12 chain radius curve on the right.
J. H. MOSS

Class 'O2' 0−4−4T No. 29 drawing a train from Sandown off the single line onto the down loop line and over the level crossing on its way to Cowes on 24th August 1936. The other home signal arm on the bracket read to the up loop line; both loop lines were bidirectionally signalled, but, as the view above shows, there was no route from the up loop line to the Ventnor West branch.
H. F. WHEELLER

'A1X' Class 0-6-0T No. 13 Carisbrooke *pulling away from Merstone with the 1.25 p.m. to Ventnor West on 16th September 1948. The Sandown line home signals can be seen above the rear coach.*
PAMLIN PRINTS

View from the driving compartment of a push/pull coach approaching Merstone down branch distant signal on 28th July 1951. In the foreground are the rail parapets of Kennerley underbridge No. 14. COLLECTION A. BLACKBURN

climbing at 1 in 200/340 before levelling out and following a straight course through a shallow cutting and then falling at 1 in 300 over Kennerley footpath crossing.

The line then negotiated a short 30 chain radius left-hand and 50 chain radius right-hand curve, climbing at 1 in 116 past Merstone down distant signal and then crossing the infant Eastern Yar by culvert No. 13 (IWCR No. 50), 8 miles 67 chains, and Kennerley underbridge No. 14 (IWCR No. 51), 8 miles 72 chains, on a section of straight track, with Little Kennerley farm to the west of the railway. The branch then negotiated a 38 chain right-hand curve, climbing 1 in 130 through a short cutting before following a straight course over Bow Bridge No. 15 (IWCR No. 52) 9 miles 31 chains, where the Newport-Godshill-Shanklin main road (later A 3020) passed under the line. Climbing at 1 in 180 across arable land, the branch crossed an occupational footpath at 9 miles 61 chains before entering Godshill station 9 miles 66 chains from Cowes. Godshill, claimed by some to be the prettiest village on the Island, was located half a mile to the east of the railway and nestling in the shadow of All Saints church. Local legend has it that when the church was being built the stones were laid on flat land at the base of the hill, but every night unknown hands took them to the top, causing local inhabitants to abandon their original plans.

The 300 ft long straight platform at Godshill, located on the up (east) side of the single line, was host to an imposing two-storey station master's house and single-storey station buildings with a half-timbered effect achieved by horizontal and vertical strips of cement on rough cast. The station building, containing

Godshill Halt, facing Merstone, in 1950. The familiar concrete SR nameboard and fencing back the platform whilst churns show that milk traffic was handled to the last. The station was downgraded to the status of a halt in 1927 and from thereon was unstaffed.
COLLECTION A. BLACKBURN

Two-coach ex-LCDR push/pull set 483 forming an SR officers special, pausing for a station inspection at Godshill in the late 1920s.

GODSHILL 1929 Track Plan

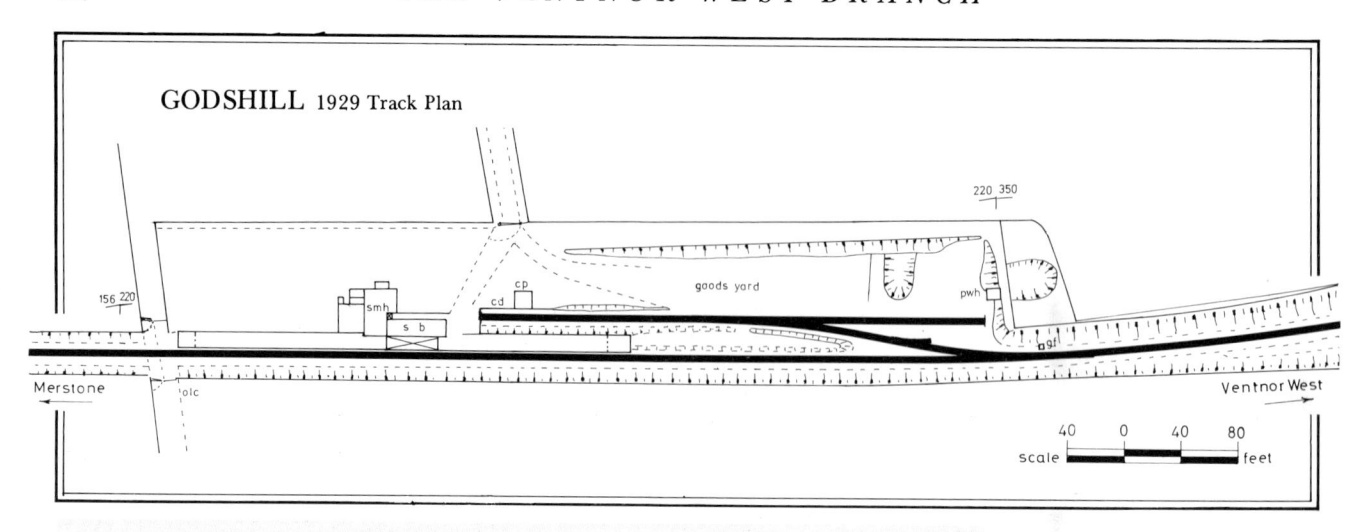

Godshill loading dock and buffer stops at the end of the 180ft siding.

View facing south from Godshill platform, showing goods yard access points and the 180ft yard siding. The 80ft headshunt is occupied by an ex-LBSCR van. The points to the siding were operated from a ground frame with lock released by Annett's Key on the train staff. The siding could only be shunted by up trains. J. H. MOSS

booking office, waiting room, toilets and staff accommodation, was fronted by a canopy spanning the platform and offering protection to passengers from adverse elements. Public access to the station from the village was along an exposed and windswept unmade road across farm fields. From the platform there were good views of the aptly named Bleak Down to the west and Rew Down to the east.

At the south end of the station, points (facing for trains proceeding to Merstone) gave access to the single goods yard siding, 180 ft in length, which ran along the back of the platform to act as a loading dock. At the opposite end of the yard was an 80 ft long headshunt which for many years was occupied by a rotting ex-LBSCR van awaiting scrapping. The station was originally equipped with up and down home and distant signals operated from a lever frame on the platform. The points to and from the siding were operated from a ground frame on the up side adjacent to the points. The point lock was released by an Annett's Key attached to the train staff.

The siding, referred to in the original company publicity as 'a modest goods yard', was served by a small unmade trackway to enable horse-drawn carts and road vehicles to load and unload merchandise from railway wagons.

No. 35 Freshwater, *near Bridge Court underbridge, climbing away from Godshill with an afternoon train formed of push/pull unit 503 on 28th July 1951. The engine was working Newport duty 16 as depicted by the headboard mounted on the top lamp bracket. The branch headcode is correct but, in true branch-line malpractice, the tail lamp was also being carried.* PAMLIN PRINTS

Leaving Godshill, the branch continued climbing at 1 in 180 for a further quarter of a mile, negotiating two short 30 chain radius left-hand curves through a shallow cutting, before the gradient eased to 1 in 300.

The railway then crossed the wrought iron Bridgecourt underbridge No. 16 (IWCR No. 53) at 10 miles $2\frac{1}{2}$ chains, and Bow Court farm underbridge No. 17 (IWCR No. 54) at 10 miles 9 chains, before climbing at 1 in 72 for a quarter mile to Nodehill (or Noddyhill) underbridge No. 18 (IWCR No. 55) at 10 miles 24 chains where the minor road from Godshill to Chale Green passed under the line. The infant Eastern Yar river kept close company on the west side of the line as the branch entered a short 41 chain radius right-hand curve to follow a straight course, climbing at 1 in 100 across undulating farmland, to Roud underbridge No. 19 (IWCR No. 56) at 10 miles 54 chains, constructed of wrought iron girders on brick parapets. Beyond the bridge the gradient stiffened to 1 in 72 for a mile, initially through a cutting where the railway was spanned by Roud footbridge No. 20 (IWCR No. 57) at 10 miles 79 chains. Continuing on a straight course, the branch then ran across a long embankment, passing over Millers Lane underbridge No. 21 (IWCR No. 58) at 11 miles 30 chains. Left-hand curves of 47 chains and 23 chains brought the railway on a converging path with the Godshill to Whitwell road which was crossed on Southford underbridge No. 23 (ICWR No. 60) at 11 miles 60 chains. Immediately beyond the bridge the branch ran through a short cutting before passing under Whitwell cart track overbridge No. 24 (IWCR No. 61), 11 miles $77\frac{1}{2}$ chains, to follow a straight course to Whitwell cattle creep No. 25 (IWCR No. 62), 12 miles 12 chains, on a rising 1 in 250 gradient, thence to enter Whitwell station at 12 miles 20 chains.

Both platforms at Whitwell were 258 ft in length. The down platform was provided with only a small waiting shelter whilst on the up side was built a two-storey half-timbered station master's house and adjacent single-storey station building, fronted over the platform by a canopy supported by strong

Roud footbridge (numbered 20 by the SR and 57 by the IWCR), spanning the branch at 10 miles 79 chains from Cowes, was constructed of wrought iron girders on brick abutments with timber decking and had a span of 35ft 2in. This view was taken looking towards Merstone.
A. BLACKBURN

The rail parapets of Southford underbridge are in the foreground of this view looking towards Godshill with the falling gradient of 1 in 72 beyond. The structure was SR No. 23, IWCR No. 60.
A. BLACKBURN

WHITWELL 1925 Track Plan

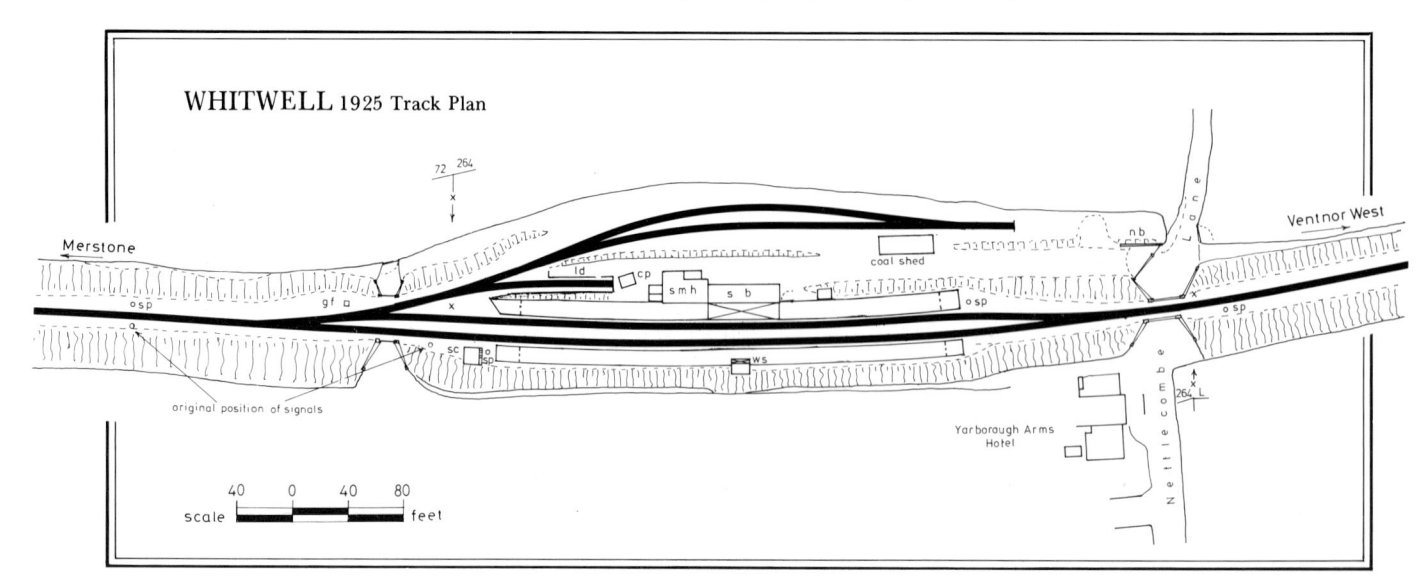

The NGSLR was taken over by the IWCR in 1913 but, despite all efforts to attract passengers, the route to Ventnor by the IWR was more popular. When the SR took over the island system in 1923, serious efforts were made to bring the railways to modern standards and economies were made. The IWCR route to Ventnor with small amounts of traffic could not justify the retention of the rarely used crossing loop at Whitwell. It was subsequently taken out of use in 1926 but remained in situ for over two years before removal. This photograph, facing Godshill and Merstone, taken on 5th November 1928, shows the signal box and signals still in place.

H. C. CASSERLEY

Whitwell station, facing Ventnor, in earlier years when the crossing loop was in use. The station master's house and single-storey station building including booking office and waiting room, were on the up side whilst the down side was provided with a small waiting shelter. In this picture a Ventnor Town to Merstone train, hauled by a 'Terrier' 0–6–0T, is entering Whitwell.

COLLECTION
A. BLACKBURN

wooden brackets. Fencing along each platform was originally wooden railings but those on the up platform were replaced by the SR which installed its standard concrete fencing. Before 1926 Whitwell was the intermediate crossing place on the branch with the up and down loop lines 520 feet in length. The points and signalling were controlled from the Saxby & Farmer-built signal box located on the down (west) side of the line at the north end of the down platform.

As part of the SR's rationalisation programme, the down loop line was taken out of use in 1926 and totally removed two years later. The goods yard was located on the east side of the line with sidings extending round the back of the station buildings. The entry points facing Ventnor-bound trains (originally controlled from the signal box) were located in the up loop line and gave access to the cattle dock siding 100ft in length, the 'Long siding' 360 feet in length and the run-round loop siding. After closure of the signal box, the points were operated from a ground frame with the facing point lock lever locked and unlocked by Annett's Key attached to the train staff. Whitwell village, taking its name from White Well (a place of pilgrimage in Medieval times), lay to the west of the railway, hugging the side of a valley of a tributary of the Eastern Yar. Access to the station and goods yard from the village was a wide approach road from Nettlecombe Lane on

The approach road from Nettlecombe Lane to Whitwell station in 1949. The van on the left stood by the buffer stops on the long siding for many years. On the right the main single line can be seen passing over Whitwell Bridge (No. 26) before curving away on 19 and 35 chain radius curves towards Dean Crossing and the Downs. J. H. MOSS

Whitwell or Nettlecombe Lane underbridge No. 26 (IWCR No. 63) and beyond the entrance gate to Whitwell station. The clearance of the structure is shown as 14ft 6in.
A. BLACKBURN

The up distant signal for Dean Crossing, seen looking back towards Whitwell on 18th May 1952. P. J. GARLAND

Dean Crossing, facing Ventnor Town, in 1920. The crossing keeper's cottage is on the left whilst the wooden hut on the right, with ornate finials, housed the ground frame which operated the gate lock and up and down protecting signals. The down home, set a good distance from the gate, can be seen in the cutting just to the right of the IWCR notice. The lattice footbridge (IWCR No. 65, SR No. 27) was installed to obviate delays to pedestrians but this was removed and transferred to Wroxall on 27th August 1926 before it received the SR number. H. J. PATTERSON RUTHERFORD

THE ROUTE DESCRIBED

the up side of the line. In the 1920s Len Cotton conveyed passengers to and from the village and Niton in his horse-drawn coach 'Victoria'.

Leaving Whitwell station on the 35 chain left-hand curve, the line crossed Nettlecombe Lane on Whitwell Bridge No. 26 (IWCR 63), 12 miles 30 chains, with the adjacent Railway Hotel (later Yarborough Arms) on the down side of the line. Beyond the bridge the line negotiated 19 and 35 chain right-hand curves across a shallow embankment, climbing at 1 in 93 over Berryl footpath crossing at 12 miles 40 chains. The line continued on a straight course with the high land of Week Down closing in on the up or east side and a fine view of the Church of St Mary and St Rhadegund and adjacent vicarage (later Youth Hostel) at the south end of the village on the down or west side. A long 63 chain radius left-hand curve across meadow land brought the line to Dean crossing, 12 miles 77 chains. The gates here were hand-operated. They were interlocked with home (later distant) signals and in later years a warning bell, operated by approaching down trains depressing a treadle, sounded when any services departed from Ventnor Town, assisting the gatekeeper by giving 7 minutes warning of the need to close the gates against road traffic. South of Dean crossing a lattice footbridge, IWCR No. 65 (SR No. 27), was installed across the line to enable pedestrians to cross when the gates were closed. This was an expensive luxury for such a minor branch, and the Southern transferred the footbridge to Wroxall station on 27th August 1926. Alongside the bridge on the up side of the line was the brick-built crossing keeper's cottage. After the crossing, the branch continued climbing at 1 in 93 on the 63 chain left-hand curve through a deepening cutting, before levelling out and entering St Lawrence or High Hat Tunnel 619 yards in length. Structure No. 28 (IWCR No. 66) was constructed of brick semi-circular arch with masonry abutments and 14 feet 11 inch square span. Immediately on entering the northern portal, the line began to fall at 1 in 55 following a straight course, before swinging left on a 14 and then 12 chain radius curve to emerge high above the village of St Lawrence and the Undercliff. St Lawrence Tunnel was reputed to be extremely damp in places and, as a precaution, train crews working the first train of the day through the portal in damp and cold weather, were advised to keep well inside the cab as there was great danger of injury from icicles hanging down from the roof of the tunnel.

A 12 chain radius left-hand curve took the branch across St Rhadegund's footpath crossing at 13 miles 44 chains before

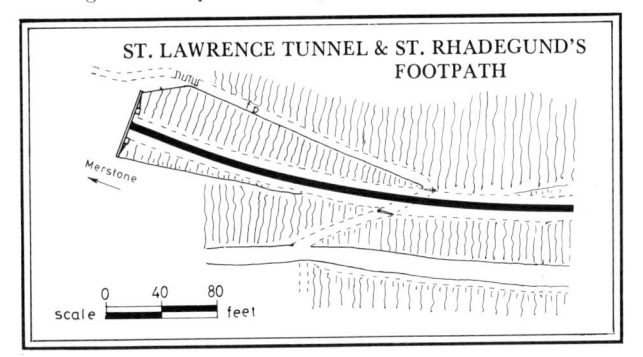

'O2' Class 0–4–4T W30 Shorwell leaving St. Lawrence Tunnel with a Cowes–Ventnor West train on 21st July 1935. After the relaying of the permanent way, 'O2' class engines usually hauled through services from Cowes, Newport or Freshwater.   S. W. BAKER

The view that made the Ventnor West branch so popular with travellers – the breathtaking panorama above the undercliff. Here 'Terrier' No. 8 Freshwater, with push/pull set No. 484, is crossing St. Rhadegund's footpath crossing after emerging from St. Lawrence tunnel on 23rd July 1935. The footpath crossing can be seen in the foreground and the post carrying its protecting warning bell.

S. W. BAKER

Facing Ventnor West from St. Lawrence Halt platform. The station signboards still carried the Southern Railway titles when this picture was taken in 1951. Beyond the bridge the line curved out of sight on a 47 chain left-hand curve. J. H. MOSS

continuing on a straight section of line, hugging close to the downland cliff on a ledge where the gradient eased to 1 in 78 falling. A 47 chain right-hand curve on a 1 in 160 falling gradient brought the line to St Lawrence station 13 miles 62 chains.

The single platform on the down side of the line, 220 ft in length, with its attendant half-timbered and Ventnor stone station master's house and station offices, was wedged between the railway and road leading from St Lawrence Shute to the village. The station building was a combined structure with the station master's accommodation on the first floor and the booking office, staff room, and a waiting room on the ground floor. Because of the steep gradient on the road, it was level with the first floor opposite the station master's front door.

St. Lawrence Halt, viewed from under the arch of St. Lawrence Shute overbridge which was constructed chiefly of Ventnor stone.

St. Lawrence station, 5 miles 44 chains from Merstone and 13 miles 62 chains from Cowes, was wedged between high downland and a public road. It had a 220ft long platform located on a 1 in 160 falling gradient and was temporary terminus of the line from 1897 to 1900. The siding serving the small goods yard can just be seen beyond the bridge. This photograph was taken in 1930 when flat-bottom track was still in use.
REAL PHOTOGRAPHS

THE ROUTE DESCRIBED

ST. LAWRENCE 1925 Track Plan

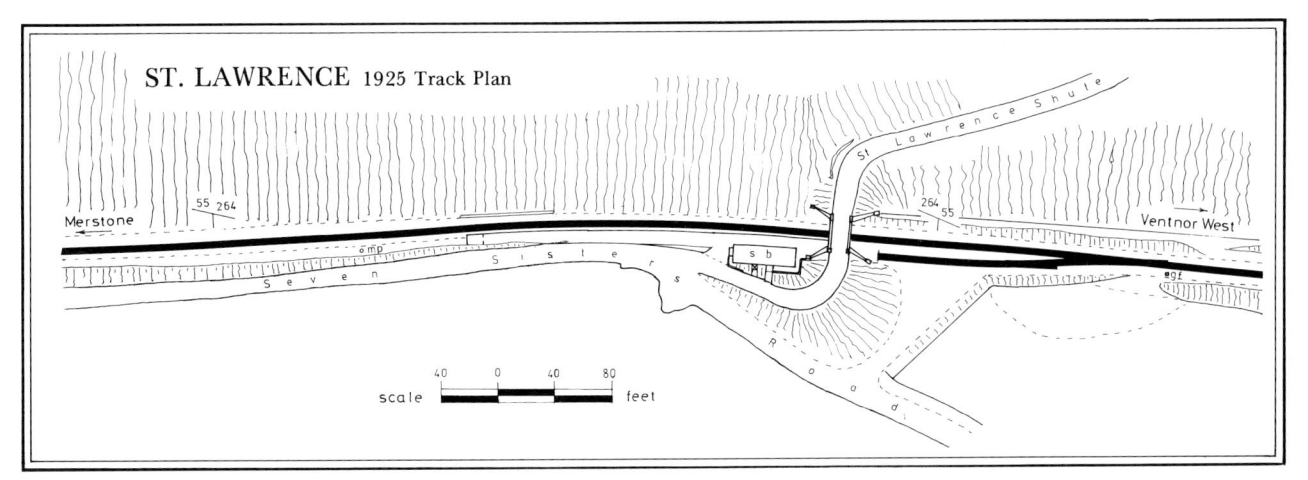

Looking towards Merstone in 1950 from St. Lawrence Shute overbridge.

Facing west towards Merstone from St. Lawrence Halt, showing the steep rise of the downland and the 1 in 78/55 rising gradient towards St. Lawrence tunnel. J. H. MOSS

THE VENTNOR WEST BRANCH

A 'Terrier' tank hauling ex-LCDR push/pull set No. 483 away from St. Lawrence Halt towards Ventnor West on 24th April 1937.
COLLECTION R. SILSBURY

From 1897 until 1900, when St Lawrence was terminus of the line, a ground frame on the platform operated a distant, home and starting signals and points to a run-round loop line located east of the station where there was also a goods yard siding. During this period, after disembarking passengers, the train was taken forward into the loop where the engine ran round the train before returning to the platform for the return journey. After extension of the line to Ventnor, the loop was removed but the single goods siding 140 feet in length remained until removed as part of the rationalisation programme in 1932. As the siding was on a 1 in 55 falling gradient, no shunting was permitted after dark or during fog or falling snow.

From the platform of St Lawrence the branch passed under St Lawrence Shute overbridge No. 29 (IWCR No. 67) before negotiating a 47 chain left-hand curve on a 1 in 55 falling gradient where the points to the goods yard siding formed a trailing connection for up trains until removed. A short straight section on a 1 in 94 falling gradient was followed by a 30 chain right-hand curve as the gradient eased to 1 in 320. Hugging the base of Week Down and continuing on the ledge above the Undercliff, the line then fell at 1 in 130 on a straight section of track where a gated footpath leading from the upper cliff to Pelham Woods crossed the line before passing over Pelham Woods underbridge No. 30 (IWCR No. 68). Beyond the bridge the line fell at 1 in 58 for nearly a mile, negotiating first a 30 chain left-hand curve passing over a footpath leading to Ventnor Quarry and then a straight section where the stone quarry, at one time owned by Percy Mortimer, was located to the north of the branch.

The points leading to the short quarry siding formed a trailing connection for up trains 28 chains from Ventnor Town station. The quarry, which at one time possessed its own narrow

IWCR 2-4-0T No. 8 passing Ventnor Town distant signal with the 10.55 a.m. to Cowes on 11th June 1910. The distant arm was painted red with white 'V' rather crudely painted on. At this period the distant signal was workable – later it was fixed at caution. The distinctive finial marks the signal out as a product of the Railway Signal Co.
LCGB/KEN NUNN COLLECTION

VENTNOR QUARRY SIDING

Quarry — *Quarry* — shed — Ventnor West — Merstone

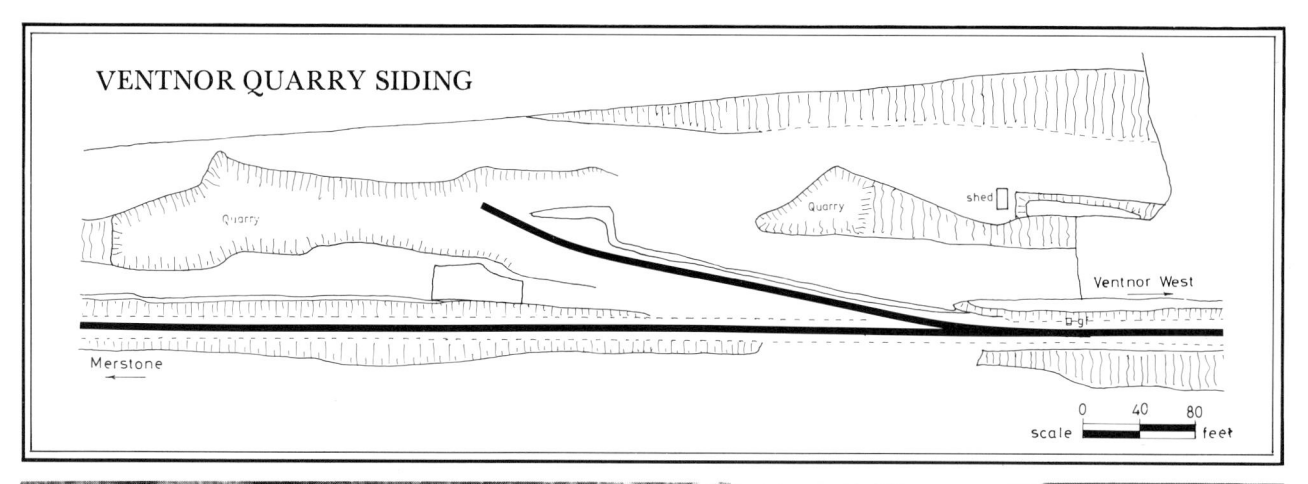

scale 0 40 80 feet

The up home signal for Ventnor Town was unusual for a passenger line. It had the arms mounted one above the other. The 'top and left' rule applied only to the two main arms, so that in order from the top, the signals read to Platform No. 1, Platform No. 2 and the goods yard.

H. F. WHEELLER

The lightweight appearance of the original flat-bottomed rail is evident in this view at Ventnor West, looking towards Merstone in June 1928. The signals and signal box were products of the Railway Signal Company. The 'hallmark' on the signal is the distinctive land around the finial. On the signal box it is the array of lower windows to the operating floor, the window high in the gable end, and the distinctive bargeboard to the end of the roof. The shed in the background was occupied by Messrs. Wood & Co. H. F. WHEELER

THE ROUTE DESCRIBED

Ventnor West station facing the buffer stops in 1930. The shed on the left of the goods yard was used by Wood & Co. (coal and coke merchants). The coal siding behind the signal box was 480ft long, and the dock road behind the down platform was 60ft long.

L & GRP, CTY. DAVID & CHARLES

'Terrier' 0–6–0T No. 10 at Ventnor West with the 2-coach ex-LCDR push/pull set in the late 1920s.

Ventnor Town station, 6 miles 68 chains from Merstone and 15 miles 6 chains from Cowes, facing the buffer stops c.1910. Two platforms were provided, each 337ft in length, but the up side, which was devoid of buildings, saw very little use as most trains terminated on the 'down' side. The IWCR originally designated the line 'down' to Ventnor Town but later altered it to 'up', a designation continued by the SR.
COLLECTION A. BLACKBURN

gauge tramway, was served by an engine propelling wagons from Ventnor Town goods yard. The siding, 280 ft in length, was removed in 1926. On the approach to Ventnor Town the branch followed a 19 chain right-hand curve over Ventnor underbridge No. 31 (IWCR No. 69), approaching the station on a 54 chain left-hand curve before entering the platforms on straight track and 1 in 215 falling gradient to the buffer stops at 15 miles 6 chains (from Cowes).

Ventnor Town (renamed Ventnor West by the Southern Railway on 1st June 1923) occupied the site of the former stables of Steephill Castle and had platforms of equal length (337 ft). On the down (or south side) platform No. 2 was the station building, which, in contrast to others on the line, was of local Ventnor grey stone. The two-storey station master's accommodation was at the west end of the structure and the single-storey building adjacent contained the booking office, refreshment room, waiting rooms and staff rooms, and had a timber canopy fronting over the platform. The up side or north platform No. 1 was devoid of buildings and remained gravelled and grass covered for most of its existence, as was the walkway connecting the platforms behind the buffer stops.

The track layout at Ventnor West consisted of a main running line with a 220 ft long run-round loop on the north side. The release crossover points were 84 yards east of the signal box. A 60 ft long dock road siding served cattle docks on the down side of the line. This siding also contained a locomotive inspection pit and an adjacent water column which enabled locomotives standing on the down platform road or dock road to replenish supplies. Access from points in the up loop line led to two sidings which served the goods yard. The northern siding, 360 ft in length known as Cliff Road, served the small timber goods shed whilst the adjacent 480 ft coal road served coal stacking grounds. Points and signals at the station were operated from the 10 ft by 10 ft timber signal box located at the west end of the up side platform. When the steam railcars worked the line, and later during push-and-pull operation, the box was only opened when trains required to shunt the goods yard or when an engine required to run-round.

In the early years the IWCR boasted that the two platforms at Ventnor Town could accommodate 20 four-wheel coaches but, with the introduction of bogie stock, six vehicles was the limit. Platform 2 was normally utilized for all workings but platform 1 on the north side was pressed into service when special workings ran on the branch, or in the inter-war years and up to 1952 annually on Ventnor Carnival Day when trains were strengthened with additional stock and extra trains ran. In the latter years when very little goods traffic was handled, the sidings were used during winter months for the storage of coaching stock.

The speed limit of trains on the branch in IWCR days was 30 mph with reduced speed required as follows:-

1. Merstone to be considered and treated as a terminal station with Up and Down trains limited to a speed of 15 mph when passing the distant signals and not more than 5 mph when passing the home signal to enable the train to be brought to a stand at the station by application of the hand brake only.
2. Whitwell station. Up trains not to pass the home signal at a greater speed than 10 mph.
3. St Lawrence Curve (between St Lawrence Tunnel and St Lawrence station). Speed of trains restricted to 10 mph from the curve in St Lawrence Tunnel for a distance of about 250 yards.
4. Ventnor Town station. Up passenger trains not to pass the distant signal at a greater speed than 15 mph and the home signal at more than 5 mph to enable the train to be brought to a stand at the station by application of the hand brake only. Up goods or coal trains were not to pass the distant signal at a greater speed than 10 mph and were required to stop at the home signal whether in the 'on' or 'off' position. The engine driver then had to await instructions from the station staff or guard as to the disposal of the train. Trains of empty coaches and other coaching stock when shunted from the platform up the gradient for the purpose of running back to the platform, after releasing the engine, were controlled by hand brake only, guards being responsible for testing the handbrake before shunting the train.
5. On entering these stations, the Westinghouse brake was to be held in reserve and used only in cases of emergency.

Unfortunately, Ventnor Town station was over a mile west of the town centre and, on takeover by the Southern Railway, the terminus was renamed more appropriately Ventnor West on 1st June 1923. The exterior of the station in the 1930s shows the fine single-storey station buildings including refreshment room and on the left the two-storey station master's house constructed of Ventnor stone. A. B. MACLEOD

A view over the buffer stops between Platforms No. 2 (on the left) and No. 1 in July 1931, with a 'Terrier' running round its short train before returning to Merstone. Note that there is a facing point lock on crossover point (No. 2 lever) in No. 1 platform, but that the point disc shown on the diagram on page 77 and in the photo on page 79 had been taken away. The holidaymakers on the left faced a long walk to the town centre and the beach. G. N. SOUTHERDEN

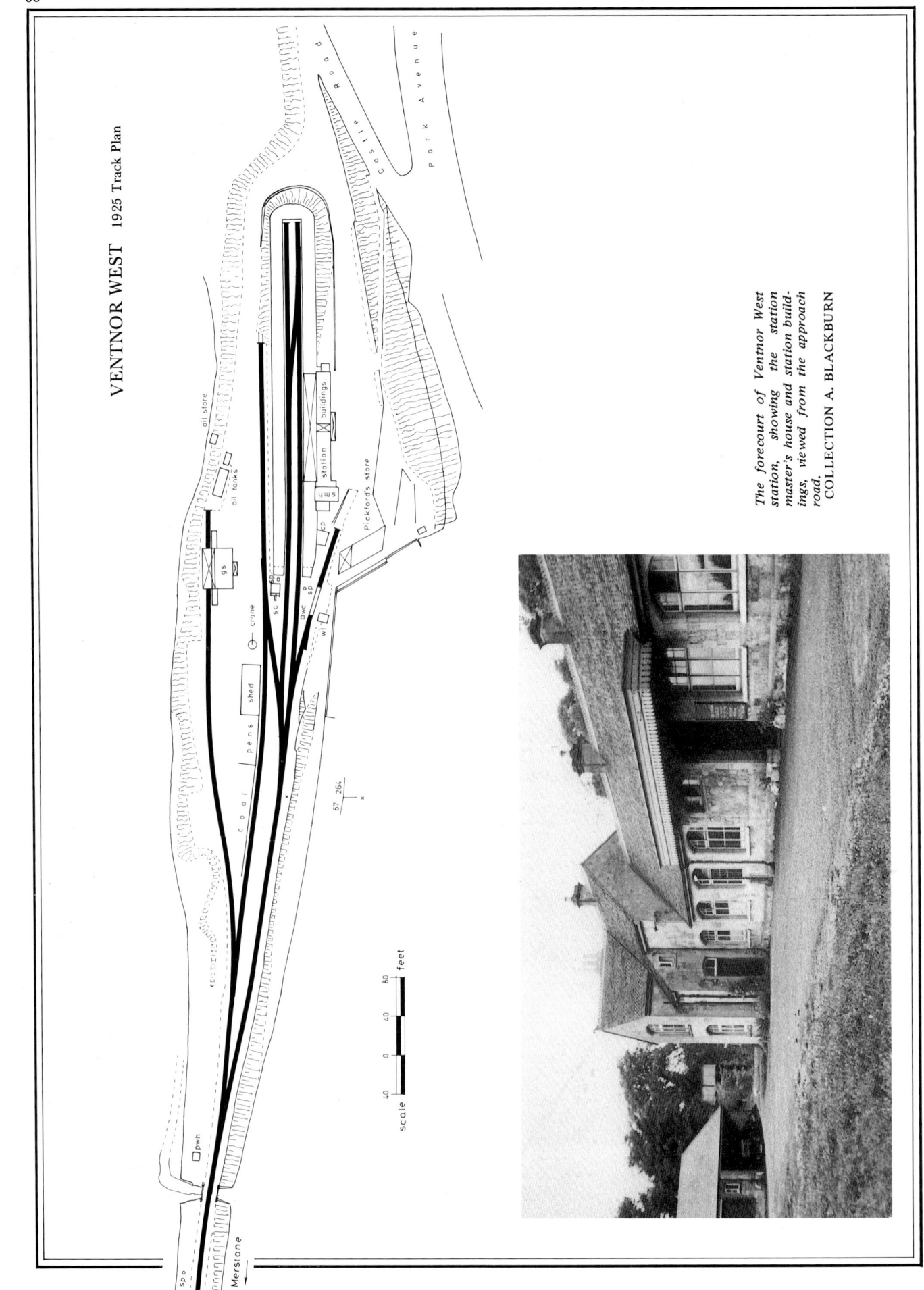

VENTNOR WEST 1925 Track Plan

The forecourt of Ventnor West station, showing the station master's house and station buildings, viewed from the approach road.
COLLECTION A. BLACKBURN

A view under the awning at Ventnor West in June 1928, revealing a substantial station, as befitted the terminus of the line. Flat-bottom track is still in place and the cover has been left off the economical facing point lock in No. 1 platform, revealing its mechanism.
H. F. WHEELLER

With the signal already off for departure, this photograph shows 'Terrier' No. W10 backing to its coaches in Platform No. 2 in June 1928, in preparation for the return journey to Merstone. The lagging on the pipework of the water column was crude but essential.
H. F. WHEELLER

Again looking towards the buffer stops with Platform 1 on the left and Platform 2 with station buildings on the right. The appendage to the Southern Railway cast concrete station nameboard denotes that Ventnor West was 168ft above sea level, 126ft lower than the former IWR terminus.
COLLECTION
A. BLACKBURN

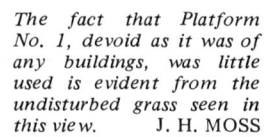

The fact that Platform No. 1, devoid as it was of any buildings, was little used is evident from the undisturbed grass seen in this view. J. H. MOSS

The 10ft square Ventnor West signal box constructed by the Railway Signal Company, shown here on 18th May 1952. The starting signal at the end of Platform 1 had acquired a cast-iron finial to its post to replace the broken one featured on page 64.
P. J. GARLAND

Right: A view of the 'steps end' of the signal box, with the usual jumble of fire buckets and tools lying under the steps. The door giving access to the locking room below the operating floor of the box can be seen through the steps. 18th May 1952.
P. J. GARLAND

The facing point at the entrance to Ventnor West station was laid out so as to give a favourable run into the right-hand platform. The economical FPL mechanism shows well in this view taken on 18th May 1952.
P. J. GARLAND

This photograph of the up platform nameboard also provides a closer view of the goods shed.
J. H. MOSS

Track relaying at Ventnor West in 1930 when 90lbs per yard rail was being installed to replace flat-bottom track. The gang are using a rail saw, jim crow, gauge and track jack.
COLLECTION J. MACKETT

Track relaying gang and trolley on the same occasion. The permanent way is formed of old IWCR flat-bottom track.
COLLECTION J. MACKETT

CHAPTER SEVEN
PERMANENT WAY AND SIGNALLING

THE permanent way on the Newport, Godshill and St Lawrence Railway was initially formed of 67 lbs per yard flat-bottom steel rails, secured by iron spikes and fang bolts to sleepers measuring 8 ft 11 ins × 10 inches × 5 inches laid on ballast stated to consist of broken stone. On inspection Lieutenant Colonel Addison found that in many places it was 'hardly distinguishable from chalk ballast'. The formation of the line varied from 16 ft to 18 ft in width. Because of the poor condition of the ballast, the inspector required complete reballasting of the whole line, a task which was ultimately completed by the IWCR. The extension to Ventnor Town was laid with 72 lbs per yard flat-bottom rails in 28 ft lengths secured by fang bolts to each sleeper with eleven sleepers under rail length. The sleepers were laid on ballast consisting of 'smashed stones'. The formation was for single track only, except at passing places or where sidings were provided, when the statutory 6 ft spacing between tracks was established. Drainage of the formation was afforded by wide ditches, and railway property was protected by post and wire fencing with the top strand of barbed wire.

When the Southern Railway absorbed the Island companies in 1923, the Ventnor Town branch permanent way was found to be substandard. Whilst the remainder of the former IWCR system had been relaid in the period 1912 to 1917, the branch was equipped with only second-hand flat-bottom rails of various weights spiked directly to the sleepers. After the Southern authorities decided the line was to be worked as a basic railway, the loop at Whitwell was secured out of use in 1926 and two years later removed when the track was totally relaid using LSWR bullhead rails of 87, 88 and 90 lbs per yard in 30 ft and 45 ft lengths. The shorter lengths were joined with 18 in 4-hole fishplates and the longer by 22 in 4-hole plates. LSWR chairs of 45 lbs supported the rails on the sleepers. In the later years British Standard rails of 90 and 95 lbs per yard were used whilst points were a mixture of standard LSWR and SR components. All rails were secondhand supplied from the mainland. Originally the ballast used by the Southern was shingle dredged from the Solent off Bembridge Ledge and loaded at St Helens Quay. From the late 1930s Blackwater gravel was used from the pits at St George's Down and forwarded from Shide.

In addition to attending day-to-day track maintenance, the permanent way gangs were responsible for cleaning toilets where no mains sewage existed as well as maintaining fences and gates. On hot and dry summer days they also patrolled the line, acting as beaters to extinguish small fires caused by stray sparks from passing locomotives. When the Merstone gang were lifting and packing the track near Godshill in June 1951, they had to leave everything after a message was received that their services were required to fight a heather and gorse fire near the junction. It appeared 'Mad' Maurice Parsons was the driver of No. 35 *Freshwater* working the branch and no further explanation as to the cause was necessary!

Maintenance of the permanent way on the branch was the responsibility of two gangs. In Southern days the section from Merstone to Whitwell was under the jurisdiction of Merstone 'B' gang ('A' gang covered Merstone to Shide) with Whitwell to Ventnor West under the Ventnor West gang. In the latter years the Ventnor West permanent way gang was formed of six men under the charge of ganger George Sibbeck. Others in the team were sub ganger J. Raw and labourers C. Punt, B. Lampard, R. Record and M. Jeffries, the last named replacing Bert Smith who had transferred to the Ventnor gang.

A near accident was averted at the last minute when the combined Ventnor West and Merstone permanent way gangs were chair scraping in St Lawrence Tunnel. Inspector Macklin, in charge of operations, had appointed Frank Buddin to act as flagman at Dean Crossing where S. Western was gatekeeper. Buddin was under strict instructions to stop all trains and advise the driver to await instructions before proceeding. Whilst in the middle of operation and with six lengths of track removed, the gang working in the inky depths of the tunnel were aghast to hear an approaching train. Immediately two or three men ran towards the locomotive shouting and waving to the driver of No. 36 *Carisbrooke* who fortunately stopped the train short of the removed rails. The train then set back out of the tunnel to await the replacements of rails and chairs. Needless to say Frank Buddin was severely reprimanded for allowing the train to proceed without authority.

SIGNALLING

Signalling on the Newport, Godshill and St Lawrence Railway line as far as St Lawrence was supplied by Saxby and Farmer Limited. The signal box at Merstone Junction was provided with a 28-lever frame with 26 working and 2 spare levers (later 25 working and 3 spares). Godshill was initially provided with a four-lever frame on the platform to work home and distant signals for each direction of travel. Points to the goods yards were operated from a ground frame released by Annett's Key attached to the train staff and this remained in use until the closure of the branch. At Whitwell the signal box of timber construction, measuring 10 ft by 10 ft with operating floor 8 ft above rail level, was equipped with a 10-lever frame with all levers working. For the three years St Lawrence enjoyed the status of terminal station, a 5-lever ground frame at the Ventnor end of the platform controlled signals and points. After extension of the line to Ventnor Town, the entry points to the single siding were operated from a ground frame which was released by Annett's Key attached to the train staff. Similar arrangements were made to control the points to the quarry siding on the approach to Ventnor. Ventnor Town signal box, with the same measurements as Whitwell, was provided with a 13-lever frame but the box and signals on this extension of the original line were provided by the Railway Signal Co of Fazakerley. Merstone Junction was protected by a distant and home signal on the branch. Godshill had working distants on 30 ft tall posts located 700 yards in rear of the home signals which had 25 ft posts. In the 1926 rationalisation programme all signals were removed. At Whitwell the crossing loop was protected by distant, home and starting signals for up and down directional movements. Dean Crossing was protected by home signals in each direction. St Lawrence, for its short period as a terminus, was provided rather strangely with a working distant located 600 yards in rear of the home signal, which itself was located on the same post as the starting signal. Ventnor West was protected by an operating (later fixed)

Whitwell station, looking towards Ventnor. The Saxby & Farmer signal cabin on the right, containing a frame for 10 levers, had an austere appearance when compared with the more ornate Railway Signal Co. cabin at Ventnor. This photograph was taken during a period of transition in the signalling at Whitwell. The down (in SR terms) right-hand line in the loop could still be used, as the shine on the rails shows, but by now it was customary for most trains to run in both directions on the up line. The signals are 'off' in both directions, with the signals which would normally apply to the down line now applying to the up line instead. The sidings on the yard had to be accessible whether the signal box was 'open' or not, so control of the running line and catch points, and the facing point lock, had been transferred to a two-lever Stevens pattern ground frame which was unlocked by a key on the train staff. The point lever in the signal box, made spare by putting the yard connection on to the ground frame, is believed to have been utilized as a 'king lever' for switching the box out, allowing the signals for both directions to be cleared at the same time, and the down direction signals to be cleared with the points set for the up line. The interlocking would normally prevent this!

distant leading to splitting home signals with a calling on arm, all accommodated on the same post. For departures both platforms were equipped with starting signals.

In SR days Dean Crossing was protected by gate distants interlocked with the crossing gates in both up and down directions. The gate lock and gate distants were operated from levers in a ground frame located in a hut beside the crossing. When Ventnor West box was closed and thus no block bell signals were being exchanged, the gatekeeper received no warning of the approach of traffic for up trains from Merstone to Ventnor West, but in the down direction a treadle-operated bell sounded when trains departed from Ventnor West, giving the gatekeeper seven minutes to open the gates and pull the distant signal.

At St Rhadegund's footpath crossing to the south of St Lawrence Tunnel, pedestrians were warned of approaching trains from the tunnel by a bell which was actuated by the wheel flanges depressing a mercury treadle inside the tunnel. The bell rang until the train passed over another treadle at the crossing.

By 1930 the arrangement at Dean Crossing was that the large gates were normally kept closed across the railway. They were closed across the road and locked against the public five minutes before a down train was due to pass and three minutes before an up train. In the event of any conditional goods, other train or light engine having to run without prior notice, the driver was warned verbally at Merstone or Ventnor West to proceed cautiously when approaching Dean Level Crossing and to be prepared to bring the train to a stand short of the gates and whistle for them to be opened.

The original signalling equipment supplied by Saxby and Farmer and the Railway Signal Co. included conventional lower quadrant home and distant signals with pitch pine posts, cedar arms and cast and wrought iron fittings. At that time the distant signals arms were painted the same red as stop signals but with a white V on the face and black V on the reverse. They showed the same red and green aspects to drivers at night. Unlike the GER and LSWR, no Coligny-Welch lamps were attached to these distant signals to assist identification at night. With the advent of the SR, the distant signals that remained in use at Ventnor West and Merstone were repainted the familiar yellow with black V (and were fitted with yellow spectacle glasses instead of red) but it is doubtful if the distants at Godshill and Whitwell were ever modified before removal. As the years progressed, several of the wooden signal posts were found to be rotting and were replaced by rail-built posts with upper quadrant metal arms. The up and down starting signals and down branch distant at Merstone and Platform 2 starter at Ventnor West were renewed in this manner. An interesting relic which survived in the goods yard at Ventnor West until closure was a 'drop flap' ground signal of Stevens pattern, probably added after the grouping.

Initially the branch was worked by Train Staff and Ticket method with Block section Merstone to Whitwell and Whitwell to St Lawrence (later Ventnor Town). When the Southern removed the signalling at Godshill, and crossing loop and

PERMANENT WAY AND SIGNALLING

IWCR 'Terrier' 0–6–0T No. 10 leaving St. Lawrence Tunnel soon after the opening of the line. The engine is carrying the normal stopping passenger train code of white disc on the lamp bracket at the top of the smokebox. To the left of the track, partly hidden by the usual warning notice board, was the post carrying the electric bell which gave warning to pedestrians of the approach of a train through the tunnel. The treadle which silenced the bell can be seen attached outside the left-hand rail.

L & GRP, CTY. DAVID & CHARLES

From Whitwell the railway climbed at a gradient of 1 in 93 for three-quarters of a mile to Dean Crossing where the road from Whitwell to Ventnor crossed the line. The downs closed in as the railway entered St. Lawrence Tunnel (619 yards) and swept downhill on a 12 chain left-hand curve high above the undercliff, with breathtaking views on the south side of coastal scenery. This scene shows the south end of St. Lawrence Tunnel and the adjacent St. Rhadegund's footpath crossing in 1920. In this picture the post carrying the pedestrian warning bell is painted white.

H. J. PATTERSON RUTHERFORD

MERSTONE

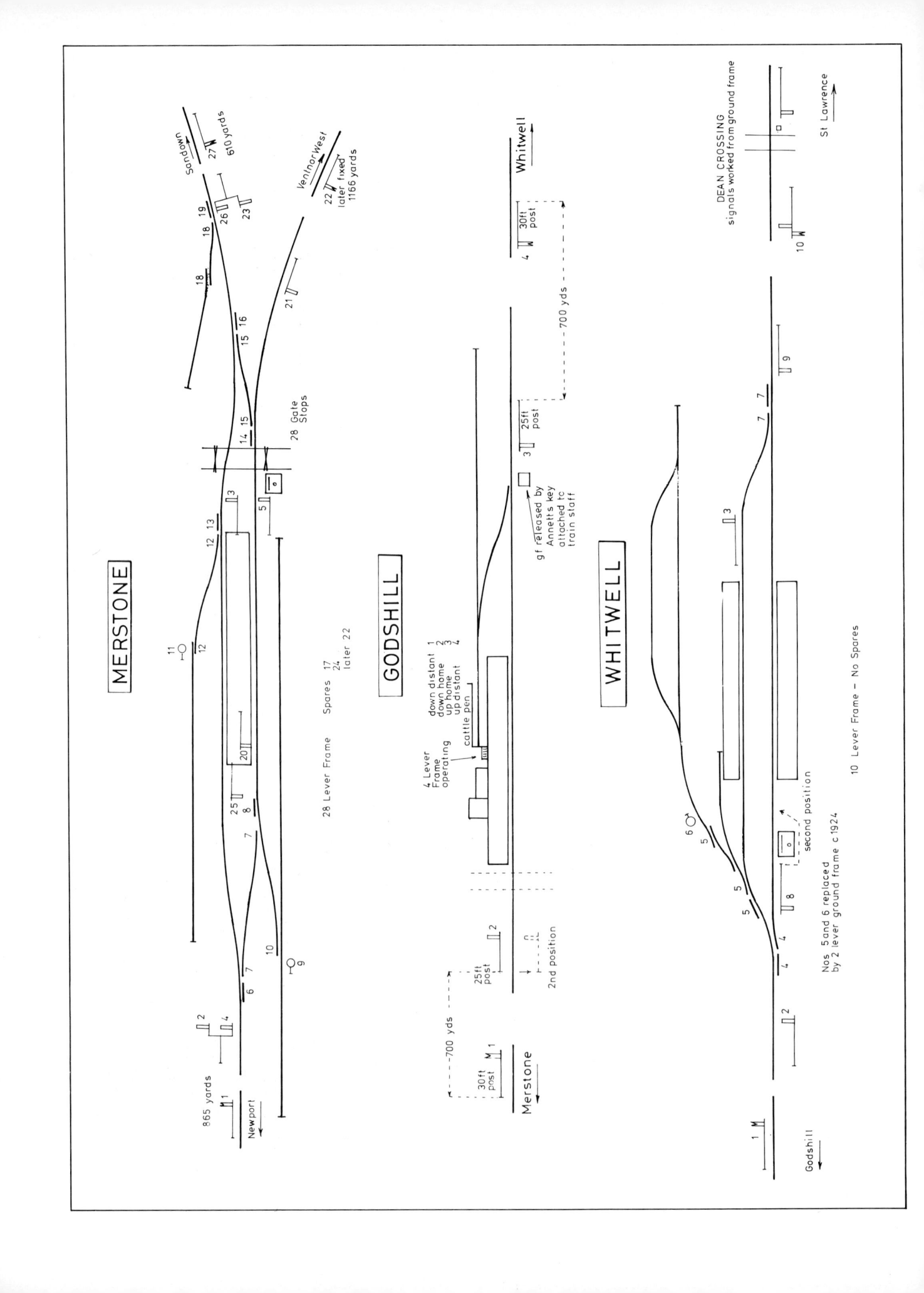

865 yards ← Newport

28 Lever Frame Spares 17, 24 later 22

Sandown 610 yards
Ventnor West later fixed 1166 yards

28 Gate Stops

GODSHILL

1 down distant
2 down home
3 up home
4 up distant

4 Lever Frame operating

cattle pen

2nd position

25ft post
30ft post
700 yds

↓ Merstone

gf released by Annett's key attached to train staff

25ft post
30ft post
700 yds

Whitwell →

WHITWELL

Nos 5 and 6 replaced by 2 lever ground frame c.1924

second position

↓ Godshill

DEAN CROSSING
signals worked from ground frame

St Lawrence →

10 Lever Frame – No Spares

ST LAWRENCE

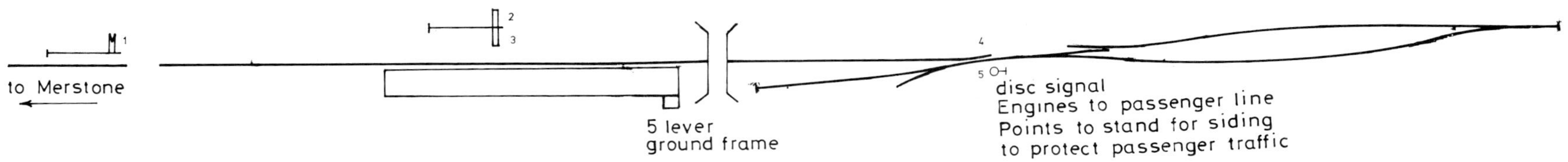

to Merstone
1
2
3
4
5
5 lever
ground frame
disc signal
Engines to passenger line
Points to stand for siding
to protect passenger traffic

1 down distant
2 down home
3 up starter
4 points
5 disc

VENTNOR WEST

fixed
originally 12
Merstone
13
10
original layout
11
replaced by
13 11 10
9
9
8
9
5
5
3
3
1
4
platform 1
2
2
2
2
platform 2
6
also 12 (see note)
7
7
7

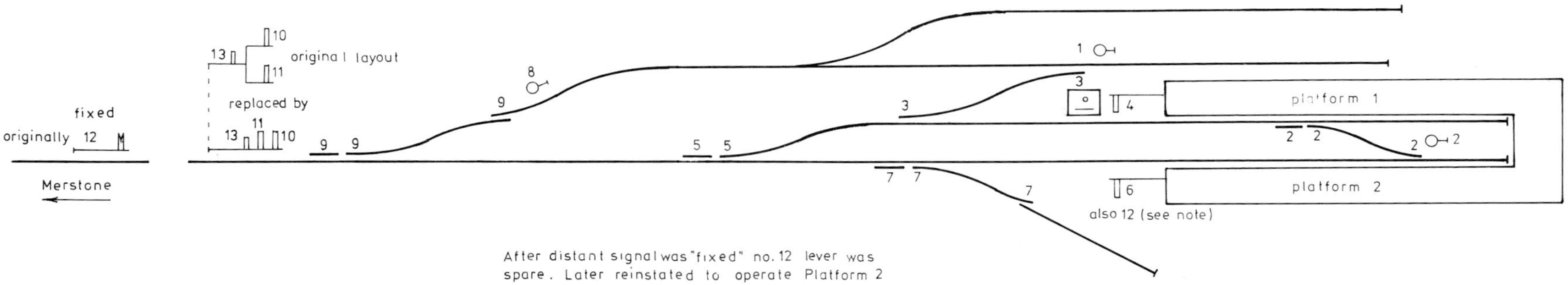

After distant signal was "fixed" no. 12 lever was spare. Later reinstated to operate Platform 2 starter when signalbox "switched out."

A delightful view of the approach to Ventnor West station, taken beside the up home signal. After the introduction of push/pull working, the locking in the box at Ventnor was changed to allow the up home to Platform No. 2 and the down from No. 2 to be cleared at the same time, and this is how they normally stood. So in this photograph both signals are off, and the home signal reads 'clear' despite the fact that there is a train in Platform No. 2.
P. J. GARLAND

PERMANENT WAY AND SIGNALLING

The rear of the up home signal. The original signal lamps had been replaced by 'seven day' lamps — a significant factor in making economies, saving the need for a man to attend every signal each day. Note that there was no back-light 'blinder' for the lower arm, that reading to the goods yard. P. J. GARLAND

Ventnor Town station from the buffer stops in 1920. The point disc signal beside the release crossover points was later removed.
COLLECTION A. BLACKBURN

related signalling at Whitwell, the complete line from Merstone to Ventnor West was worked as one section on the 'one engine in steam' principle with Train Staff Only. Preece's two-position one-wire instruments were provided, but only at Merstone were the instruments and staff box located in the signal box. At Whitwell, St Lawrence and later Ventnor Town, the instruments and the staff box were accommodated in the booking office where they could readily be operated by the station master (or porter).

Even before closure, Whitwell signal box could be switched out to allow the line to be worked as one long section. In later years the locking at Ventnor West signal box was rearranged to allow the points to be set for the No. 2 platform road and the relevant up home and down starting signals to be lowered simultaneously. This permitted the push-and-pull train service to arrive and depart with the driver in possession of the long section staff and with the signal box unattended. The locking

Drop flap ground signal at Ventnor West on 26th March 1949. This Stevens-pattern signal has had an SR balance weight added. In the original signalling installation at Ventnor, two out of the four 'shunt signals' were actually point discs working with the points rather than independent discs, worked by wire from the signal box, as this signal was. When moved to 'clear', the red-painted face of this signal fell 90 degrees forward to a horizontal position, moving the red glass from in front of the white light. White was often used as a 'clear' indicator in shunt signals long after green was substituted for 'clear' in main line running signals. As the old saying goes, 'White is right and red is wrong'.
COLLECTION A. BLACKBURN

and release of these signals (Nos. 11 and 6) was effected by a king lever released by Annett's Key attached to the Long Section Staff. After the closure of Whitwell signal box, the Long Section Staff was utilized in connection with the 'one engine in steam working'. Just prior to the closure of the crossing loop at Whitwell, the porter/signalman had given the single line staff to the driver of a special goods train working to Ventnor West on the understanding that a 'quick shunt' would take place so that the engine and brake van could return to Whitwell in time to cross the up branch passenger train. Unfortunately, unbeknown to the porter/signalman, the shunting at Ventnor West was taking longer than expected and the branch passenger train duly arrived at Whitwell from Merstone. Urgent phone calls to Ventnor West revealed that shunting would take some considerable time to complete. Unable to issue a ticket to the driver of the up passenger train, the porter/signalman was forced to pedal his cycle furiously to the terminus and back to obtain the staff to allow the passenger train forward to Ventnor West. Needless to say, the passenger train was delayed over one hour at Whitwell, and 'please explain' notices were issued from the office at Newport.

At the junction in IWCR days a No. 6 Tablet Instrument was used on the single line section from Merstone to Shide but the SR substituted a Key Token Instrument from Merstone through to Newport South. Between Merstone and Sandown both IWCR and SR utilised the Train Staff and Ticket method of operation with an intermediate block post without passing place at Newchurch.

During fog or falling snow the following signals were provided with fog-signalmen to place detonators on the line to warn approaching trains: Merstone down distant from Ventnor Town, Whitwell up and down homes, and Ventnor Town up distant and up home signals.

Dean Crossing gates after the branch was closed and before the rails were lifted. 28th July 1953. A. BLACKBURN

A telephone circuit was established linking Merstone station and Merstone signal box, Godshill station, Whitwell station, St Lawrence station and Ventnor Town station, although curiously Dean Crossing gatehouse was omitted.

The Telephone Bell Code was:

Merstone station	3 short
Merstone signal box	2 short 1 long
Merstone station master's house	2 short 4 long used after station closed for the night
Godshill station	1 long 4 short
Whitwell station	1 long 3 short
St Lawrence station	1 long 2 short
Ventnor town station	1 long 1 short

The train staff for the section Ventnor Town to Whitwell. At the left-hand end is the Annett's Key to unlock the intermediate ground frames. The squared section at the opposite end of the staff could be inserted into the ticket box and, when turned, unlocked the lid to allow the signalman to take out a train ticket. It is easy to see why it was generally reckoned that any SR ticket box could be opened with the point of the office poker!
COLLECTION M. CHRISTENSEN

CHAPTER EIGHT
TIMETABLES AND TRAFFIC

THE construction of the railway south of Merstone to St Lawrence and ultimately Ventnor, essentially as a rival route to the Isle of Wight Railway, and in the hope of encouraging travellers from the Midlands and the West of England via Southampton and Cowes, meant the line was built with little thought of attracting local passenger traffic. Despite the estimated catchment population figure of 40,000 quoted at the Lords Select Committee hearings, the branch played only a small part in the lives of local villages. The truth may be gauged from the figures which C.N. Anderson recorded as the approximate population figures for places served in 1923. They were only 52.5 per cent of the census of 1951 (excluding Ventnor), the year before the line closed.

	1923	1951
Merstone	170	350
Godshill	300	1,029
Whitwell	740	763
St Lawrence	180	506
Ventnor	6,000	7,314
Total excluding Ventnor	1,390	2,648
Total including Ventnor	7,390	9,962

Most of the area served by the branch formed part of large agricultural estates or downland and consequently the majority of the populace were employed on the land. Local industry was almost non-existent and therefore rail travel to and from work was minimal. In 1923 Godshill and Whitwell could muster 5 season ticket holders apiece, with 2 from St Lawrence and 6 from Ventnor West. The line carried the majority of its passengers on Tuesdays, Newport market day. Other traffic, except during the holiday season, was spasmodic and usually long distance to and from destinations on the mainland. The generous timetables offered in the early years contrasted with much reduced frequencies in the latter years of the Southern Railway and under nationalisation, when the service was sparse but adequate, especially during the winter months.

The initial timetable operated by the IWCR from 20th July 1897 comprised ten trains in each direction on weekdays and four on Sundays.

1897 TIMETABLE

Weekdays

		am	am	am	*A* pm	pm	pm	pm	*B* pm	pm	pm
Newport	dep	7.50	9.02	10.18	12.00	1.00	3.00	5.17	6.25	7.45	8.55
Merstone	dep	8.00	9.13	10.28	12.10	1.12	3.13	5.25	6.35	7.56	9.06
Godshill	dep	8.05	9.18	10.33	12.15	1.17	3.18	5.31	6.40	8.01	9.11
Whitwell	dep	8.12	9.25	10.40	12.22	1.24	3.25	5.38	6.47	8.06	9.18
St Lawrence	arr	8.17	9.30	10.45	12.27	1.29	3.30	5.43	6.52	8.13	9.22

A through train from Cowes dep 11.45 am
B through train from Cowes dep 5.05 pm

		am	am	*C* am	pm	pm	*D* pm	pm	*E* pm	pm	pm
St Lawrence	dep	8.21	9.35	10.50	12.32	2.25	3.35	5.47	7.05	8.18	9.25
Whitwell	dep	8.27	9.40	10.55	12.37	2.30	3.40	5.52	7.10	8.24	9.33
Godshill	dep	8.33	9.46	11.01	12.42	2.36	3.46	5.57	7.16	8.30	9.39
Merstone	arr	8.37	9.50	11.05	12.46	2.40	3.50	6.01	7.20	8.35	9.43
Newport	arr	8.55	10.05	11.17	12.57	2.59	4.08	6.20	7.32	8.47	9.54

C through train to Cowes arr 11.32 am
D through train to Cowes arr 4.27 pm
E through train to Cowes arr 9.05 pm

Sundays

		am	pm	pm	pm
Newport	dep	9.17	12.55	2.47	8.16
Merstone	dep	9.23	1.06	3.00	8.29
Godshill	dep	9.33	1.13	3.05	8.34
Whitwell	dep	9.40	1.20	3.12	8.41
St Lawrence	arr	9.45	1.25	3.17	8.46

		am	pm	pm	pm
St Lawrence	dep	10.30	2.10	4.40	9.00
Whitwell	dep	10.35	2.13	4.45	9.05
Godshill	dep	10.41	2.21	4.51	9.11
Merstone	arr	10.45	2.25	4.55	9.15
Newport	arr	11.00	2.36	4.59	9.27

1898 TIMETABLE

Weekdays		Parl am	am	pm	pm	pm	pm	pm	SO pm
Merstone	dep	9.13	10.28	12.10	1.12	3.13	5.28	7.58	9.10
Godshill	dep	9.18	10.33	12.15	1.17	3.18	5.33	8.03	9.15
Whitwell	dep	9.25	10.40	12.22	1.24	3.25	5.40	8.10	9.22
St Lawrence	arr	9.30	10.45	12.27	1.29	3.30	5.45	8.15	9.27

Sundays		am	pm	pm	pm
Merstone	dep	9.28	1.08	3.00	8.29
Godshill	dep	9.33	1.13	3.05	8.34
Whitwell	dep	9.40	1.20	3.12	8.41
St Lawrence	arr	9.45	1.25	3.17	8.46

Weekdays		Parl am	am	am	pm	pm	pm	pm	pm	SO pm
St Lawrence	dep	8.25	9.35	10.46	12.32	2.30	3.40	5.50	8.20	9.35
Whitwell	dep	8.30	9.40	10.50	12.37	2.35	3.45	5.55	8.25	9.40
Godshill	dep	8.36	9.46	10.56	12.42	2.41	3.51	6.01	8.31	9.46
Merstone	arr	8.40	9.50	11.00	12.46	2.45	3.55	6.05	8.35	9.50

Sundays		am	pm	pm	pm
St Lawrence	dep	10.30	2.10	4.40	9.00
Whitwell	dep	10.35	2.15	4.45	9.05
Godshill	dep	10.41	2.21	4.51	9.11
Merstone	arr	10.45	2.25	4.55	9.15

1900 TIMETABLE

		am	am	am	pm	pm	pm	pm	SO pm
Cowes	dep	8.45	10.00	11.45	12.40	2.43	5.05	7.28	8.30
Newport	dep	9.02	10.18	12.00	1.00	3.00	5.17	7.45	8.55
Merstone Jnc	dep	9.13	10.28	12.10	1.12	3.12	5.28	7.58	9.08
Godshill	dep	*	*	*	*	*	*	*	*
Whitwell	dep	9.22	10.37	12.19	1.22	3.22	5.37	8.07	9.17
St Lawrence	dep	*	*	*	*	*	*	*	*
Ventnor Town	arr	9.30	10.45	12.27	1.30	3.30	5.45	8.15	9.25

* calls if required by request

		am	am	am	pm	pm	pm	pm	SO pm
Ventnor Town	dep	8.30	9.45	10.50	12.32	2.30	3.40	5.50	8.20	9.30
St Lawrence	dep	*	*	*	*	*	*	*	*	*
Whitwell	dep	8.38	9.55	10.59	12.40	2.39	3.49	5.59	8.29	9.39
Godshill	dep	*	*	*	*	*	*	*	*	*
Merstone Jnc	arr	8.45	10.02	11.06	12.47	2.46	3.56	6.06	8.36	9.46
Newport	arr	8.57	10.15	11.17	12.59	2.59	4.09	6.20	8.48	9.58
Cowes	arr	9.17	11.15	11.32	1.18	3.17	4.27	6.37	9.05	

* calls if required by request

1901 TIMETABLE

Weekdays		am	pm	pm	† pm	pm	pm	SO pm	Sundays am	pm
Merstone Jnc	dep	9.13	12.10	1.12	–	5.28	7.58	9.08	9.28	8.28
Godshill	dep	*	*	*	*	*	*	*	*	*
Whitwell	dep	9.22	12.19	1.22	*	5.37	8.07	9.17	9.37	8.37
St Lawrence	dep	*	*	*	*	*	*	*	*	*
Ventnor Town	arr	9.30	12.27	1.30	4.10	5.45	8.15	9.25	9.45	8.45

* calls if required
† 3.30 pm ex Cowes, 3.45 pm ex Newport

Weekdays		am	am	pm	pm	† pm	pm	pm	SO pm	Sundays am	pm
Ventnor Town	dep	8.30	10.50	12.32	2.30	4.45	5.50	8.20	9.30	10.35	9.00
St Lawrence	dep	*	*	*	*	*	*	*	*	*	*
Whitwell	dep	8.38	10.59	12.40	2.39	4.53	5.59	8.29	9.39	10.44	9.08
Godshill	dep	*	*	*	*	*	*	*	*	*	*
Merstone Jnc	arr	8.46	11.06	12.47	2.46	–	6.06	8.36	9.48	10.52	9.16

* calls if required
† to Newport and Cowes

VENTNOR LINE.

DOWN. WEEK-DAYS. SUNDAYS.

Miles			1	2	3	4	5	6	7	8		9	Sundays 1	Sundays 2
			Goods	Mixed	Pass.	Pass	Pass.	Exprs	Pass	Mixed		Pass	Mixed	Pass
			a.m.	a.m.	a.m.	noon	p.m.	p.m.	p.m	p.m.		p.m.	a.m.	p.m.
	MERSTONE Jct.	dep	7 0	9 18	10 32	12 10	1 20	pass	5 35	8 15	Saturdays	9 24	9 30	8 34
1¼	Godshill A	dep	7 15	9 22	10 36	12 13	1 25	4 4	5 39	8 19		9 28	9 35	8 39
4	Whitwell	,,	7 45	9 29	10 41	12 18	1 31	4 A9	5 45	8 24		9 33	9 40	8 45
5¼	St. Lawrence A	,,	7 55	9 35	10 45	12 22	1 35	4 A12	5 50	8 31		9 37	9 45	8 50
6¾	VENTNOR Town	arr	8 5	9 40	10 50	12 25	1 40	4 15	5 55	8 35		9 40	9 50	8 55

A. Stops by Signal.

N.B. All Passenger Trains must stop momentarily outside Ventnor Home Signals—Goods Trains to stop dead.

NOTES. Week-days.

No. 1 Take all Ventnor Line Wagons Must work to time. Shunt Ventnor Yard on arrival. Load Sand when required. | N.B.—See Main Line Sheet for Branch Engine W..king.
No. 3, 4, 6. & 8 Through Trains Cowes to Ventnor Town.
ELECTRIC BLOCK· Merstone Junction, Godshill, Whitwell, Ventnor Town
TELEPHONE. Same, including St. Lawrence.

UP. WEEK-DAYS. SUNDAYS

Miles			1	2	3	4	5	6	7	8		9	Sundays 1	Sundays 2
			Mixed	Pass	Pass.	Pass	Mixed	Pass.	Pass	Pass		Pass	Mixed	Pass
			a.m.	a.m.	a.m.	noon	p.m.	p.m.	p.m.	p.m.		p.m.	a.m.	p.m.
	VENTNOR Town	dep	8 25	9 45	10 55	12 30	2 35	4 45	6 0	8 40	Sats. only.	9 45	10 35	9 0
1¼	St. Lawrence	A	8 30	9 50	10 59	12 34	2 39	4 49	6 4	8 44		9 49	10 39	9 4
2¾	Whitwell	dep.	8 35	9 55	11 3	12 38	2 43	4 53	6 8	8 48		9 53	10 44	9 8
5¼	Godshill	A	8 40	9 59	11 7	12 42	2 47	4 57	6 12	8 52		9 57	10 48	9 12
6¾	MERSTONE Jct.	arr.	8 45	10 2	11 10	12 46	2 50	4 59	6 15	8 55		10 0	10 52	9 15

NOTES.—Week-days. A Calls by Signal.

No. 1 to bring all Ventnor Line Wagons Heavy Engine. Must run to time.
No. 3 4. & 6 Must run to time. Through Trains to Cowes.
STAFF SECTION. Merstone Junction to Whitwell. Whitwell to Ventnor Town.

N.B.—Every effort must be made to work the Branch Trains to time, so that delay may not result to the Main Line T..ns.

1909 TIMETABLE

The passenger timetable for August 1898 showed a reduction in services with seven SX and eight SO in the down direction, and eight SX and nine SO in the up direction on weekdays, and four trains each way on Sundays.

With the opening of the extension to Ventnor from 1st June 1900 the service operated without an increase in the number of trains and Godshill and St Lawrence were reduced to conditional stopping points.

On Sundays trains departed Ventnor Town at 10.35 am, 2.10 pm, 4.40 pm and 9.00 pm matched by four trains in the down direction.

The winter timetable showed a further reduction in the number of trains although Sunday services were still offered. The timetable for December 1901 was typical of the period.

Of especial interest were the 3.30 pm ex Cowes and 4.45 pm return ex Ventnor Town which were booked to run non stop through Merstone.

The optimistic confidence of the directors that the new line would poach traffic from the monopolistic IWR route to Ventnor proved to be false hope. The IWCR made a spirited bid in competition and during 1900, 1901 and 1902 ran a through service from Cowes to Ventnor and return, completing the journey in 40 minutes, forming part of an advertised 4½ hour LSWR express timing from Waterloo via Southampton and Cowes. This longer route from London could not, however, compete with the faster journey offered by the LBSCR from Victoria or LSWR from Waterloo to Portsmouth and connecting IWR service from Ryde Pier Head to Ventnor. Traffic from the North and West Midlands via Cheltenham and the MSWJR never reached expectations and the promoters of the NGSLR were left in no doubt that their route had lured very little traffic away from their competitors. Local traffic was also below expectations and the outlook was extremely bleak.

Having endured an operating loss in the first three years, the IWCR quickly curtailed the service to run from Newport to Ventnor Town only. To effect further economies, not only on the Ventnor line but on the remainder of the system, the IWCR obtained a steam rail-motor in 1906 and then formed a second out of a diminutive 0–4–2 saddle tank shunting locomotive and a clerestoried 12-wheel coach bought from the Midland Railway. Neither was operationally successful but both spent a considerable part of their working life on the Ventnor Town line. The problems with water capacity precluded their use on long runs and both had to have their tanks topped up at Ventnor and Merstone or Newport after each trip. The operational inconvenience was soon realised and in 1907 the IWCR terminated most services at Merstone.

In 1909 the IWCR working timetable showed one goods, two mixed, four passenger and one express passenger in the down direction on Mondays to Fridays with an additional passenger train on Saturdays. The morning goods 6.30 am ex-Newport called at all stations on the branch and was diagrammed for a 'heavy engine'. The 10.32 am ex-Merstone conveyed through coaches from Cowes, departing 10.00 am as did the 12.10 pm ex-Merstone (11.45 am ex-Cowes). The afternoon express passenger from Cowes at 3.35 pm ran fast from Newport to Ventnor Town, calling at Godshill, Whitwell and St Lawrence by request only, with arrival at the terminus at 4.15 pm. In the evening the 7.40 pm mixed train conveyed through coaches for the branch, departing Merstone at 8.15 pm, arriving at Ventnor Town 20 minutes later. The additional Saturday train departed the junction at 9.24 pm. On Sundays the branch engine hauled the down 8.50 am goods from Newport to Merstone before working the 9.30 am mixed train to Ventnor Town, whilst in the afternoon the engine worked the 5.15 pm goods from Newport to Sandown returning with the 6.30 pm goods ex-Sandown to Merstone, before working the 8.34 pm passenger to Ventnor Town.

In the up direction two mixed and six passenger trains formed the Monday to Friday service with the additional passenger train on Saturday. The first up mixed train at 8.25 am ex-Ventnor Town cleared the branch of all goods wagons requiring transit, either loaded or empty. The 10.55 pm, 12.30 pm and 4.45 pm conveyed through coaches for Cowes. On Saturday the additional train departed the terminus at 9.45 pm. On Sundays trains departed Ventnor Town at 10.35 am (mixed) and 9.00 pm (passenger) to Merstone, connecting with the Sandown line services.

The timetable pattern remained unchanged the following year and by 1913 (when the IWCR absorbed the smaller company) seven passenger and goods trains ran each way on weekdays with two passenger trains on Sundays. In the years prior to grouping the winter timetable was further reduced to five trains each way on weekdays and two on Sundays. In contrast to working timetables, the public books continued to show trains calling at Godshill and St Lawrence only by request.

The first summer passenger timetable operated by the Southern Railway on weekdays only was: *[see below]*

As will be noted, the new regime required all trains to call at all stations.

In contrast the winter timetable for 1926 showed the service reduced to six trains each way SX, although the additional late Saturday trains continued to run. By this date the Southern Railway authorities had renamed Ventnor Town station 'Ventnor West'.

The summer timetable for 1927 consisted of ten passenger trains and one freight in each direction but again no Sunday services.

The passenger timetable from 22nd September 1930 showed six trains in each direction, departing from Merstone at 7.51 am, 10.42 am, 12.42 pm, 2.42 pm, 4.42 pm and 6.50 pm, returning from Ventnor West at 8.18 am, 11.17 am, 1.17 pm, 3.17 pm, 5.17 pm and 7.46 pm. On Saturdays an additional train departed Merstone at 9.18 pm, returning from Ventnor West at 9.44 pm. No trains ran on the branch on Sundays. As in earlier Southern timetables, the railway company attempted to attract additional traffic to the line by advertising Godshill Halt as the station for Sandford, $1\frac{1}{2}$ miles distant, Whitwell for Niton $1\frac{3}{4}$ miles and Chale $4\frac{1}{2}$ miles and St Lawrence Halt for Blackgang $3\frac{1}{2}$ miles.

The following summer, ten SX and eleven SO passenger services ran each way along with the mandatory freight train in each direction. This was reduced to six passenger and one freight train each way in the winter timetable. The winter service 1934/5 continued to offer the same number of trains

SUMMER 1923 TIMETABLE

UP

		am	am	am	pm	pm	pm	pm	SO pm
Merstone	dep	8.06	9.36	11.06	12.36	3.36	5.06	6.36	9.06
Godshill	dep	8.09	9.40	11.10	12.40	3.40	5.10	6.40	9.10
Whitwell	dep	8.12	9.46	11.16	12.46	3.46	5.16	6.46	9.16
St Lawrence	dep	8.15	9.51	11.21	12.51	3.51	5.21	6.51	9.21
Ventnor Town	arr	8.19	9.55	11.25	12.55	3.55	5.25	6.55	9.25

DOWN

		am	am	am	pm	pm	pm	pm	SO pm
Ventnor Town	dep	8.45	10.20	11.45	1.20	2.45	4.20	5.45	7.20	9.30
St Lawrence	dep	8.49	10.24	11.49	1.24	2.49	4.24	5.49	7.24	9.34
Whitwell	dep	8.53	10.28	11.53	1.28	2.53	4.28	5.53	7.28	9.38
Godshill	dep	8.59	10.34	11.59	1.34	2.59	4.34	5.59	7.34	9.44
Merstone	arr	9.02	10.37	12.02	1.37	3.02	4.37	6.02	7.37	9.47

WINTER 1926 TIMETABLE

UP

		am	am	pm	pm	pm	pm	SO pm
Merstone	dep	7.51	10.42	12.42	2.42	4.42	6.46	9.07
Godshill	dep	7.54	10.45	12.45	2.45	4.45	6.49	9.10
Whitwell	dep	8.00	10.51	12.51	2.51	4.51	6.55	9.16
St Lawrence	dep	8.05	10.56	12.56	2.56	4.56	7.00	9.21
Ventnor West	arr	8.10	11.01	1.01	3.01	5.01	7.05	9.26

DOWN

		am	am	pm	pm	pm	pm	SO pm
Ventnor West	dep	8.16	11.22	1.22	3.22	5.22	7.38	9.35
St Lawrence	dep	8.19	11.25	1.25	3.25	5.25	7.41	9.38
Whitwell	dep	8.23	11.29	1.29	3.29	5.29	7.45	9.42
Godshill	dep	8.29	11.35	1.35	3.35	5.35	7.51	9.48
Merstone	arr	8.32	11.39	1.39	3.39	5.39	7.55	9.52

No Sunday services were offered.

TIMETABLES AND TRAFFIC

with an additional late run in each direction on Saturday evenings.

The May 1935 timetable was identical, but from July 1935 eleven up and twelve down trains were advertised Monday to Fridays with additional services each way on Saturdays, departing Merstone at 9.20 pm and returning from Ventnor West at 9.52 pm. Three trains ran in each direction on Sundays *[see table]*.

The working timetable for the summer of 1939 showed the last regular Sunday services to run on the branch until after World War Two.

In the absence of run-round facilities in the platform at Whitwell, the engine hauling the SXQ freight ran round the wagons and brake van in the loop siding in the goods yard.

After the outbreak of World War Two, services were drastically reduced and by the autumn of 1940 only three trains ran in each direction SX, departing Merstone at 7.40 am,

1935 SUNDAY SERVICE

UP

		am	pm	pm
Merstone	dep	10.02	1.54	8.45
Godshill	dep	10.07	1.59	8.50
Whitwell	dep	10.14	2.05	8.57
St Lawrence	dep	10.20	2.10	9.03
Ventnor West	arr	10.25	2.15	9.08

DOWN

		am	pm	pm
Ventnor West	dep	10.30	2.21	9.30
St Lawrence	dep	10.34	2.25	9.34
Whitwell	dep	10.39	2.30	9.39
Godshill	dep	10.46	2.37	9.47
Merstone	arr	10.51	2.42	9.53

1939 TIMETABLE

WEEKDAYS
UP   FN   SX   SO
                                                                                      LE&BQ

	M.Ch		am	am	am	am	am	pm	pm	pm	pm	pm	pm	pm	pm	pm
Merstone	0.00	dep	6.30	7.40	9.12	10.35	11.25	12.25	1.25	2.25	4.25	5.25	7.30	8.30	9.25	9.25
Godshill Halt	1.49	dep		7.45	9.17	10.39	11.30	12.30	1.30	2.30	4.30	5.30	7.35	8.35		9.30
Whitwell	4.03	dep		7.52	9.24	10.45	11.37	12.37	1.37	2.37	4.37	5.37	7.42	8.42	9.35	9.37
St Lawrence Halt	5.45	dep		7.57½	9.29½	10.49	11.42½	12.42½	1.42½	2.42½	4.42½	5.42½	7.47½	8.47½		9.42½
Ventnor West	6.69	arr	6.50	8.01½	9.33½	10.53	11.46½	12.46½	1.46½	2.46½	4.46½	5.46½	7.51½	8.51½		9.46½

FN   Freight ex Newport dep 6.10 am
LE&BQ   Light Engine and Brake runs if required SX

DOWN   F   SX   SO
                                                                                   FQ

	M.Ch		am	am	am	am	am	pm	pm	pm	pm	pm	pm	pm	pm	pm
Ventnor West	0.00	dep	7.00	8.15	9.40	10.58	11.55	12.55	1.55	2.55	4.55	6.20	7.58	8.58		9.58
St Lawrence Halt	1.24	dep		8.19½	9.44½	11.02½	11.59½	12.59½	1.59½	2.59½	4.59½	6.24½	8.02½	9.02½		10.02½
Whitwell	2.66	dep	7.15	8.25	9.50	11.08	12.05	1.05	2.05	3.05	5.05	6.30	8.08	9.08	9.45	10.09
Godshill Halt	5.20	dep		8.32	9.57	11.14	12.12	1.12	2.12	3.12	5.12	6.37	8.15	9.15		10.16
Merstone	6.69	arr	7.27	8.36½	10.01½	11.19½	12.16½	1.16½	2.16½	3.16½	5.16½	6.41½	8.19½	9.19½	9.55	10.20½

F   Freight
FQ   Freight runs if required SX

SUNDAYS

                     N   C

UP		am	pm	pm		DOWN		am	pm	pm
Merstone	dep	9.52½	1.51½	9.09½		Ventnor West	dep	10.28	2.30	9.36
Godshill Halt	dep	9.57½	1.56½	9.14½		St Lawrence	dep	10.32½	2.34½	9.40½
Whitwell	dep	10.04½	2.03½	9.21½		Whitwell	dep	10.38	2.40	9.47
St Lawrence	dep	10.10	2.09	9.27		Godshill Halt	dep	10.45	2.47	9.54
Ventnor West	arr	10.14	2.13	9.31		Merstone	arr	10.49½	2.51½	9.58½
								FR	C	

N   through train from Newport dep 9.40 am
C   through train from Cowes dep 1.26 pm

FR   through train to Freshwater arr 11.51 am
C   through train to Cowes arr 3.20 pm

1.23 pm and 5.25 pm, returning from Ventnor West at 8.15 am, 2.00 pm and 5.57 pm. On Saturday additional trains ran at 8.22 pm from Merstone, returning from Ventnor West at 8.50 pm. By July 1941 three trains ran each way SX and five each way SO as under:

UP		am	pm	SO pm	pm	SO* pm
Merstone	dep	7.40	1.24	2.26	5.22	8.22
Godshill	dep	7.44	1.28	2.31	5.26	8.27
Whitwell	dep	7.51	1.35	2.38	5.33	8.34
St Lawrence	dep	7.57	1.40	2.43	5.38	8.39
Ventnor West	arr	8.02	1.46	2.49	5.44	8.45

ex Cowes

DOWN		am	SO pm	pm	pm	SO pm
Ventnor West	dep	8.15	2.00	3.00	5.49	8.50
St Lawrence	dep	8.19	2.04	3.05	5.52	8.54
Whitwell	dep	8.24	2.09	3.09	5.58	9.00
Godshill	dep	8.31	2.16	3.16	6.05	9.07
Merstone	arr	8.36	2.22	3.20	6.11	9.11

From 1942 the Southern Railway reduced the service to three each way on Mondays to Fridays and four on Saturdays during winter months with an extra train on Saturdays during the summer.

1942 TIMETABLE

UP		am	pm	pm	SO pm
Merstone	dep	7.40	1.25	5.22	8.22
Godshill	dep	7.44	1.29	5.26	8.27
Whitwell	dep	7.51	1.36	5.33	8.34
St Lawrence	dep	7.57	1.41	5.38	8.39
Ventnor West	arr	8.02	1.47	5.44	8.45

DOWN		am	pm	pm	SO pm
Ventnor West	dep	8.15	1.55	5.59	8.50
St Lawrence	dep	8.19	1.58	6.03	8.54
Whitwell	dep	8.24	2.04	6.08	9.00
Godshill	dep	8.31	2.11	6.15	9.07
Merstone	arr	8.36	2.16	6.21	9.11

After hostilities, services gradually increased but in 1946 only one through train ran from Ventnor West to Newport, the 1.55 pm. The stock then worked to Cowes to form the 3.56 pm to Sandown, returning thence to Merstone to resume branch working. All other trains were confined to the branch.

In the summer of 1947 the Southern Railway made a valiant attempt to attract extra patronage by offering holidaymakers and local people a vastly improved service with later departures and through trains to and from Newport on Sundays.

1947 TIMETABLE

Weekdays

		am	am	am	pm	pm	pm	pm	pm	SO pm	SO* pm
Merstone	dep	7.35	9.12	11.27	1.25	4.25	5.27	6.27	7.27	8.27	9.27
Godshill	dep	7.39	9.16	11.31	1.29	4.29	5.31	6.31	7.31	8.31	9.31
Whitwell	dep	7.46	9.23	11.38	1.36	4.36	5.38	6.38	7.38	8.38	9.38
St Lawrence	dep	7.52	9.29	11.44	1.42	4.42	5.44	6.44	7.44	8.44	9.44
Ventnor West	arr	7.57	9.34	11.49	1.49	4.47	5.49	6.49	7.49	8.49	9.49

27th September and 4th October only

		am	am	am	pm	pm	pm	pm	pm	SO pm	SO* pm
Ventnor West	dep	8.12	9.40	12.00	2.00	4.57	5.57	6.57	7.57	8.57	9.57
St Lawrence	dep	8.16	9.44	12.04	2.04	5.01	6.01	7.01	8.01	9.01	10.01
Whitwell	dep	8.22	9.49	12.09	2.09	5.06	6.06	7.06	8.06	9.06	10.06
Godshill	dep	8.29	9.56	12.16	2.16	5.13	6.13	7.13	8.13	9.13	10.13
Merstone	arr	8.35	10.01	12.21	2.21	5.19	6.19	7.19	8.19	9.19	10.19

27th September and 4th October only

Sundays until 21st September

		N am	N pm	Y pm
Merstone	dep	9.52	1.51	9.06
Godshill	dep	9.57	1.56	9.10
Whitwell	dep	10.04	2.03	9.17
St Lawrence	dep	10.09	2.08	9.23
Ventnor West	arr	10.14	2.13	9.28

		N am	N pm
Ventnor West	dep	10.28	2.30
St Lawrence	dep	10.32	2.34
Whitwell	dep	10.37	2.39
Godshill	dep	10.44	2.46
Merstone	arr	10.49	2.51

N Through train from Newport
Y Connection off through train from Freshwater dep 8.05 pm

N Through train to Newport

1950 TIMETABLE

UP	M.Ch		Pass am	Pass am	Freight am	Pass am	Pass pm	Pass pm	Pass pm	Pass pm	Pass pm
Merstone	0.00	dep	7.35	9.12	10.10	11.27	1.27	4.25	5.27	6.27	7.27
Godshill Halt	1.49	dep	7.40	9.17	CS	11.32	1.32	4.30	5.32	6.32	7.32
Whitwell	4.03	dep	7.47	9.24		11.39	1.39	4.37	5.39	6.39	7.39
St Lawrence Halt	5.45	dep	7.52½	9.29½		11.44½	1.44½	4.42½	5.44½	6.44½	7.44½
Ventnor West	6.69	arr	7.56½	9.33½	10.30	11.48½	1.48½	4.46½	5.48½	6.48½	7.48½

CS Stops when required

DOWN	M.Ch		Pass am	Pass am	Freight am	Pass am	Pass pm	Pass pm	Pass pm	Pass pm	Pass pm
Ventnor West	0.00	dep	8.12	9.40	10.40	11.57	2.00	4.57	5.57	6.57	7.57
St Lawrence Halt	1.24	dep	8.16½	9.44½		12.01½	2.04½	5.01½	6.01½	7.01½	8.01½
Whitwell	2.66	dep	8.23	9.50		12.07	2.10	5.07	6.07	7.07	8.07
Godshill Halt	5.20	dep	8.30	9.57		12.14	2.17	5.14	6.14	7.14	8.14
Merstone	6.69	arr	8.34½	10.01½	11.18½	12.18½	2.21½	5.18½	6.18½	7.18½	8.18½

These Sunday services were to be the last operated on the branch before closure of the line.

In the first year of nationalisation British Railways operated eight passenger trains in each direction departing Merstone at 7.35 am, 9.12 am, 11.27 am, 1.25 pm, 4.25 pm, 5.27 pm, 6.27 pm and 7.27 pm, returning from Ventnor West at 8.12 am, 9.40 am, 12.00 noon, 2.00 pm, 4.57 pm, 5.57 pm, 6.57 pm and 7.57 pm. The freight train ran at 10.10 am from Merstone, calling at Godshill (if required) and returning from Ventnor West at 10.40 am, calling at Whitwell to shunt the yard from 10.50 am to 10.58 am during winter months only, chiefly to pick up sugar beet traffic and drop off empty wagons.

The Working Timetable for the Summer of 1950 showed a weekdays only service.

As before, the down freight train called at Whitwell 10.50 am to 10.58 am during the winter months. This timetable remained in operation until closure of the line on 13th September 1952.

FARES AND EXCURSIONS

The fares charged by the IWCR from Newport to stations on the Newport Godshill and St Lawrence Railway on the opening of the line were:

	Single			Return		
Class	1st	2nd	3rd	1st	2nd	3rd
Godshill	1/3	10d	5d	1/11	1/3	10d
Whitwell	1/10	1/3	7½d	2/3	1/11	1/3
Ventnor (St Lawrence)	2/3	1/6	9d	3/5	2/3	1/6

After the opening the IWCR was soon advertising 'The new and direct route to Ventnor' on posters and in local newspapers with the boast that a saving of 6 miles and an acceleration of 25 minutes had been effected on journeys to Ventnor from Newport, Cowes, Southampton, Freshwater, Lymington and Yarmouth. Fares from Newport to Ventnor were then reduced by

	1st Class	2nd Class	3rd Class
Single	1/3	1/2	6d
Return	1/9	1/7	1/4

with proportional reductions from other places.

'Well appointed conveyances' were advertised 'meeting all trains at St Lawrence station' for onward journey to Ventnor, whilst the return departed from 22 Pier Street half an hour prior to the advertised departure time of all trains from Ventnor (St Lawrence), with the fare one way 6d per head and luggage free. For Ventnor travellers 'ask for tickets via Godshill' was the new catchphrase.

To supplement the normal fare structure the IWCR also included the new line in its 500 mile Weekly Tourist Ticket which with the FYNR embraced 40 route miles of island railway. Fares were 12/6 1st Class, 10/– 2nd Class, with children half fare. For those not so ambitious, half-day excursion cheap tickets were offered to Godshill (for Sandford), Whitwell (for Niton) and Ventnor (St Lawrence) from Newport, Cowes, Ryde, Sandown, Yarmouth and Freshwater on Wednesdays and Thursdays. Cheap Tickets were also available from the branch stations to all IWR stations. Summer evenings by the sea were also available from Newport to Ventnor (St Lawrence) by the 5.27 pm and 6.25 pm trains for 1/–, with last return journeys possible on the 8.18 pm SX and 9.28 pm SO trains from St Lawrence.

From Monday, 26th May 1900, cheap excursion tickets were available on Mondays only by all trains up to 6.30 pm and between any two stations on the IWCR and NGSLR line with a zonal fare arrangement based on distance,

	1st Class	3rd Class
Not exceeding 6 miles	9d	6d
Not exceeding 13 miles	1/6	1/–
Not exceeding 21 miles	3/–	2/–

the latter including stations on the FYNR. Similar fares were also available to or from IWR stations at the common rate of 3/– 1st class, 2/– 3rd class. The IWCR also issued Weekly Tourist Tickets which included the St Lawrence line stations at 12/6 1st class and 10/– 3rd class with children at half fare.

The IWCR continued to offer passengers the Weekly Tourist Tickets until the grouping of 1923. The cheap day returns were an attempt to counteract the habit of passengers from Cowes and Newport travelling via Sandown to Ventnor.

By 1924 the Vectis Bus Company was providing a tolerably good service which for local traffic proved a formidable rival.

The only way the Southern authorities could improve matters was to introduce a more generous service with cheaper fares. To this end cheap tickets permitting a return journey for single fare were introduced for travel after 10 am and as a result often the railway return fares were cheaper than the single bus fares.

Despite the competition C.N. Anderson recorded the following receipts for 1923:

	Merstone	Godshill	Whitwell	St Lawrence	Ventnor West
	£ s d	£ s d	£ s d	£ s d	£ s d
Passenger	268 12 7	263 10 5	531 18 1	196 16 10½	1420 16 0
Parcels	399 18 1	122 1 7	209 4 6	55 19 5	31 5 6½
Goods	4 14 9	23 9 3	14 6 0	17 0 5	24 0 2
Valuables	15 8 0	13 4 1	6 18 0	5 3 8	54 4 1
Total	688 13 8	402 15 4	762 16 7	274 18 7½	1530 5 9½
Wage Bill	599 12 9	160 0 0	160 0 0	nil	265 0 0
Monthly passengers booked (heaviest)	724	1375	2181 August	1182	4507
Monthly tickets collected (heaviest)	674	1445	2781 August	8159	2215

The All Island Weekly Season Ticket was also issued during the summer months at 10/6 1st class and 7/6 3rd class embracing 33 stations and 55½ miles of route. Sales reached 35,000 in the 1930 season.

The cheap day tickets and Runabout facilities were withdrawn during World War Two but, with the introduction of special market tickets after hostilities, traffic increased considerably and on more than one occasion, on Tuesdays, the driver of a down train had to stop the engine at the end of Godshill and Whitwell platforms to advise intending passengers to stand away from the edge. In the latter years passengers departing Ventnor West could return to Ventnor and tickets were interchangeble. By 1949 the All Island 5-day (Monday/Friday) Holiday Runabout Ticket was available at 15/- 1st class and 10/- 3rd class. Cheap day tickets were also available daily by all trains and a sample of fares showed:

	Merstone	Godshill	Whitwell	St Lawrence	Ventnor West
Cowes	1/10	2/1	2/7	2/10	3/3
Freshwater	3/3	3/7	4/2	4/6	4/9
Godshill	6d	—	6d	—	2/1
Mill Hill	—	251	2/5	2/10	3/1
Newport	11d	1/2	1/8	2/1	2/4
Ryde St Johns Rd.	2/2	2/7	3/1	—	—
Ventnor West	—	1/2	8d	—	—
Whitwell	1/-	6d	—	—	8d
Yarmouth	—	3/3	3/7	4/2	4/5

Children 3–14 years were half fare.

In IWCR days specific instructions were issued regarding the examination of tickets. At Ventnor Town 'on every possible occasion the train, is to be gone through before starting and the tickets examined'. In the up directions tickets for Ventnor Town were to be collected at St Lawrence 'except by the last train Newport to Ventnor on Saturday nights when they are to be collected at Ventnor Town'. Tickets to other stations were to be collected at destination stations.

GOODS TRAFFIC
Before the advent of the railway, local carriers carts were a common sight on the roads linking St Lawrence, Niton, Chale, Whitwell and Godshill with Newport and Ventnor. With the competitive service offered by the IWCR many of these direct carriers services were withdrawn, and the operators concentrated their efforts, providing a feeder service to and from the branch line stations. Mr Sprake was the local carrier conveying goods from Whitwell station yard to Niton and Chale.

In addition to the traditional root vegetable crops conveyed to Newport (potatoes, carrots, swedes and turnips), from the early 1920s sugar beet increasingly was grown in the area served by the branch and especially during World War Two. Until closure of the line, horse-drawn waggons and motor lorries conveyed considerable loads to the goods yard at Godshill, Whitwell and Merstone. The produce was taken by special trip working or local freight train to Medina Wharf for forwarding to the mainland, where the ultimate destinations were the beet processing factories at Peterborough, Selby and Kidderminster. In the late 1940s often three trains of 19 wagons and brake van were despatched daily from Merstone in the growing season.

Milk was regularly despatched from all stations on the branch but later only Godshill and Whitwell handled the traffic, conveying the valuable liquid to dairies at Newport and Cowes in the familiar 17 gallon churns. Two consignments were sent daily during the summer months, the first by the early morning train and then again in the late afternoon. During winter months the milk was forwarded by the early morning train only. Unlike many locations on the mainland, not all the milk traffic was lost to road carriers, and milk traffic continued to be conveyed in small quantities until the closure of the line. In 1923 the daily despatches of churns were

	Summer	Winter
Merstone	19	20
Godshill	4	3
Whitwell	7	5

From the outset the livestock traffic handled on the branch was minimal, a fact reflected in the small number of cattle wagons operated by the IWCR and Southern Railway (8 and 7 respectively). The principal consignments appear to have been sheep reared on the downland around Whitwell and St Lawrence. Pigs and cattle were conveyed in such small numbers that sometimes ordinary covered vans were used. Possibly the largest import of livestock came on 24th May 1925 when over 200 baskets of homing pigeons were delivered to Ventnor West for station staff to release at the start of a race.

Coal traffic (and to a lesser extent coke) was handled at all station yards, where merchants quickly established coal grounds. All coal was routed from the mainland via Medina Wharf for distribution throughout the Island and, prior to the

The north end of Merstone station on 28th July 1951 with a Cowes to Sandown train approaching on the main single line. 'O2' No. 35 Freshwater is in the holding siding waiting to pull into the platform with the connecting service to Ventnor West. PAMLIN PRINTS

opening of the Ventnor extension in 1900, the IWCR had the audacity to increase the coal conveyance rates from the wharf to the branch stations. The rate to Whitwell went up from 2/- to 2/3 per ton and St Lawrence 2/5 to 2/6 per ton. Typical receipts during 1923 were Godshill 40 tons per annum, Whitwell 96 tons, St Lawrence 15 tons and Ventnor West 400 tons. In later years much of the traffic transferred to road but Merstone, Whitwell and Ventnor West received small consignments until 1952.

Other commodities carried included Ventnor stone despatched from the quarry near Ventnor Town from 1909 until closure of the establishment in 1926. The IWCR authorised a locomotive to propel not more than 5 wagons from Ventnor Town station to the Quarry siding at a speed not exceeding 10 mph. The siding was worked by special trip from the terminus with the locomotive at the lower end of the train and not by the branch goods service.

In the late 1920s and early 1930s many of the Island roads remained unmetalled - dust tracks in summer or muddy morasses in wet weather. A programme of road improvements carried out involved levelling the surface before covering with granite chippings and tarmacadam. Much of this material was delivered by rail from Medina Wharf to the branch stations where it was offloaded and taken to site by horse and cart. The granite and tarmacadam was then levelled by steamroller.

Although not situated in a prolific fruit growing area, the branch passenger and freight trains regularly conveyed produce in the early years but most had been transferred to road transport well before World War Two. Gooseberries, raspberries and apples were despatched to Newport and occasionally to the mainland, the soft fruit between June and August and the apples thereafter to the end of the autumn.

General goods and 'smalls' traffic was conveyed by ordinary goods train or in the brake vans of passenger services but tonnages were low. In 1923 Godshill received 2 tons, Whitwell forwarded 2 tons and received $3\frac{1}{2}$ tons, St Lawrence received 1 ton, whilst Ventnor West forwarded 14 tons and received 50 tons. From 1936 the SR decided to transfer all general goods traffic arriving from the mainland to Messrs Pickford's wharf at Cowes for onward delivery by road. As the company was railway owned, traffic internal to the Island was also conveyed by road, and railway goods trucks and vans were declared surplus to requirements. Thereafter only parcels were conveyed in brake vehicles of passenger services, with the guard or travelling porter preparing consignment notes en route. Miscellaneous traffic for Godshill was offloaded at Merstone or Whitwell whilst St Lawrence traffic was taken through to Ventnor West for distribution. After Whitwell became unstaffed all parcels traffic was taken to Ventnor West for road distribution by Pickfords.

The following facilities were available for goods and livestock traffic at the branch stations.

Merstone	1 loading gauge
Godshill	1 loading dock
Whitwell	1 loading dock
Ventnor West	1 loading dock
	1 loading gauge
	1 goods shed
	1 goods crane 5 tons capacity

By 1943 the 5 ton crane at Ventnor West was partly dismantled to provide spares for other cranes located at more strategic positions on the Isle of Wight.

The classification and maximum loads for engines on the branch in IWCR days was:

	Mineral Wagons	Goods Wagons	Empties Wagons	Passenger Vehicle Coaches
Merstone to Ventnor Town				
Class A engine	16	25	30	12
Class B engine	11	16	24	10
Class C engine	10	16	22	9

Ventnor Town to Merstone

Class A engine	10	15	20	12
Class B engine	9	14	20	10
Class C engine	8	12	17	9

3 minerals were equal to 5 goods, 3 empties to 2 goods and Brake Van equal to one goods vehicle.

Engines were classified as follows
Class A   Nos 6 and 7
Class B   Nos 9, 10, 11 and 12
Class C   Nos 4, 5 and 8

Soon after takeover the Southern Railway restricted the working of the branch to engines W1, W2, W3, W4, W9, W10, W11 and W12 with loads of passenger and freight trains as under:

Merstone to Ventnor West	*Passenger*	*Freight*
Class A engine	131 tons	25 loaded goods
Class B engine	85 tons	16 loaded goods
Class C engine	65 tons	12 loaded goods
Ventnor West to Merstone		
Class A engine	125 tons	20 loaded goods
Class B engine	80 tons	14 loaded goods
Class C engine	60 tons	10 loaded goods

The permitted engines allowed on the branch were classified

Class A   nil
Class B   W1, W4, W9, W10 and W12
Class C   W2, W3 and W11

After the relaying of the permanent way the maximum loadings of passenger and freight trains were amended as follows:

Merstone to Ventnor West	*Passenger Tons*	*Freight Vehicle limit 30*
Class A engine	150	25 loaded goods
Class B engine	135	18 loaded goods
Class C engine	90	16 loaded goods
Ventnor West to Merstone	*Tons*	*Vehicle limit 30*
Class A engine	150	30 loaded goods
Class B engine	135	20 loaded goods
Class C engine	90	14 loaded goods

Engines were classified as follows

A	Class E1	Nos 1 to 4 inclusive
B	Class O2	Nos 14 to 33, and after transfer away of A1X class, 34 to 36
C	Class A1X	No 8, 11 and 13

TRAFFIC STAFF

For the opening of the line the IWCR employed station masters at all stations. They dealt with signalling of trains and booking office duties in addition to administrative duties; for the mundane duties a porter was also employed. The first porter at St Lawrence, Thomas Silsbury, was initially employed as a boy labourer digging St Lawrence Tunnel. On completion of the work he left the contractors and joined the IWCR, and for the official opening of the line was supplied with a uniform jacket with silver buttons. Immediately after the ceremony the coat was retrieved for the silver buttons to be replaced by cloth buttons. One of the earliest station masters at St Lawrence was Philip Corrick, renowned for shooting rabbits on the cliff opposite the platform, his prizes being consumed for dinner or given to train crews in return for illicit supplies of coal.

In 1908 Mr Urry held the post of station master at Whitwell with a salary of £1 2s 6d per week. He was subsequently promoted to Freshwater to replace F. Newland, who in turn was demoted to Whitwell for neglect of duties at the terminal station. The luxury of two staff at each station could not be maintained and during World War One reductions were made by IWCR management. Thereafter Godshill and Whitwell were reduced to one man stations whilst Ventnor Town enjoyed the services of station master and lad porter. St Lawrence was manned in part by a member of staff sent down from Ventnor Town. When C.N. Anderson, the traffic assistant appointed by the Southern, made a survey in 1923, little had changed. Merstone had three staff (station master and 2 porter signalmen) with an annual wage bill of £599-12s-9d. Godshill and Whitwell each enjoyed the services of a grade one porter at an annual cost of £160 each. The station master and lad porter at Ventnor West cost the company £265 annually but by this time St Lawrence was totally unstaffed, although it was not officially registered as such until 1927. In the same year Godshill was permanently unstaffed and down-rated to status of halt under the SR rationalisation programme. From 16th March 1928 Whitwell was also reduced to a halt, being staffed during the summer months only, existing as such until 1st July 1941 when it was fully unstaffed. The last resident grade one porter during the summer periods was Sam Wells who transferred from temporary porter's post at Bembridge.

Further rationalisation took place after World War Two when control of Ventnor West came under the station master at Ventnor Station. One of the occupants of the joint post was Mr Dew. Signalmen who served at Merstone from the 1940s until closure of the branch included Ronald Bennett, Len Sheath, Sydney Dennett, Jess Wheeler, George 'Chocolate Soldier' Hunt and Harold 'Wrecker' Blundey. Gordon Porter was grade one porter/signalman for a period and part of his duties included relief in the signal box during the period between the early turn signalman booking off duty and his late turn counterpart booking on.

Isle of Wight Central train crews were always responsible for working the branch services, and guards in the early years were supplied with their own personal issue tail lamp with brass fittings which they used on all trains they worked. The Ventnor West line was always ranked for a junior man taking up duty and when, in 1938, Percy Primmer joined the SR as a guard, his first working after passing his Rules and Regulations exam was on the push-and-pull from Merstone, issuing tickets in addition to the operational functions. Mrs May Joyce, who commenced on the railway in 1945, was one of eight women employed by the SR to cover vacancies created by permanent staff away with the armed forces. Whilst acting as guard on the branch she met her future husband Ted, who was a driver at Newport and regularly employed on the Ventnor West trains. The workload of the conductor-guard working the branch trains was quite considerable, especially during the summer months, and on one occasion an influx of scouts from a neighbouring camp joined the train at St Lawrence for the short journey to Ventnor West. The elderly guard had his work cut out issuing 50 or so half-fare tickets in the three minutes allowed.

CHAPTER NINE
LOCOMOTIVES AND ROLLING STOCK

THE substantial construction of the Newport Godshill and St Lawrence Railway, at least by Isle of Wight standards, allowed all IWCR locomotives to operate over the line with no prohibitions. After grouping only eight locomotives were permitted on the branch as the line was the last to receive attention from the Civil Engineer. The only dispute came when the SR considered introducing 'O2s' on push-pull workings in 1925. The engineer questioned the wisdom of the motive power authorities but agreed to a test on the restricted route which proved that the locomotives were far too heavy for the track, and the 'Terriers' continued to work the branch. Later, after 1928 when the permanent way had been relaid with heavier bullhead rails, the 'O2s' were allowed on the branch. All engines could then work between Merstone and Ventnor West.

The contractor for the Bembridge Railway used two locomotives during the construction of that line, *Bembridge* (a six coupled Manning Wardle Class M saddle tank) and *St Helens*, an aged 2–4–0 well tank, rebuilt from a main line engine with a haystack firebox. After the opening of the Bembridge line *St Helens* was only steamed when the regular branch engine was receiving repairs or maintenance, and in September 1893, after several years in store, it was sold for £650 to Charles Westwood, the contractor of the Newport Godshill and St Lawrence Railway. Westwood renamed the engine *St Lawrence* and employed it on the building of the new line. By 1897 the locomotive was considered beyond repair and offered to the IWCR for £10 for possible conversion to a mobile tar wagon. The cost of conversion was, however, prohibitive and the offer was refused. *St Lawrence*, in a rapidly declining state, spent several months dumped at Whitwell siding, where she was subsequently broken up in the summer of 1898. During 1896 she was recorded working spoil trains between Merstone and Dean Crossing.

Due to the condition of *St Lawrence*, Westwood and Winley purchased a replacement engine in May 1897, a small 0–6–0 saddle tank with 14 in by 18 in cylinders, 3 ft 3 in coupled wheels and 11 ft 2½ in wheelbase and named her *Godshill*. The locomotive had been built by the Worcester Engine Company in October 1863 and then rebuilt in December 1895 by Kerr Stuart and Company at whose works in Stoke-on-Trent it was used carrying the name *California*, until sale for use on the Island.

Early in 1898 *Godshill* was on hire to the IWCR to work (without any great success) the branch passenger services, because the locomotive ordered by the Central company on 16th December 1896 from Beyer Peacock (IWCR No. 8) was not delivered until 26th May 1898. Motive power resources were therefore at a premium and during one period of hire including January 1898 *Godshill* was employed continuously for 45 days on shunting duties whilst the IWR 2–4–0T *Sandown* covered the passenger work. After removal from the Island, the 0–6–0 saddle tank ended her days on construction work on the Great Central Railway line between Marylebone and St John's Wood tunnels.

The third contractors engine to work on the Newport Godshill and St Lawrence Railway was a small 0–4–0 saddle tank engine with 8 in by 15 in cylinders and 2 ft 6 in wheels, built in June 1888 by Hudswell Clarke (Makers No. 302) for T. A. Walker, a contractor for the Manchester Ship Canal. On the Godshill company contract the engine was chiefly utilized for the movement of spoil trains from St Lawrence Tunnel, but after the opening of the line to Ventnor Town it was employed by the IWCR for a short period shunting Medina Wharf. After useful service on the Island the engine, named *Weaste*, was employed by the same contractor (J. T. Firbank) on the construction of the Basingstoke and Alton Light Railway.

The withdrawal of the former IW (NJ) Railway 2–2–2WT locomotive *Newport* in July 1895 and the impending opening of the Newport Godshill and St Lawrence Railway resulted in the IWCR board seeking tenders on 21st October 1896 for a locomotive similar in tractive effort to their Black Hawthorn 4–4–0 tank No. 6. Of the five manufacturers who replied, with costs ranging from £2,400 to £1,950, the company awarded the contract to Beyer Peacock and Company on 16th December 1896 after they had tendered the lowest price for a 2–4–0 tank engine akin to IWCR Nos. 4 and 5. The new locomotive No. 8 was not delivered until 26th May 1898, a considerable time after the opening of the Godshill line. On arrival it was found that the engine weighed 4 tons more than the two earlier tanks, with a minor increase in coal and water capacity. Other alterations included steel boiler, deeper cab side sheets, steam sanding and increased boiler pressure of 150 lbs psi. Because of the poor state of the finances of the IWCR, the engine was initially paid for by the Southern Counties Rolling Stock Company and agreement was reached for the total build and delivery cost of £2,033 to be paid off over ten years with monthly instalments of £21 17s 0d. Once delivered, No. 8 ran trouble-free for 27 weeks covering some 18,053 miles before being stopped for repairs.

IWCR No. 8 performed regularly on the Ventnor Town line but unfortunately came to grief one day on an up working with a bent valve spindle. The authorities at Newport sent a fitter from the locomotive shed to attend to the casualty, and the ever adaptable fitter tried to make the locomotive serviceable by using one cylinder only and disconnecting the side rod. An attempt was then made to move the engine but, much to the consternation of the footplate crew, the front of the cylinder blew out, fortunately with no resultant injury. A further message was forwarded to Newport and a second fitter was sent to the branch with a locomotive to haul the train back to Merstone and then return to Newport with No. 8 for the necessary attention and repairs.

No. 8 had the following dimensions:

Cylinders	14 in by 20 ins
Leading wheels	3 ft 4 ins
Coupled wheels	5 ft 1 in
Wheelbase	12 ft 2 ins
Boiler diameter	3 ft 6¾ ins
length	8 ft 9½ ins

Firebox length	3 ft 7 ins
Heating surfaces	
Tubes (116 × 2 ins)	552 sq.ft.
Firebox	53 sq.ft
Total	605 sq.ft
Boiler pressure	150 lbs psi
Grate area	10.5 sq.ft
Water capacity	520 gallons
Coal capacity	16 cwt
Weight in working order	30 tons 17 cwt
Max. axle loading	11 tons 18 cwt

Before their withdrawal the former Cowes and Newport 2-2-2 well tanks Nos. 1 and 2 were often employed on the Ventnor Town or Sandown branches of the IWCR. The engines, built by Slaughter Gruning at a cost of £1,960 each, were landed at Medham Hard on 24th September 1861 and hired by the contractor building the C&N line. Painted in light blue livery with black bands and fine red lining, the pair operated the passenger services on and from 16th June 1862. In 1884 Nos. 1 and 2 were fitted with tapered stove-pipe chimneys, cabs, and boiler-top mounted cylindrical sandboxes and, together with No. 3, were purchased in September 1887 for £1,695 from H.D. Martin who, as director and controller of the C&N, had originally purchased the engines and worked the line under contract. By 1898 both were restricted to light duties but then received minor repairs before being laid aside in scrap condition on 30th August and 17th January 1901 respectively.

The leading dimensions were:

Cylinders (outside)	13½ ins by 16 ins
Leading wheels	3 ft 6 ins
Driving wheels	5 ft 3 ins
Trailing wheels	3 ft 6 ins
Wheelbase	11 ft 4 ins
Boiler diameter	3 ft 4 ins
length	8 ft 3 ins
Firebox length	3 ft 6 ins
Heating surfaces	
Tubes	496 sq.ft
Firebox	53 sq.ft
Total	549 sq.ft
Grate area	8.75 sq.ft
Boiler pressure	120 lbs psi
Water capacity	390 gallons
Coal capacity	6 cwt
Weight in working order	19 tons 5 cwt

In 1879 the C&N and R&N Joint Committee took over the administration of the Isle of Wight (Newport Junction) Railway and, with their new asset and the growing importance of Medina Wharf, found motive power at a premium. The directors duly authorised Martin to purchase a suitable second-hand tank engine for a sum not exceeding £1,000. Unfortunately, the usual sources of second-hand material, the LSWR and LBSCR, had nothing available but the North London Railway offered a 19-year old 4-4-0 tank engine for £750. The engine was inspected at Bow Works on 28th January 1880 and was duly accepted as mechanically sound on 25th February. The 4-4-0 had been designed by William Adams and built by Slaughter Gruning and Company at a cost of £2,650 in October 1861 (works number 443) being numbered 35A on the NLR duplicate list. It was named *Whippingham* on arrival on the Island. The engine had been rebuilt at Bow Works in March 1875 with a larger boiler, 16½ in cylinders and cab. H.D. Martin actually bought the locomotive and was reimbursed by monthly payments of £18 12s 6d. In October 1887 the Joint Committee settled their debt by paying £594 to Martin. *Whippingham* was usually rostered for the Sandown-Newport line duty and became No. 7 under the IWCR, who removed the name the following year. After the opening of the Ventnor Town line, No. 7 was included in the general rostering on the services with other IWCR engines. No. 7 failed with a burst tube when working the 9.30 am Ryde St Johns Road-Newport goods on 23rd July 1906 and when inspected was found to be beyond economical repair and was laid up for scrap.

The principal dimensions of the ex-North London Railway 4-4-0T were:

Cylinders	16½ in by 22 ins
Bogie wheels	3 ft 2 ins
Coupled wheels	5 ft 3 ins
Wheelbase	18 ft 9½ ins
Boiler diameter	4 ft 0½ ins
length	9 ft 9 ins
Firebox length	5 ft 0 ins
Heating surface	
Tubes (178 × 2 in)	815 sq.ft
Firebox	81 sq.ft
Total	896 sq.ft
Boiler pressure	120 lbs psi
Grate area	13.75 sq.ft
Water capacity	845 gallons
Bunker capacity	1 ton
Weight in working order	36 tons 19 cwt
Max axle load	14 tons 5 cwt

After vain efforts by the Ryde and Newport Railway to purchase second-hand tank engines, that company ordered two 2-4-0 tank engines from Beyer Peacock and Company at a cost of £1,765 each on 14th July 1875. Initially they were named *Cowes* and *Osborne* but on the formation of the IWCR in July 1887 their names were obliterated and the pair became Nos. 4 and 5. After the opening of the Godshill Railway to St Lawrence and later Ventnor Town, they were regularly utilized on both passenger and freight services and proved popular with footplate crews.

The dimensions of Nos. 4 and 5 were:

Cylinders	14 in by 20 ins
Leading wheels	3 ft 3 ins
Coupled wheels	5 ft 0 ins
Wheelbase	12 ft 2 ins
Boiler diameter	3 ft 6¾ ins
length	8 ft 9½ ins
Firebox length	3 ft 7 ins
Heating surfaces	
Tubes (116 × 2 in)	552 sq.ft
Firebox	53 sq.ft
Total	605 sq.ft
Boiler pressure	120 lbs psi
Grate area	10½ sq.ft
Water capacity	480 gallons
Coal capacity	15 cwt
Weight in working order	26 tons 8 cwt
Max axle load	9 tons 15 cwt

The poor initial receipts from the Ventnor Town branch, with little hope of early increase in traffic, forced the IWCR directors

IWCR railmotor No. 1 at Ryde Esplanade during trial running over the IWCR system.
COLLECTION R. SILSBURY

to seek ways of cutting operational costs. Around the turn of the century many of the mainland railway companies were introducing steam or petrol-engined railcars on branch and cross-country services where traffic was light. Various companies successfully introduced this new breed of traction on their systems including the LSWR and LBSCR and this persuaded the IWCR Board to contemplate the employment of a steam railcar on the Merstone–Ventnor Town services. The idea was first mooted on 20th January 1904 but matters did not make real progress until 18th May, when the secretary was requested to seek advice from the GWR and LSWR before seeking tenders. The Chairman and Mr Conacher subsequently visited Swindon Works on 22nd June and later journeyed on the LSWR Basingstoke and Alton Light Railway on 13th July 1904. First impressions were favourable and Conacher inspected a Pickering rail-motor at Rolvenden on the Rother Valley Railway on 11th November. Twelve days later tenders were sought from Hurst Nelson & Company, the Metropolitan Carriage Company, Birmingham Carriage & Wagon Company and Kitson & Company for the provision of a steam rail-motor capable of conveying 50 passengers and designed to negotiate the relatively sharp curves of the IWCR system including the Ventnor line.

The submissions were duly discussed by the board on 29th March 1905 when, after careful deliberation, Hurst Nelson's tender for £1,450 for the carriage was accepted. Hurst Nelson & Co had sub-contracted the work for the locomotive portion to R&W Hawthorn & Co. The rail-motor was due for delivery in June 1906 but the locomotive portion did not arrive at the Motherwell Works of Hurst Nelson & Co until 24th September. After the uniting of the two sections, the rail-motor worked south under its own power from Motherwell to Southampton Docks where a temporary line of rails was laid to a barge which conveyed it across the Solent for offloading at St Helens on 4th October 1906.

The new acquisition was numbered 1 in the IWCR fleet and was painted in the company's standard livery of crimson lake which extended to the lower carriage panelling with the upper portion painted cream. The locomotive was fitted with Walschaerts valve gear, together with a copper-capped chimney and side tanks which extended from the cab to the smokebox front. The standard Westinghouse brake was fitted. The passenger compartment lighting was initially rape-oil lamps. So keen were the directors to put the rail-motor to revenue-earning service that preliminary trials were conducted between Merstone Junction and Ventnor Town on 5th October 1906 with the manufacturer's representatives supervising operations.

Robert Guest, later reporting to the Institute of Mechanical Engineers, stated that during the trials on the branch the rail-motor consumed 16 lbs of 'Nixons Navigation' coal per mile. The coach portion suffered no effects of vibration from the locomotive even when passengers travelled in the front of the third class compartment. Guest attributed this to the two units being separated by large indiarubber washers encircling the engine bogie pin. At the loose joints or rail subsidences, oscillation was apparent although decreasing to the rear of the coach. The short wheelbase made the footplate an uncomfortable ride for the enginemen. A trial was subsequently made on the Freshwater line where clearance difficulties required minor modifications to the vehicle at a cost of £20, paid by the FYNR.

The dimensions of the rail-motor were:

Cylinders (outside)	14 in by 9 ins
Coupled wheels	3 ft 6 ins
Wheelbase (engine)	8 ft 0 ins
Boiler diameter	3 ft 6 ins
length	4 ft 6 ins
Firebox length	2 ft 6 ins
Heating surfaces	
Tubes	289 sq.ft
Firebox	40 sq.ft
Total	329 sq.ft
Boiler pressure	160 lbs psi
Grate area	7.5 sq.ft
Water capacity	400 gallons
Coal capacity	12 cwt
Carriage length	44 ft 6 ins
Seating 1st Class	6
2nd Class	44

IWCR railmotor No. 1 was ordered from Hurst Nelson & Co of Motherwell at a price of £1,450. The locomotive portion was built by R. & W. Hawthorn. Theoretically suitable for the Merstone–Ventnor Town branch, it was an operator's nightmare and was only used for a few years after delivery in October 1906.
R. SILSBURY

After trials on the Ventnor Town branch IWCR railmotor No. 1 was transferred to the FYNR where traffic was of equally light loadings. The railmotor is here seen at Freshwater.
G. W. TRIPP

Initially impressed by the economic operation of railmotor No. 1, the IWCR sought to purchase a second unit. However, prices quoted were too expensive and the company decided to modify their ex-C & NR 0–4–2T No. 3 with an ex-Midland Railway clerestory coach. Work, including purchase of the coach and conversion of vehicle and locomotive with mechanical push/pull gear was £437 9s 5d. As railmotor No. 2, the new unit proved a liability and often failed in service. It is seen here at Newport in 1910. M. BARNSLEY

Weight in working order
Engine	15 tons 12 cwt
Carriage	16 tons 11 cwt
Total	32 tons 3 cwt

Subsequently further trials were conducted over the entire IWCR network and, on satisfactory completion, No. 1 commenced regular work on the Ventnor Town branch on 2nd November 1906. The following month trials were instituted on the branch to compare operating costs of the rail-motor with Terrier 0–6–0T locomotive No. 11 hauling six coaches. For these special runs rail-motor No. 1 was coupled to three four-wheeled carriages and a brake van which were thought by the IWCR authorities to be a comparable load relative to the size of motive power. As a result, rail-motor No. 1 proved the more efficient unit, burning 13.2 lbs of coal per mile compared with the 17.8 lbs of the Terrier tank, with respective costs per mile of 1.4d and 1.9d. After two years in regular service on the branch, rail-motor No. 1 was transferred to the Freshwater line in October 1908.

Impressed by the economic operation of their new acquisition, the IWCR board instructed Conacher to investigate the possibility of working the Sandown-Newport line with a similar unit. Conacher advised that this operation was possible and on his recommendation the directors authorised the ordering of a second rail-motor on 12th February 1907. Hurst Nelson and Company were asked to quote for the provision of a 65-seat car with a third more power than available on No. 1. Their tender of £2,040, received on 27th February, was considered exorbitant and alternatives were proposed. On 27th March 1907 the board, after lengthy discussion, decided to modify 0–4–2 tank locomotive No. 3 to work with a high capacity bogie coach. Tenders for such a vehicle received from manufacturers ranged from £1,125 to £2,398 and were again considered excessive, so a search was made for a suitable second-hand vehicle. On 25th September 1907 a composite bogie carriage complete with electric lighting and Westinghouse brake was purchased from the Midland Railway at a cost of £250 including conversion but not delivery. The authorities hoped No. 3 would be rebuilt before Easter 1908 but more urgent repairs to other locomotives meant that a 'Terrier' tank coupled to the Midland coach had to deputise on the Merstone-Ventnor Town services whenever No. 1 was out of service (and after its transfer to the Freshwater line) until May 1909 when No. 3 was completed and available to work with its ex-MR carriage. The work, including the purchase of the coach, cost a total of £437 9s 5d and was carried out at Newport Works. The alterations including encasing No. 3's boiler and cab, the fitting of mechanical push-and-pull gear and close-coupling it to the carriage, which was also modified and fitted with a driving compartment at one end.

Principal dimensions of No. 3 were:

Cylinders (outside)	10 in by 17 ins
Coupled wheels	3 ft 3 ins
Trailing wheels	2 ft 4 ins
Boiler diameter	3 ft 0 ins
length	8 ft 0 ins
Firebox length	2 ft 6 ins
Heating surfaces	
Tubes	272 sq.ft
Firebox	32 sq.ft
Total	304 sq.ft
Grate	6 sq.ft

Boiler working pressure	140 lbs psi
Bunker capacity	10 cwt
Water capacity	400 gallons
Wheelbase	10 ft 3 ins
Weight in working order	15 tons 10 cwt

As rail-motor No. 2, the new unit, however, proved a liability and often failed in service. Between May 1909 when it entered service and June 1912 when it was put into store, the vehicle ran only a total of 6,892 miles. The ex-Midland Railway carriage portion was soon converted for normal service but the engine portion remained in store for a further eleven months when, with much casing removed, the 0–4–2T returned to traffic as No. 3, used on menial shunting duties at Medina Wharf.

After the withdrawal of the rail-motors (No. 1 in November 1910 and No. 2 in June 1912), the Ventnor Town branch services were usually operated by one of the 'Terrier' 0–6–0 locomotives and a set of four-wheeled carriages, with the locomotive running round its train at each end of the journey. The 'Terrier' tanks which worked the branch had a long and varied history and before detailing their involvement with the line it is necessary to trace how the IWCR came to possess such useful machines.

By the time Beyer Peacock No. 8 was delivered, the St Lawrence line services were being handled by any suitable locomotive that was available including the original Slaughter Gruning 2–2–2 well tank engines Nos. 1 and 2 of the Cowes and Newport Railway which were restricted to light branch duties or shunting. Conacher recommended that the pair be scrapped but, because of the uncertainty of the motive power availability, the board authorised (on 14th September 1898) some patch-up repairs for both until a suitable second-hand

IWCR 0–4–2ST No. 3 coupled to former Midland Railway clerestory 12-wheel bogie coach forming steam railmotor No. 2 working the Ventnor Town service between the terminus and St. Lawrence.

IWCR No. 3, which formed the locomotive portion of railmotor No. 2, shown after removal of cladding.
REAL PHOTOGRAPHS

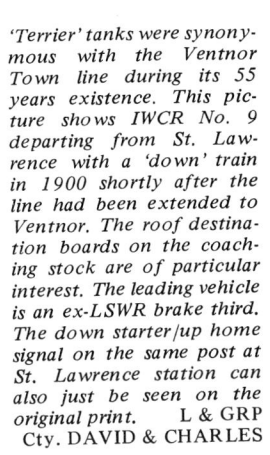

'Terrier' tanks were synonymous with the Ventnor Town line during its 55 years existence. This picture shows IWCR No. 9 departing from St. Lawrence with a 'down' train in 1900 shortly after the line had been extended to Ventnor. The roof destination boards on the coaching stock are of particular interest. The leading vehicle is an ex-LSWR brake third. The down starter/up home signal on the same post at St. Lawrence station can also just be seen on the original print. L & GRP Cty. DAVID & CHARLES

locomotive could be purchased from a main line company. Approaches were made to the LSWR and LBSCR for engines and subsequently the former offered a Manning Wardle saddle tank of 1862 for £550 and 'Ilfracombe Goods' 0-6-0 built by Beyer Peacock in 1873 for £750 with tender or £685 without. The Brighton offered one of their 'Terrier' 0-6-0 tank engines No. 75 *Blackwall* at £800. Conacher wanted the 0-6-0 'Ilfracombe Goods' but weight restrictions and the fixed wheelbase would have restricted the engine to the Ryde–Cowes line and so the 'Terrier' was subsequently accepted after an independent assessor, J.M. Budge of the GNR Doncaster Works, had inspected the engine and found it in good mechanical order. Thus the first of the Brighton 'Terriers' which were to become the regular motive power on the Ventnor West services for four decades found its way to the Island. Numbered 9 by the IWCR, the engine was (like No. 8) the subject of hire purchase via the Southern Counties Rolling Stock Finance Company at £9 8s 10d per month over ten years.

The 'Terrier' tank was immediately popular with footplate crews and mastered most duties so that when the old Cowes and Newport Railway 2-2-2Ts Nos. 1 and 2 were withdrawn, the IWCR took the opportunity to purchase three more 0-6-0Ts from the LBSCR. The first to arrive, No. 69 *Peckham*, came in April 1900 complete with a new pair of 14 in × 20 in cylinders fitted a year earlier. On transfer the Central numbered the engine 10. Nearly two years elapsed before the famous No. 40 *Brighton* was purchased at a cost of £600. She had a pair of 13 in by 20 in cylinders fitted as a condition of the sale. *Brighton* became No. 11 in the IWCR fleet. This purchase was followed by that of a third 'Terrier' in November 1903; No. 84 *Crowborough*, fitted with 14 in by 20 in cylinders, was number 12 but this time the purchase was made by the IWCR and then transferred to the Southern Counties Rolling Stock Finance Company to permit Nos. 1 and 2 to be broken up. Nos. 10 and 11 were both the subject of hire purchase from the finance company.

The principal dimensions of the Terrier tanks were:

	Original A1 on arrival on the Island	*A1X*	*No. 2 (Drummond type)*
Cylinders	13 in or 14 in by 20 ins	14 in by 20 ins	13 in by 20 ins
Coupled wheels	4 ft 0 ins	4 ft 0 ins	4 ft 0 ins
Wheelbase	12 ft 0 ins	12 ft 0 ins	12 ft 0 ins
Boiler diameter	3 ft 6 ins	3 ft 6 ins	3 ft 4½ ins
Boiler length	7 ft 10 ins	8 ft 1¼ ins	7 ft 9½ ins
Firebox length	4 ft 1 in	4 ft 1 in	4 ft 0½ in
Heating surface			
Tubes	(118 × 1¾) 456 sq.ft	(119 × 1¾) 433 sq.ft	424 sq.ft
Firebox	55 sq.ft	55.5 sq.ft	53 sq.ft
Total	511 sq.ft	488.5 sq.ft	477 sq.ft
Boiler pressure	140 lbs psi	150 lbs psi	150 lbs psi
Grate area	10 sq.ft	10 sq.ft	11¼ sq.ft
Water capacity	500 gallons	500 gallons	500 gallons
Coal capacity	12 cwt	1 ton 10 cwt	1 ton
Weight in working order	27 tons 10 cwt	28 tons 15 cwt	26 tons 3 cwt
Max axle loading	10 tons 3 cwt	10 tons 8 cwt	9 tons 17 cwt

When on 6th February 1889 the IWCR agreed to take over the working of the Freshwater, Yarmouth and Newport Railway, the board estimated that one additional engine, six carriages and eleven wagons would be required to cover the agreed service. Once again the LBSCR and LSWR had no suitable second-hand engines available and so approaches were made to private contractors. Of the four replies received, three offered 2–4–0 tank engines with costs ranging from £1,790 to £2,550. Black Hawthorn and Company, however, offered a 4–4–0 at £1,845 with delivery within six months. None of the other manufactuers could offer such advantageous delivery and so, with the proviso that the wheel diameter was reduced to 5 ft 3 ins and cylinders enlarged to 16 in diameter, the contract was signed on 18th December 1889. Construction was completed on 19th March 1890 but delivery was delayed until 7th June 1890 by a strike. Registered as No. 6 on the IWCR stock list, the engine was robustly built but rough riding on the indifferent permanent way. No. 6 was duly allocated to work the inaugural special train on the Newport Godshill and St Lawrence Railway.

Principal dimensions of No. 6 were:

Cylinders (outside)	16 in by 24 ins
Bogie wheels	3 ft 0 ins
Coupled wheels	5 ft 3 ins
Wheelbase	17 ft 9 ins
Boiler diameter	4 ft 0 ins
length	10 ft 6 ins
Firebox length	5 ft 0½ in
Heating surface	
Tubes (170 × 2 in)	806 sq.ft
Firebox	81 sq.ft
Total	887 sq.ft
Boiler pressure	140 lbs psi
Grate area	14.5 sq.ft
Water capacity	700 gallons
Coal capacity	1 ton 10 cwt
Weight in working order	40 tons
Max axle load	14 ton 18 cwt

As a replacement for the ex-NLR tank No. 7, the IWCR again perused the second-hand locomotive market, being offered a D class 0–4–2T and E class 0–6–0T by the LBSCR at £995 and £940 respectively. A third locomotive offered at the much cheaper price of £695, was a Midland and South Western Joint Railway Beyer Peacock 2–4–0T No. 6, which was duly purchased. The engine reached the Island on 2nd December 1906 and commenced working on 7th December as IWCR No. 7. The engine was originally delivered to the Swindon, Marlborough and Andover Railway in July 1882 and for loading purposes on the IWCR was put in the same class as the 4–4–0T No. 6.

Principal dimensions of the ex MSWJR 2–4–0 tank engine were:

Cylinders	16 in by 24 ins
Leading wheels	4 ft 0 ins
Coupled wheels	5 ft 6 ins
Wheelbase	14 ft 6 ins
Boiler diameter	4 ft 0.7/8 ins
length	9 ft 10 ins
Firebox length	5 ft 6 ins
Heating surfaces	
Tubes (166 × 2 in)	880 sq.ft
Firebox	72 sq.ft
Total	952 sq.ft
Boiler pressure	120 lbs psi
Grate area	14.75 sq.ft
Water capacity	800 gallons
Coal capacity	1 ton 15 cwt
Weight in working order	35 tons 5 cwt
Max axle loading	14 tons 10 cwt

The engine was finally withdrawn in April 1926.

After unsuccessful attempts to purchase locomotives from the LSWR, LBSCR, M&SWJR and Great Western Railway, the IWCR obtained a powerful 0–4–4 tank engine on 30th June 1909 from Frazer and Son, Hebburn-on-Tyne for £850. She was delivered to the Island on 11th July and numbered 2 in the Central fleet. The engine had originally been built at Seaham Harbour for the Marquis of Londonderry's Railway in April 1895. As No. 21 on the private railway, the engine was absorbed into North Eastern Railway stock in 1900 but was almost immediately placed in store and finally sold to Frazer and Son for £650 on 19th May 1909. Despite the fact that No. 2 weighed 45 tons 15 cwt, the IWCR put the new locomotive to work on all lines, only to find that on many lightly laid sections the track spread. She subsequently entered Newport Works where the side tanks were shortened and other fittings removed. With a limit of 1½ tons of coal in the bunker, a reduced weight of 40 tons was achieved but even then No. 2 was officially restricted to Cowes-Ryde services. In truth, however, she again visited all lines, including the Ventnor Town branch. More trouble than she was worth, the locomotive was finally laid aside in store at Newport in October 1914 where she remained for almost three years before sale to Sir W.G. Armstrong Whitworth and Company of Elswick for £1,200 in August 1917. The new owners numbered the engine 26.

When delivered to the Island No. 2 had the following dimensions:

Cylinders	17 ins by 24 ins
Coupled wheels	5 ft 4½ ins
Trailing wheels	3 ft 0 ins
Wheelbase	22 ft 3 ins
Boiler diameter	4 ft 1 in
length	10 ft 0 ins
Firebox length	4 ft 9 ins
Heating surfaces	
Tubes	812 sq.ft
Firebox	83 sq.ft
Total	895 sq.ft
Boiler pressure	140 lbs psi
Grate area	13 sq.ft
Water capacity	1075 gallons
Coal capacity	2 tons 10 cwt
Weight in working order	45 tons 15 cwt
Max axle loading	16 tons 5 cwt

After the grouping a further 'Terrier' tank, ex-FYNR No. 2, was rostered with others of the class to work the branch. No. 2 was built at Brighton Works as No. 46 *Newington* in December 1876 and was subsequently sold to the LSWR in March 1903 for working the Axminster–Lyme Regis Light Railway. When the FYNR broke off relations with the IWCR the engine was initially hired by the Freshwater Company from the LSWR until being purchased outright in February 1915. It served on the FYNR as No. 2 until the company was absorbed by the Southern Railway in August 1923. Since No. 2 was only fitted with the vacuum brake, it could find little work except on the Freshwater branch. In March 1924 it was painted Maunsell Green and equipped with Westinghouse brake and larger

To prove that the push/pull ex-LCDR sets were not used exclusively on the Ventnor West branch, 'Terrier' A1 class No. W2 before naming, is shown here with set No. 484 at Freshwater station.

bunker, akin to her IWCR sisters. At the next general repairs in January 1927 (now numbered W2) the engine received steam carriage heating equipment and was fitted for motor train working. Twenty-two months later she received the name *Freshwater*, the nameplates being affixed on the side tanks beneath the SR lettering and above the W prefix and number. Just over a year later, in November 1929, the nameplate was lowered and the numerals and W prefix located on the bunker. By this time she had taken up duties with the other 'Terriers' turn-and-turn-about on the Ventnor West branch and in April 1932 she was renumbered W8, and fitted with a hooter and Drummond pattern copper-capped chimney.

In April 1925 the Southern Railway authorities wanted to introduce motor train operation on the branch and sub-

SR 'Terrier' A1 Class No. 2 Freshwater *standing in Platform 1 at Ventnor West. Built at Brighton in December 1876 as No. 46* Newington, *it was later purchased by the LSWR in March 1903 for the Lyme Regis branch. Renumbered 734 and provided with a Drummond pattern boiler at Eastleigh in 1912, she was later hired by the FYNR at £1 6s 8d per day before being purchased outright for £900 in 1915. She entered service with the Southern in 1923, retaining the number 2 and was later renumbered 8. After fitting with push/pull gear, she was regularly used on the Ventnor West services.*

This 'Terrier' was transferred to the Isle of Wight by the Southern Railway in May 1927 as W3 complete with enlarged bunker, but in April 1932 was renumbered W13, by which time it was named Carisbrooke. *The locomotive received motor train equipment in 1930 and is shown at Ventnor West with a fireman making a last minute check along the side of the train before departing for Merstone.*

COLLECTION R. SILSBURY

'A1X' W4 Bembridge *was transferred to the island in May 1929, receiving the name* Bembridge *before entering service. The engine received push/pull equipment in 1930 and was used on Ventnor West services. She was renumbered in April 1932 to W14 but became surplus to requirements after additional transfers of 'O2' class locomotives, and was sent back to the mainland in 1936 where she later saw use as 2678 with SR and later as 32678 in BR days.*

sequently the newly commissioned 'O2s' Nos. 23 and 24 equipped for push-pull working arrived with two sets of SE&CR bogie push-pull coaches. Because of weight problems the locomotives were officially barred from the Ventnor West and Bembridge branches where push-pull was the desired method of working. In February and March 1926 'Terrier' tanks W9, 10, 11 and 12 were equipped with push-pull equipment for working the Ventnor line and Brading–Bembridge branch with ex-LC&DR four-wheel two-coach sets. The two 'O2s' were subsequently transferred from Newport to Ryde. 'Terrier' Ws 11 and 12 were additionally equipped with carriage steam heating equipment in October 1927 to provide some comfort to the branch passengers in the winter months.

By 1927 there was acute shortage of locomotives to work the lightly laid lines from Newport to Freshwater and the Bembridge and Ventnor West branches. 'Terrier' W9 was condemned with a defective fire-box in April 1927 and several of the IWR Beyer Peacock tanks were withdrawn with nothing available to cover as standby. To ease the situation three further ex-LBSCR 'Terrier' tanks were transferred to the Island in the next three years.

W3 (ex-B667), which had been in store at Brighton since September 1925, was sent to Eastleigh Works in April 1927 for repairs and the fitting of an extended bunker before being transhipped to the Island in May. It was later named *Carisbrooke* and in April 1932 renumbered W13 to make way for the transfer of the ex-LBSCR 'E1' class. The second of the trio, W4 (ex-B678), was also laid aside in store from September 1925 but in April 1929 was sent to Eastleigh for similar treatment to W3 and transferred to the Island the following month. Before entering service, W4 received the name *Bembridge* and was subsequently renumbered W14 in April 1932. The second 'Terrier' to bear the number W9 (ex B650) was the last of the batch and received similar treatment to the other two locomotives at Eastleigh but in addition received motor train equipment before being transferred in May 1930 with the name

'A1X' 0–6–0T No. 8 Freshwater waiting at Merstone with the branch train to Ventnor West.
A. BLACKBURN

The original IWCR 'Terrier' tank No. 9 was purchased from the LBSCR in 1898 for £800 and arrived on the island in March of the following year. She saw regular use on the Ventnor Town branch but was scrapped in April 1927. This picture shows the engine awaiting the cutter's torch.

The second 'A1X' class 0–6–0T W9 Fishbourne was often used on Ventnor West services during her short stay on the island.

The second SR 'W9' (ex-B650) was the last 'Terrier' tank to receive a larger bunker and motor train equipment at Eastleigh before being shipped to the island in May 1930. She was allocated to Newport for Ventnor West services but, with the upgrading of permanent way and influx of additional 'O2' tank engines, she became surplus to requirements and was transferred back to the mainland in May 1936. The engine later became service locomotive DS515 and finally BR 32650.

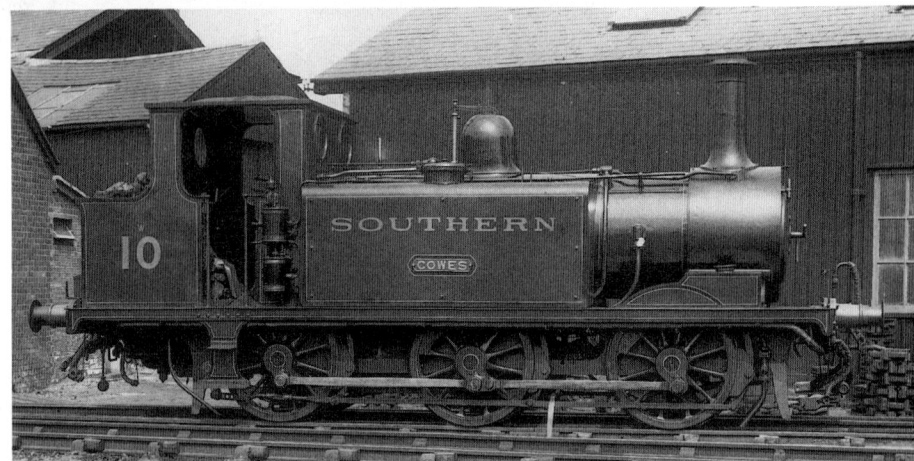

'Terrier' tank W10 Cowes, shown here at Newport, was a regular locomotive on the Ventnor West push/pull trains.

'Terrier' tank class 'A1X' No. W12 Ventnor was another regular performer on the Ventnor West push/pull services.

Fishbourne. W3 and W4 were later fitted with motor train equipment, removed from 'O2s' W23 and W24, at Ryde Works.

The allocation of 'Terriers' in 1930 included W9, W10 and W13 at Newport for working the Ventnor West and Freshwater services and W11 and W12 at Ryde for the Bembridge branch. However with the upgrading of permanent way on the Freshwater and Bembridge lines and associated easing of restrictions, coupled with a further influx of 'O2' 0–4–4Ts, several of the 'Terriers' became surplus to requirements. W12 *Ventnor* was withdrawn in October 1935 and, with W9 *Fishbourne*, W10 *Cowes* and W14 *Bembridge*, was despatched to Eastleigh Works in May 1936. W10 and W12 were stored until October 1940 when they were dumped in the scrap yard and cannibalised until the remnants were cut up in March 1949. W14 was condemned in December 1936 but later reprieved and returned to traffic as No. 2678 in June 1937. W9 was stored at Eastleigh until April 1937 when she was repaired and transferred to service stock as 515S employed at Lancing Carriage Works. After renumbering to DS515, she was returned to operational service as 32650.

After the 1936 transfers to the mainland, only three 'Terriers' (W8 *Freshwater*, W11 *Newport* and W13 *Carisbrooke*) remained at work on the Island. All were shedded at Newport and, being equipped for motor train operation, shared the operation of the Merstone–Ventnor West branch, with pilot duties and trip workings to Medina Wharf and Cement Mills Siding.

On the outbreak of World War Two an emergency timetable was introduced with much reduced train services. As a result several engines were stored including W11 at Ventnor with 'E1' Class W4 and 'O2' Class W29. As the situation eased so services improved but locomotives were still stored until August 1944. During the war years all three 'Terrier' tanks shared the Ventnor West branch duties although when W8 was stored several 'O2s' deputised when W11 or W13 were unavailable.

Before the cessation of hostilities, Ryde Works commenced painting locomotives Malachite Green, No. 13 being the first Island locomotive to receive this livery. With the wartime closure of Cement Mills Siding, the need for three 'Terrier' tank locomotives to work the Ventnor West branch was considered excessive and so the decision was taken to return one engine to the mainland. No. 11 *Newport* was duly chosen and was conveyed from the Island with 'O2' W29 *Alverstone* on the floating crane on 22nd February 1947 after E4 0–6–2T No. 2510 had been delivered to Medina Wharf for trials on the Island railway system. No. 11 was duly repaired and renumbered 2640 and sent to work on the Hayling Island branch. Later she saw service on the Kent and East Sussex line and at Brighton before

'A1X' No. 13 Carisbrooke *sandwiched between the two ex-LCDR 2-coach push/pull sets 483 and 484, restarting the branch train out of St. Lawrence on 20th August 1936.*
H. F. WHEELLER

being condemned from Eastleigh in September 1963. She was duly replaced by 'O2' No. 34 which acquired the name *Newport* in May 1947.

Nos. 8 and 13 finally returned to the mainland, without nameplates, in May 1949, having been ousted by the new 'O2s' Nos. 35 and 36. After several weeks of inactivity at Eastleigh, they both entered the works for attention before emerging as Nos. 32646 and 32677 to work on the Hayling Island branch. No. 32677 was subsequently withdrawn in September 1959 whilst 32646 worked the services turn-and-turn-about with other 'Terriers' until the branch closed in November 1963. She is now back on the Island as W8, alongside W11, at the Haven Street Steam Centre.

The 'O2' class tank locomotives so synonymous with the Isle of Wight railways after the takeover by the Southern Railway in 1923, were only used irregularly on the Ventnor West branch until the latter years when all the 'Terrier' tanks had been returned to the mainland. In the closing months of 1922 officials of the LSWR toured the Island railway system to evaluate the state of each line and to recommend where immediate improvements were required. As might be expected, additional and more powerful locomotives were of the highest priority. Because of weight and permanent way restrictions, the new regime sought spare tank locomotives for transfer to the Island. The South Eastern (ex-SECR) and Central (ex-LBSCR) had no suitable engines available, but fortunately the Western (ex-LSWR) section possessed a number of surplus 'O2' 0–4–4 tank engines made redundant by the London area electrification in 1915 and 1916. Accordingly, in April 1923, Nos. 206 and 211, still in LSWR livery, were fitted with Westinghouse brake equipment and the following month shipped by Admiralty Floating Crane from Portsmouth to Ryde Pier Head.

Happy memories at Ventnor West with 'A1X' No. 13 Carisbrooke.

COLLECTION J. MACKETT

'O2' 0–4–4T No. 31 Chale, *still retaining small bunker and fitted with Drummond type boiler with safety valves in the dome, is seen here leaving Merstone with a Cowes to Sandown train in the summer of 1932. The train is an LSWR 3 set with a centre van brake third, a composite and an ex-PDSWJ brake third. The engine is carrying the Sandown line headcode of one white light or disc over the left-hand buffer.*

The two engines were immediately allocated to work the heavy Ryde Pier Head–Ventnor trains, replacing the IWR Beyer Peacock 2–4–0Ts. Under the separate island numbering scheme, No. 206 was renumbered W19 and No 211 to W20 in February 1924 when they were also repainted in Maunsell green by Ryde Works. Two more 'O2s' (Nos. W21 and W22) were transferred in June 1924, dismantled and shipped by barge to St Helens Quay before being reassembled at Ryde Works by fitters sent across from Eastleigh. In April 1925 two more (Nos. W23 and W24) were landed by the Southern Railway floating crane at Medina Wharf, to be followed by W25 and W26 in June of the same year.

In addition to the Westinghouse air pump bolted to the left-hand side of the smokebox with long cylindrical air reservoir on top of the left-hand side tank, Nos. W23 and W24 were fitted with motor train gear for possible working of the Ventnor West and Bembridge branches. After an initial test between Merstone and Ventnor West, wiser counsels prevailed and transferred the locomotives from Newport to Ryde to work the lucrative main line to Ventnor. The motor train gear was not removed from W23 and W24 until March 1930 when it was transferred to 'Terriers' W3 and W4.

The 'O2s' carrying Adams type boilers had the following dimensions:

Cylinders	$17\frac{1}{2}$ ins by 24 ins
Coupled wheels	4 ft 10 ins
Trailing wheels	3 ft 0 ins
Wheelbase	20 ft 4 ins
Boiler diameter	4 ft 2 ins
length	9 ft 5 ins
Firebox length	5 ft 0 ins
Heating surfaces	
Tubes ($119 \times 1\frac{3}{4}$)	898 sq.ft
Firebox	89 sq.ft
Total	987 sq.ft
Boiler pressure	160 lbs psi
Grate area	13.75 sq.ft
Water capacity	800 gallons
Coal capacity	2 tons
Weight in working order	46 tons 18 cwt
Max axle loading	16 tons 8 cwt

Nine boilers were supplied to Drummond pattern with dome top lock-up safety valves, and six 'O2s', transferred to the Island between March 1926 and May 1928, Nos. W27 to W32 inclusive, carried these boilers on arrival. The tube layout and heating surfaces differed.

Tubes ($180 \times 1\frac{3}{4}$)	785 sq.ft
Firebox	87 sq.ft
Total	872 sq.ft
Grate area	14.9 sq.ft

The Drummond pattern boilers failed to produce the output of the Adams boilers, and W27–W32 suffered from priming and erratic steaming. Therefore between June 1936 and September 1938 Adams boilers were substituted. In September 1932 a larger bunker was fitted to W19 *Osborne*. After some modifications had been made to the design, larger bunkers were fitted to all the 'O2s', commencing with W26 *Whitwell*. This increased the carrying capacity to 3 tons of coal, but increased the weight of locomotives in working order to 48 tons 8 cwt, with maximum axle loading on the trailing wheels of 18 tons 8 cwt.

A class which rarely saw service on the Ventnor West branch, but must be included for their odd excursion on the line, were the ex-LBSCR Class 'E1' 0–6–0s. Although goods traffic on the Island lines was generally relatively light, there were considerable movements of coal between Medina Wharf and Newport and bagged cement from Cement Mills, both for distribution throughout the Island. The 'Terrier' tanks were underpowered for such duties so the Southern Railway authorities decided, after the upgrading and relaying of the Island permanent way, to transfer four of the Class 'E1' to the Island, three in July 1932 and the fourth in June 1933. Before transfer all were taken into Eastleigh Works to be fitted with replacement boilers, injectors, sight feed lubricators and Drummond

'E1' 0–6–0Ts made occasional forays over the Ventnor West branch, usually with ballast trains. This view shows No. 3 Ryde at Newport shed on 11th June 1946.
IAN L. WRIGHT

pattern chimneys. B136 became W1 *Medina*, B152 was renumbered W2 *Yarmouth* and B154 became W3 *Ryde*. B131 received the number W4 and name *Wroxall*. Leading dimensions were:

Cylinders	17 in by 24 ins
Coupled wheels	4 ft 6 ins
Wheelbase	15 ft 3 ins
Boiler diameter	4 ft 0 ins
length	10 ft 2 ins
Firebox length	5 ft 2 1/8 in
Heating surface	
Tubes (174 × 1¾ ins)	841 sq.ft
Firebox	83 sq.ft
Total	924 sq.ft
Boiler pressure	170 lbs psi
Grate area	15.5 sq.ft
Water capacity	900 gallons
Coal capacity	2 tons 5 cwt
Weight in working order	44 tons 3 cwt
Maximum axle loading	15 tons 18 cwt

In 1946 the Southern Railway authorities gave considerable thought to the use of more powerful locomotives on the Island and in particular, the possibility of using push-pull trains on the Ryde–Ventnor line. In December 1946 ex-LBSCR Billinton large radial 0–6–2T Class 'E4' No. 2510 was taken into Eastleigh Works for modification to the Island loading gauge which included the fitting of a shorter chimney. On 22nd February 1947 No. 2510 was shipped across the Solent from Southampton Docks to Medina Wharf and entered trial service from Newport shed a few days later. During the initial tests the locomotive ran on all lines with Walter Gear as nominated driver.

Unfortunately, the long coupled wheelbase, tight clearances and poor braking, combined with heavier coal consumption when compared with the more flexible 'O2' class locomotives, meant No. 2510 was soon relegated to the position of spare engine at Newport shed, with use restricted to the Sandown to Cowes line. The engine was seldom steamed and returned to the mainland on 14th April 1949.

Principal dimensions were:

Cylinders	18 in by 26 ins
Coupled wheels	5 ft 0 ins
Radial wheels	4 ft 0 ins
Wheelbase	21 ft 6 ins
Boiler diameter	4 ft 3 ins
length	10 ft 7¼ ins
Firebox length	5 ft 8¼ ins
Heating surfaces	
Tubes (242 × 1 5/8 ins)	1106.5 sq.ft
Firebox	93.0 sq.ft
Total	1199.5 sq.ft
Grate area	17.25 sq.ft
Boiler pressure	160 lbs psi
Water capacity	
Side tanks	1000 gallons
Well tank	408 gallons
Total	1408 gallons
Coal capacity	2.25 tons
Weight in working order	52 tons 12 cwt
Maximum axle load	14 tons 15 cwt

In May 1947 an additional 'O2' No. 34 *Newport* (ex-No. 201) was shipped across to the Island as a replacement for 'Terrier' 0–6–0T No. 11 which had been despatched to the mainland on 22nd February. With No. 34 came sister engine No. 29 *Alverstone* returning from works overhaul at Eastleigh and painted in malachite green livery.

At nationalisation British Railways inherited the four Class 'E1' 0–6–0Ts Nos. 1–4, two 'Terrier' 0–6–0Ts Nos. 8 and 13, and twenty-one Class 'O2s' Nos. 14–34. Although the 'Terriers' usually found occupation on the Ventnor West branch, there was little else for them to do. At the end of 1948 the motive power authorities agreed it was uneconomic to retain a class of two locomotives with associated spares on the Island when useful duties could be found for them on the mainland. Two 'O2' class engines surplus to requirements, Nos. 30181 and 198, were sent to Eastleigh Works in March 1949 and fitted with Westinghouse brakes and large bunker. Renumbered 35 and

36, the engines were sent via Southampton to the Island on 13th April 1949. During conversion the pair were fitted with motor train equipment and, before embarkation, the former worked the Winchester–Alton push-pull trains in place of an 'M7' 0–4–4T. After arrival at Ryde, the works fitted No. 35 with the nameplates removed from 'Terrier' No. 8 *Freshwater* whilst No. 36 inherited the name *Carisbrooke*. The engines were stationed at Newport and immediately took over the Ventnor West workings from the smaller Brighton tanks which were returned to Eastleigh in May 1949. Unlike some of her sister engines, No. 35 was painted lined black by Eastleigh and this heralded the painting of all 'O2' tanks in similar livery. No. 36 was, however, initially in unlined black. The pair continued to work the Ventnor West branch turn-and-turn-about on a regular basis until closure of the line. In the event of both being out of traffic, an unfitted 'O2' deputised on the line and No. 27 *Merstone* worked the branch services on the final day of operation, 13th September 1952, because *Merstone* was considered a more appropriate name with its local association than either *Freshwater* or *Carisbrooke*.

The Ventnor West branch was always worked by an engine on daily duty from Newport shed, usually working a goods from Newport to Merstone to take up the branch workings before returning again to Newport in the evening with a late evening freight. Two crew rosters were involved with the first set working the engine out and the early run, before being relieved by the late turn set of men who worked the engine back to shed. After the legislation on footplate crews' hours, the workings were covered by three sets of men. The Ventnor West line was always a favourite with enginemen for it was the most scenic on the Island and 'off the beaten track'. Officialdom was nearly always fully occupied dealing with the more lucrative parts of the system and handling crises at Newport or Ryde, so for many days the running of the branch was left to the respective train crews and any available local station staff. Consequently, exploits were numerous including the picking of mushrooms from Farmer Choat's fields and the purloining of cabbages, lettuces, turnips and swedes and other vegetables from lineside fields. In the early years a few of the drivers carried shotguns to bag rabbits and gamebirds which strayed near the railway.

In 1950 the branch working was covered by one locomotive duty, departing Newport at 6.15 am or 6.25 am with a freight for Merstone. The engine then hauled Ventnor services, commencing with the 7.35 am to Ventnor West and finishing with the 2.00 pm from Ventnor West to Merstone. After a short standover when engine crews were changed and the fire cleaned, the engine worked the 3.10 pm freight to Sandown and

'A1X' class No. 13 Carisbrooke *at Merstone with the 1.25 p.m. to Ventnor West on 16th September 1948.*   PAMLIN PRINTS

'O2' 0-4-4T No. 27 Merstone, in malachite green livery and lettered 'British Railways', running round its train at Ventnor West on 17th September 1948. The branch duty code 22 is shown on the plate mounted on the centre lamp bracket above the buffer beam.
PAMLIN PRINTS

return before once again taking up branch duties commencing with the 4.25 pm Merstone to Ventnor West. After terminating with the 7.57 pm ex Ventnor West due at Merstone at 8.18½ pm, the engine worked back to Newport with a freight train, departing the junction at 8.33 pm. The total daily mileage of 144, or 134 if the Sandown trip was excluded, equated to a weekly mileage of 800. In SR and BR days it was customary for the locomotive to carry the duty number on a board mounted on the lamp bracket. Duties incorporating work on the branch included 16 in 1951, 20 in 1946 and 22 in 1947/8.

Drivers on the branch were always on the lookout for free meals and on many occasions an engineman, noting that a pheasant had been hit between Godshill and Merstone, requested the signalman's permission to return along the line to collect the trophy. The signalman usually obliged if there was enough time available and handed the staff to the driver to allow the locomotive to enter the single line section. The arrangement was on the understanding that occasionally a gamebird would grace the signalman's dining table.

For refreshments the locomotivemen visited the signal box at Merstone during standover to make a can of tea and pass the time of day with the signalman. Locomotivemen working the branch in Southern Railway and BR days included drivers Eddie Pragnell, Alec Bailey, with his fireman Cyril Eason, 'Mad' Maurice Parsons, Harold Lacey, Bill Miller, Ted Joyce (who considered the line his favourite), Walter Gear, Jim Hunnybun, Maurice Prouter, also Len Harvie with fireman Andrew Ross, Arthur Turner and fireman Hugh Snow, Ernie Chiverton with fireman George Ellis, and Montie Harvey with fireman Bob Church. Jack Sewell with fireman L. Harris worked the last branch train to Ventnor West and return on Saturday, 13th September 1952, on Newport duty 16 with 'O2' Class No. 27 *Merstone*.

The headcode carried during IWCR days (described as seen when a train approached, not as seen from the footplate), was one white light over the left-hand buffer for passenger and mixed trains, one white light over the right-hand buffer for light engines, and one white light over both buffers for goods and coal trains. After grouping the Southern Railway introduced a route coding, and between Merstone and Ventnor West the locomotive carried one disc or lamp above the right-hand buffer for any class of train. In IWCR days the locomotive also often conveyed a red destination board with white lettering at the base of the chimney or on the lamp bracket on the bunker.

Watering facilities for locomotives working the branch were provided by water cranes at the south end of each platform face at Merstone, fed from a 2,000 gallons capacity static tank which was fed from the flooded subway. At Ventnor West the water crane located at the departure end of the up platform was fed from a 200 gallon capacity tank (the smallest on the Island). The down side column at Merstone was later moved to a point at the centre of the down loop. Inspection pits were available at Ventnor West (short siding) and Merstone (No. 1 siding) to enable drivers to inspect their locomotive or oil up.

In the event of any accident on the branch Newport breakdown van and its attendant crew were responsible for attending the mishap. Included in their equipment were two double

'O2' 0–4–4T No. 35 Freshwater with push/pull unit 503 at Ventnor West on 3rd September 1952. This engine arrived on the island in 1949 as a replacement for 'Terrier' tank No. 8 and was push/pull fitted especially for use on the Ventnor West services.
R. M. CASSERLEY

Push/pull fitted 'O2' 0–4–4T No. 36 Carisbrooke in unlined black livery at Newport shed on 27th June 1953. Together with sister locomotive No. 35, it was regularly utilized on the Ventnor West branch trains until closure of the line.
H. C. CASSERLEY

rerailing ramps, two traversing jacks and a hand screw jack. If necessary for rerailing purposes a 10 ton capacity travelling crane was available at Ryde St Johns and 5 ton crane at Newport.

The whistle codes used on the branch included:

Merstone Junction

to or from Newport and Ventnor	1 long
to or from Newport and Sandown	3 long
to or from Newport and Sandown via loop	2 long and 1 short
to or from Loop and Dead End	1 long and 2 short
to or from No. 2 Siding	1 short 1 crow (IWCR)
	1 short 1 long (SR)

Ventnor West

No. 1 Platform Road	1 short
No. 2 Platform Road	2 short
from No. 1 to No. 2 Platform at lower crossover	3 short

In addition drivers were required to sound the engine whistle when approaching station level crossings and the undermentioned crossings:

Footpath on the Ventnor side of Merstone			
Down Distant signal at	9 miles	0 chains	
Merstone end of Godshill platform	9 "	61	"
Dean crossing	12 "	77	"
St Lawrence footpath	13 "	44	"
Footpath Ventnor side of St Lawrence Station	14 "	2	"
Ventnor Quarry	14 "	41	"

COACHING STOCK

From 1897 the IWCR worked the Newport Godshill and St Lawrence Railway with existing coaching stock and, although Conacher advised in 1900 that the company had purchased five vehicles specifically for the Ventnor express traffic, the coaches were never dedicated to the Ventnor line and became general user. The IWCR stock consisted mainly of second-hand four-wheeled vehicles, purchased from the London & North Western, London & South Western, London Brighton & South Coast, Great Eastern and North London Railways, together with two composites and a third acquired from the IW(NJ)R. The branch train in the early years was usually a

IWCR 2-4-0T No. 5 built by Beyer Peacock (ex-R & NR Osborne) approaching Ventnor Town distant signal with a train of six 4-wheel coaches in 1900 soon after the opening of the line from St. Lawrence to the terminus.
A. BLACKBURN

mixture of four-wheel coaches from the various companies and no specific stock was allocated to the service. Formation normally consisted of 2 thirds, a composite and brake third or full brake. The poor financial return experienced after the opening of the line forced the IWCR to seek ways of cutting operational costs and thoughts were turned to the purchase of a steam railcar to work the Ventnor Town services.

Negotiations to find suitably low tenders lasted almost a year until 1905 when Hurst Nelson quoted £1,450, a figure that was acceptable. The quoting firm only built the carriage portion, with the locomotive unit supplied by R & W Hawthorn (Works No. 2663). Delivery was made on 4th October 1906 and the railmotor duly entered service on the Ventnor Town branch on 5th October. As delivered the vehicle provided accommodation for 6 first class and 44 third class passengers together with one ton of luggage. The unit was equipped with Westinghouse brake, and passengers had the benefit of oil lighting. The railmotor proved economical in service and was quoted to run at 60 per cent of the cost of a locomotive and two carriages. After trials on the Ventnor Town services, the railcar received minor modifications in 1907 to enable it to work on the Freshwater, Yarmouth and Newport line. Recurring problems of locomotive axleboxes overheating were finally overcome in September 1908 and during 1910 acetylene lighting replaced oil in the passenger saloon. In the same year the vehicle returned for a short period to regular service on the Ventnor Town branch but in November 1910 the railmotor was laid aside, and soon afterwards the coach was separated from the traction portion and equipped with a second set of bogies, renumbered 52 in the IWCR carriage fleet and placed in ordinary service. When the Southern Railway took over in 1923 the coach was downgraded to a brake third, given the number 4103 and allocated diagram No. 217. During the 1930s the wood panelling was replaced by steel sheeting and it partnered ex-LBSC saloon No. 6986 as part of the set used on the 'Tourist' through train from Shanklin (later Ventnor) to Freshwater. It was finally withdrawn in April 1949 and converted to Tool Van DS 1782 for use on the mainland.

Early in 1909 the IWCR formed a second railmotor No. 2 by coupling ex-Cowes and Newport 0-4-2ST No. 3 (Black, Hawthorn & Co. No. 116 of 1870) with the 12-wheel ex-Midland Railway clerestory brake composite purchased in 1907 for £250. The locomotive was fitted with casing to match the outline of the carriage and a mechanical form of push-pull control. The railmotor was completed in April 1909 and entered service in May 1909 having cost £437 9s 5d for conversion, including the price of the carriage. Railmotor No. 2 worked on the Ventnor Town branch but was only employed spasmodically and was not popular with train crews or maintenance staff. In June 1912 the unit was taken out of service. The carriage was returned to traffic as No. 7 in the IWCR coaching fleet. The locomotive, with sheeting removed, went back to its former duties at Medina Wharf. In 1917 the carriage was converted to ride on 4-wheel bogies and the clerestory was removed. It was renumbered by the Southern Railway No. 6988 in 1925. Withdrawal from stock came in 1937.

After the unsuccessful attempts to cut operating costs using the rail-motor principle, the IWCR was forced to revert to the normal locomotive-hauled formation for the branch. Trains again reverted to anything from two to four coaches and this arrangement remained until after the grouping in 1923. On takeover the Southern authorities were quick to realise that early action was needed to reduce the operational costs of branch working in the face of encroaching competition from the Vectis Bus Company. Push-pull working was the answer, using locomotives and suitable hauled rolling stock instead of railmotors.

On 31st August 1924 the new regime transferred to the Island, via St Helens Quay, two push-pull sets Nos. 483 and 484, formed of ex-London Chatham & Dover Railway 6-wheel stock, converted to 4-wheel when modified for push-and-pull working. Set 483 consisted of Brake Third 4111 converted

Motor train working was a feature of the Ventnor West branch for many years. Ex-LCDR 4-wheel push/pull set No. 483 formed of brake third No. 4111 and composite No. 6368, and set No. 484, brake third No. 4112 and composite No. 6369, sandwich 'Terrier' class 'A1X' 0–6–0T No. 8 Freshwater at Ventnor West on 20th August 1936. The destination board on the side of No. 4111 reads 'Merstone, St. Lawrence, Ventnor West'. The push/pull sets were withdrawn in 1938. H. F. WHEELLER

Class 'A1X' 0–6–0T No. 13 Carisbrooke *taking water at Ventnor West on 20th August 1936. In the foreground is the locomotive inspection pit and alongside a pile of ashes as evidence that crews cleaned the fire during stopover at the terminus.* H. F. WHEELLER

from First Saloon No. 22 and dating from 1888, together with Composite 6368, built in 1887 and converted from First Saloon No. 18. Set 484 was formed of Brake Third 4112 converted from Brake Third No. 219 of 1898 and Composite No. 6369 built in 1887 as First Saloon No. 20. Nos. 4111, 6368 and 6369 (being converted from First Saloons) were 28 feet in length whilst 4112 was 9 inches longer. Modification of the vehicles did not follow a standard pattern for Brake Third No. 4111 was converted by turning the small compartment and part of the saloon into the driving compartment and guard's van. The other Brake Third No. 4112 had the guard's van altered to include the driving compartment whilst the three passenger compartments were opened out into a single saloon with two doors either side, the original centre compartment doors being sealed up but retaining their droplights. The two sets were employed on the Freshwater line until 'Terrier' tanks were equipped for motor-train working in January/February 1926 after which they were used on the Ventnor West and later Bembridge branches.

In June 1938 both sets were withdrawn from traffic and the underframes of 4111 and 6368 were subsequently sent to Lancing as works flats 1290S and 1291S. Both carriage bodies were sold to H. B. Joliffe Ltd, Cowes, for use as offices or huts. Of set 484, the body of 4112, complete with corridor connection, was transferred to serve as a chalet at Gurnard Marsh whilst 6369 body was used as a summerhouse in a garden at Newtown. No record exists of the underframe disposal.

Fortunately, both bodies have been recovered and after considerable attention have been mounted on 4-wheel underframes at Haven Street, and together with W8 are representative of the Ventnor West push-pull train on the Isle of Wight Steam Railway operating between Smallbrook Junction and Wootton.

On Sunday, 26th April 1925, four ex-South Eastern and Chatham rail-motor coaches, converted to pairs of open bogie coaches, were transferred to the Island for push-pull working on the Bembridge and Ventnor West branches. Designated Sets 481 and 482, the former consisted of Composite 6366 and Driving Brake Third 4110, and the latter Composite 6367 and Driving Brake Third 4109. The vehicles were accompanied on the crossing by Class 'O2' locomotives W23 and W24, a horse-box and 4-wheel inspection saloon. The locomotives were piped for push-pull working and, despite weight restrictions on the Ventnor West line, an experiment was undertaken on the branch with W24 and a two-coach ex-SECR set manned by a Newport driver and Ryde fireman, accompanied by a locomotive inspector. The late Percy Vallender, who acted as fireman on the trip, remembered the gingerly progress made by the train from Merstone to Ventnor West and return. The experiment was not repeated and as both branch lines intended for working by these units were prohibited to the 'O2' engines, the coaches were used in normal hauled formations although seldom to Ventnor West where the LCDR sets reigned supreme. With the shortage of push-pull sets on the Eastern

EX-LCDR PUSH/PULL SET No. 484

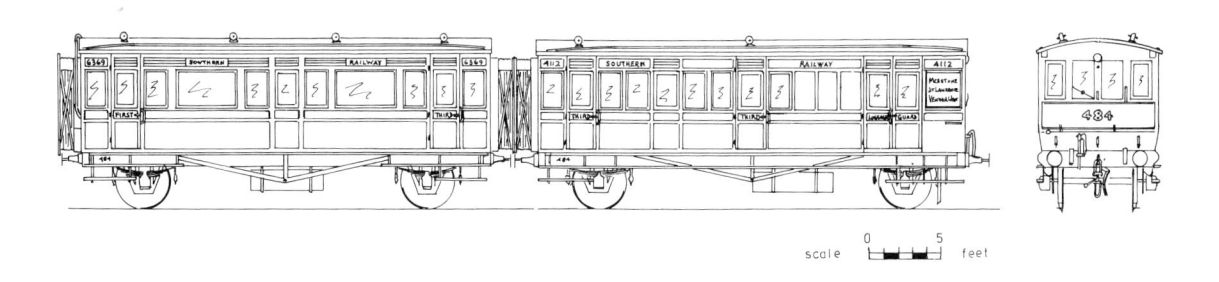

The former coach portion of steam railmotor No. 1 shown in Southern Railway days as brake third No. 4103 to Diagram 217 on the 'tourist' train in May 1934.
COLLECTION
R. A. SILSBURY

Former IWCR ex-Midland Railway brake composite, SR No. 6988, at Ryde St. Johns Road as a Ryde–Ventnor train. The vehicle was withdrawn from stock in 1937.
COLLECTION
R. A. SILBURY

The driver and porter pass the time of day at Ventnor West alongside 'Terrier' tank No. 8 Freshwater and the one-coach branch train driving push/pull composite No. 6987 on 18th April 1949. The destination board on the side of the vehicle denotes 'Merstone, St. Lawrence, Ventnor West'.
J. H. ASTON

'O2' class No. 27 Merstone pulling into Whitwell with push/pull set No. 503. Formed of ex-LBSCR vehicles, the nearer coach is composite 6367 dating from 1911, whilst the driving brake third 4169 is next to the engine. The set, together with single coach composite No. 6987, was transferred to the island in 1938 to replace the withdrawn ex-LCDR 4-wheel push/pull sets 483 and 484.
COLLECTION R. A. SILSBURY

Push/pull set 503 with 'O2' class 0-4-4T at Ventnor West on 28th July 1951.   PAMLIN PRINTS

Section of the Southern, the vehicles were returned to the mainland in May 1927.

In the event of non-availability of the push-pull sets, ordinary stock was substituted with the locomotive running round the train at each end of the journey. Most coaches were 4-wheelers of LCDR and LBSCR origin, the former originally 6-wheelers.

On the mainland by the mid-1930s some of the older LBSCR push-pull bogie coaches were being withdrawn and scrapped as ex LSWR vehicles were adapted for similar work. Electrification reduced the push-pull duties on the Central section and with suitable ex-LBSC air-controlled stock less than 30 years old, the Southern authorities decided to transfer three vehicles to the Isle of Wight enabling withdrawal of the ex LCDR 4 wheel sets. Two required minor modification before entering service. The coaches were

Brake Third	3828	Built 1911	Set 731 to IW	renumbered 4169	Set 503
Composite	6204	Built 1911	Set 731 to IW	renumbered 6367	Set 503
Composite	6238	Built 1921	Set 715 to IW	renumbered 6987	Single coach

On the mainland, Set 731 was one of a batch of corridor push-pull sets designed for use on the busy Brighton to Worthing service. The two coaches were gangwayed with the corridor along one side of each vehicle but without partition between corridor and seating. The unit comprised a guard's-/driver's compartment, 14 ft 2 in in length, with sliding doors at the extreme end of the vehicle, 5 third class compartments each 5 ft 5 ins wide, a corridor partition followed by one 5 ft 5 in third compartment and one of 5ft $11\frac{3}{4}$ in. Seating was spartan with restricted leg room. A standard underframe with motor train pipes was used for two sets of double accumulator racks (for the electric lighting) at the inner end with a dynamo at the brake end. For use on the Isle of Wight, the sliding door was removed, the sides made good, and a double set of outward opening doors was substituted centred 5 ft 8 in from the end of the vehicle. The driving end was altered from timber panelling to steel sheet but the original style was retained with four large windows and electric sockets for head/tail lamps. Drop lights were fitted in the sides adjacent to and opposite the driving position. The air brake system, installed by the LBSCR and altered to vacuum by the SR, was reinstated on return to the Island.

The composite trailer 6367 was arranged so that from the gangway end the accommodation was one 5 ft $5\frac{3}{4}$ in Third compartment, five 5 ft $11\frac{3}{4}$ in Thirds, corridor partition, two 6 ft 6 in Firsts, corridor partition and one 6 ft 6 in First. Originally electrically connected by jumper to the Brake Third and having no accumulators, the trailer was fitted with single racks both sides at the First class end of the underframes but no dynamo. Mansell wood centre wheels were retained on both coaches.

Composite 6238 was from a later build and had formed part of Set 715 which was separated in 1938. Originally a trailer composite with five Thirds and four First compartments, it was converted for Island use to have driver's/guard's compartment 12 ft 9 in in length, two 6ft $4\frac{1}{2}$ in First compartments partition, five 5 ft 5 in Third compartments, followed by a gangway connection, which, although retained, was regularly locked out of use. The underframe was generally similar to 6367 and the brake/driving end similar to 4169. On conversion 6987 retained all 18 torpedo-shaped roof ventilators which were fitted to the compartments. The pair of vehicles and single brake composite worked the Ventnor West line for most of their life but unexpected problems were encountered when 'O2' class Nos. 35 and 36 commenced push-pull duties on the branch, for it was discovered that the larger bunker fouled 6987's gangway. The gangway was subsequently removed and a single panel substituted. No. 6987 was considered part of Set 503 but it is not known whether the vehicle ran with 6367 and 4169 in service to form a three-car set. In 1940/1 6987 was shown allocated to Newport for the Ventnor West branch although in BR days it worked on the Bembridge branch for a short time. All three coaches were officially withdrawn in December 1955 and were broken up at St Helens Wharf.

In 1947 a second push-pull set similar to 503 was transferred to the Island, essentially for service on the Bembridge branch though it ran for short periods to Ventnor West. The set consisted of:

Brake Third	3825	Built 1911	Set 728 to IW	renumbered 4167	Set 505
Composite	6201	Built 1911	Set 728 to IW	renumbered 6366	Set 505

The only distinguishable feature between the two sets was a minor difference in the van side panels, accumulator boxes and complete absence of torpedo ventilators. In 1950 set 505 was split but was then reformed to continue service on the Bembridge branch. Like Set 503, vehicles 4167 and 6366 were withdrawn in December 1955 and broken up at St Helens Wharf.

For through journeys to and from Cowes and Freshwater normal hauled stock was utilised and trains were formed of bogie carriages of LBSCR origin introduced on the Island from 1936 and ex-SECR from 1948. With little demand for separate vehicles for parcels traffic, few vans ran on the branch but types available and used irregularly included ex-LSWR and LCDR 4-wheelers and bogie guards vans, and ex-LSWR, LCDR and SR 4-wheel luggage vans.

Side destination boards showing names of terminal stations and certain of the intermediate stops were fixed or slotted on the side of each brake coach on all Island lines during Southern and BR days. The Ventnor West branch was no exception and the lettering on the boards used allowed for trains starting from Merstone or Newport. The boards read 'Merstone, St Lawrence, Ventnor West' on one side and 'Newport, Merstone, Ventnor West' on the reverse.

WAGONS

The IWCR provided all goods vehicles for the line, but, in deference to the working arrangements made with the FYNR, purchased no additional wagons specifically for the NGSLR. 8-ton and 10-ton capacity open wagons used for coal, coke and manure traffic were of the 5-plank type, varying in length from 13 ft 6 in to 15 ft 0 in, with a few 6-plank wagons equipped with dumb buffers. Many of the earlier wagons were purchased second-hand from rolling stock dealers, but later purchases were made from the Great Eastern and Midland Railways. Wagons were painted grey with white lettering but, just before or after World War One, the company commenced painting the freight stock all-over black with large white letters 'IWC' spread across the full width of the wagon.

Covered goods vans for the conveyance of perishable produce, fruit and flowers provided by the company included rather squat 8- and 10-ton capacity ex-Midland Railway vans of 9 ft 0 in wheelbase, 17 ft 11 in length over buffers and overall height of 9 ft 11 3/8 in. Between 1904 and 1909 over 20 ex-GER covered goods vans were also acquired, again with 9 ft 0 in wheelbase but height of 10 ft $7\frac{1}{2}$ in. For conveyance of livestock the IWCR possessed only 8 cattle wagons of which the majority were acquired from the GER, which was a useful source of vehicles fitted with Westinghouse brake, which was standard on the IWCR. The vehicles had 16 ft 8 in body length, 9 ft 0 in wheelbase, and height of 10 ft $10\frac{1}{2}$ in, but saw infrequent use on the Ventnor Town branch.

The IWCR owned three goods brake vans, one 10-ton ex-Midland vehicle purchased in July 1911, and two 7-ton Brake and Transit Vans of local hybrid construction on LBSCR frames. Other vehicles included seven ballast wagons, of which four were 3-plank dropside ballast wagons purchased from the

Ex-LCDR Van No. 1010 at Merstone on 24th August 1936, typical of vans used occasionally on the branch for parcels traffic.
H. F. WHEELLER

This SR 4-wheel tool van utilized by the Engineering Department's bridge section was believed to have been built by the IWCR in 1911 on the underframe of an old coal wagon. The vehicle was sold to the FYNR in 1913, became covered goods van No. 15 and SR No. 47033 in March 1927. Weighing 4 tons 11 cwt and capable of conveying a load of 8 tons, it was transferred to service stock in August 1930. Shown standing at Whitwell, the van was withdrawn in 1939.
COLLECTION R. SILSBURY

Midland in 1911 (which were utilised on the branch to clear debris from a chalk fall at St Lawrence in July 1912), six carriage trucks, twelve timber wagons, a tar tank and two water tanks. During independent days wagons of the IWR and FYNR also conveyed goods and merchandise to stations on the line.

To achieve standardisation of stock and introduce improvements, the Southern Railway withdrew nearly all the former Island railway wagons as they became due for repair. The majority of new wagons transferred across the Solent were of LBSCR design but the brake-vans and some car-trucks were LSWR vintage, whilst ballast wagons were from the SECR. In 1936 it was decided to transfer all the general goods traffic to Messrs Pickford's wharf at Cowes for onward delivery by road and thenceforth only departmental, ballast and coal was conveyed by goods trains to Island stations. However, sugar beet and some root vegetable traffic required conveyance in open wagons. The covered goods vans were either broken up as surplus to requirements or transferred back to the mainland to serve as stores vans. Even the six cattle wagons registered in the early 1930s were reduced to three when the SR converted three to passenger luggage vans in 1935. Only coal traffic in small quantities and sugar beet remained on the branch in the latter years, conveyed in the ubiquitous 5-plank ex-LBSCR or 8-plank SR open wagons.

All repairs and maintenance of coaching stock and wagons used on the Ventnor West line was undertaken at Newport.

For some years LBSCR 10 ton van No. 46939 languished in the siding at Godshill as shown here in 1950. The vehicle was originally built for 8 ton capacity in 1900 but was transferred to the island as a 10 ton van. The strengthening bar across the end of the van is of particular interest. PAMLIN PRINTS

The Southern Railway transferred ten 20 ton LBSCR dropside ballast wagons to the island to assist the Civil Engineer in track maintenance. No. 62810, shown here in No. 1 siding at Merstone, was built in 1904 and was withdrawn in 1955.
PAMLIN PRINTS

'A1X' 0–6–0T No. 13 Carisbrooke pushing 2-coach push/pull set No. 503 towards the junction at Merstone with the 2.00 p.m. ex-Ventnor West on 16th September 1948.
PAMLIN PRINTS

CHAPTER TEN
NATIONALISATION AND CLOSURE

'A1X' class 0–6–0T No. 13 Carisbrooke, *in malachite green with black and yellow lining and British Railways lettering, with the branch train at Ventnor West on 21st March 1949. Within two months the locomotive was returned to the mainland.* R. DAY

THE nationalisation of the railways from 1st January 1948 brought few changes to the appearance of the Ventnor West branch which retained its Southern Railway atmosphere until closure. Some stocks of SR tickets remained in use although those in greatest demand, and Holiday Runabout tickets, were replaced by those bearing the legend 'Railway Executive'. Locomotives working the line soon lost the 'Southern' identity from their side tanks to be replaced by 'British Railways' although the malachite green livery was retained on 'Terrier' tank No. 13 until it returned to the mainland in May 1949. O2 and E1 locomotives were also green. Black became the standard livery with cream and red lining and the lion and wheel emblem. Coaching stock also retained the malachite livery for a brief period before being painted in red livery.

British Railways made few alterations to the timetable, and all branch services connected with Sandown to Cowes line trains at Merstone. Cheap day tickets were offered to all destinations on the Island and in connection with special events but, despite these offers, passenger loadings were poor except for the few weeks of high summer. Freight traffic was almost non-existent except for small flows of coal and coke to fuel merchants at Whitwell and Ventnor West, and sugar beet from Godshill and Whitwell in season. The goods sidings at Godshill and Whitwell gradually succumbed to weeds and wild flowers. Ventnor West yard, because of its sheltered position, was used for winter storage of coaches and wagons, or vehicles waiting condemnation.

The line still suffered from operating 'incidents'. On one occasion driver Jim Hunnybun was taken off shed duties to cover for driver Fred Radford who was sick. His mate for the early turn was a passed cleaner who had worked nights and was on overtime. After taking 'Terrier' tank No. 13 light engine to Merstone, the pair took up duty on the branch. The trip to Ventnor West was uneventful but on the return working with the engine pushing, Jim told his novice to leave everything in the cab until after St Lawrence. Unfortunately, after leaving the first station, the lad pulled the regulator wide open and promptly lost most of the fire from the firebox through the chimney. After stopping at Whitwell, Hunnybun decided the only way of making Merstone was to omit the call at Godshill. Fortunately, no passengers were waiting on the platform and the train rattled through at full speed. Merstone was reached with the fire on No. 13 almost non-existent. After various expletives addressed to the poor passed cleaner, the two footplate men and Len Sheath, the signalman, pulled down part of a fence and used some spare sleepers to build the fire up for the next round trip.

By 1949 the new regime considered the retention of two 'Terrier' 0-6-0 tank locomotives, Nos. 8 and 13, an expensive luxury since their only regular duty after the withdrawal of the Pan Pit to Cement Mills traffic in 1944 was on the Ventnor West branch. A decision was made to standardise the passenger locomotives to the 'O2' class and so the two 'A1X' locomotives were transferred to the mainland where there was urgent requirement for their services. Their places were taken by two 'O2' engines Nos. 35 and 36, painted in the BR black (the former lined out and the latter unlined) and fitted with push and pull gear for the branch working. Not many months after their arrival an unusual incident occurred when the train propelled by 'O2' No. 35 came to an abrupt halt north of Whitwell station and then reversed back to the station. The

The 1.25 p.m. Merstone to Ventnor West train at Whitwell hauled by 'O2' No. 27 Merstone on 17th September 1948. The 'O2' was deputising for the usual 'Terrier' tank. PAMLIN PRINTS

driver in the leading coach had played no part in these proceedings and promptly returned to the engine to find what, if anything, was mechanically amiss. The reason was soon evident. The fireman, riding alone on the locomotive and operating all controls except the regulator and brake, had noticed an attractive young lady waving an umbrella as the train departed. Without further thought, he disconnected the regulator control, stopped the train, reversed the engine and set back to the station to enable the lady to join the train. The driver admonished his mate in no uncertain terms about this dangerous practice, although in fact he had to acknowledge the lady was worth returning for!

The branch was a favourite for scenic value with passengers especially holidaymakers, and when the occasion permitted (and often as the result of a small tip), the drivers halted the train just beyond the south portal of St Lawrence Tunnel so that travellers could enjoy the view across the English Channel from the high position the railway occupied on the side of the Downs. On one occasion naval exercises were being conducted close to shore and the train was subjected to considerable delay as the crew were overawed by the event. The train reached Ventnor West when they should have been at St Lawrence on the return working. A high spirited run on the return journey, however, made up most of the time and connections were maintained at Merstone.

With only remedial maintenance during the war years and resources and materials in short supply afterwards, permanent way on the branch was in poor condition by 1950. Routine maintenance was carried out but little else had been done since the relaying programme of 1928. The new regime at Waterloo found from traffic returns that except for the twelve weeks of high summer, patronage ranged from sparse to non existent as the branch train often completed a round trip from Merstone to Ventnor West and back for the sole purpose of employing the engine crew and guard. Investigations were made by local management as to the likelihood of an upsurge in traffic, but passengers were abandoning the railway in favour of bus and private car for door-to-door service. As there was no possibility of a transformation or justification for heavy expenditure on renewal of the track and other worn assets, the management deemed the branch a candidate for closure. The first intimation came in July 1950 when several members of the Island staff visiting Waterloo were alarmed to learn that the authorities were taking the first steps to effect withdrawal of all services on the Merstone-Ventnor West branch. Confirmation of the decision came when the Southern Region Civil Engineer and Signal Engineer gave instructions for the maintenance work on St Lawrence Tunnel to cease and for the signalling renewal programme at Ventnor West to be cancelled.

In 1951 there were hopes that the rumours were unfounded as the usual early summer traffic increased the branch receipts. Closure proposals were, however, placed before the IW County Council on 6th June. Despite the gloomy outlook, the value of the branch to some local folk was recognised and at Christmas the family atmosphere among the regular travellers prevailed for on 24th December 1951, when Bill Miller halted No. 35 and her train at Godshill, the local choir were singing carols on the platform. So appreciative were the passengers that Bill held the train until the singers had finished the carol. Little did those gathered on the platform and in the train know that this was to be the last Christmas for the branch. Ironically the coal shortage during the winter of 1951, almost closed the line. Services to Ventnor West were much reduced and on the Bembridge branch suspended altogether.

The Newport branch meeting of the National Union of Railwaymen held on Friday, 1st February 1952, was of considerable importance for H.W. Franklin, president of the NUR, addressed the meeting specifically on the problems associated with the future of the Isle of Wight railways. After formal introduction by F. Sheath, the chairman, Franklin announced that British Railways had made no further progress concerning the suggested closure of the complete Island system except for the Ryde-Ventnor line and certainly appeared to be in no hurry to examine the problem. It was not the Union's duty to tell the Executive to hurry with their deliberations or decisions. At the conclusion of the disclosure the President surprised the gathering by reiterating it was the Union's opinion the Island railwaymen should help themselves by formulating arguments for opposing closure. He concluded 'Unity House could not wave a magic wand' to prevent withdrawal of services.

Late in March 1952 a heavy blizzard swept across the South Coast of England leaving a mantle of white several feet deep and snow blocked many roads on the Isle of Wight. Most of the railways remained open with difficulty but at one time the Ryde–Ventnor line succumbed to the elements. The Ventnor West branch became the life support for Godshill, Whitwell and Ventnor until the roads were gradually reopened. Traffic during the period increased considerably as Ventnor was without bus services for some days.

On 18th May 1952 the Railway Correspondence and Travel Society organised a tour of the Island Railway. After visiting Cowes behind 'E1' 0–6–0T No. 3 *Ryde*, engines were changed at Newport where 'O2' No. 32 *Bonchurch* in malachite livery with British Railways lettering and in the charge of driver Walter Gear, took over for the visit to the Freshwater and Ventnor West branches.

After rumours and counter rumours, the closure of the branch was confirmed in a letter dated 4th June 1952 from the District Traffic Superintendent, Woking, to Ventnor Urban District Council. The withdrawal of services immediately became the main topic for discussion on the agenda when details of the correspondence was announced. The Railway Executive considered that after exhaustive investigation into the economic circumstances of the Merstone to Ventnor West line, it was felt there were no grounds for maintaining the passenger and freight services. The statement attached to the letter was also forwarded to the Transport Users Consultative Committee for the South Eastern area as evidence of the poor passenger loadings on the branch. During a typical summer week in 1951, on any one day, maximum loadings of passengers travelling from Merstone to Ventnor were 122 on the 5.27 pm, 60 on the 4.25 pm and 45 on the 11.27 am, declining to 6 on the 4.25 pm and 6.27 pm, 3 on the 7.27 pm and 1 on the 1.25 pm. In the reverse direction 122 joined the 9.40 am ex Ventnor West but no other train carried more than 38 passengers, whilst totals declined to 4 on the 7.57 pm, 3 on the 6.57 pm and 2 on the 5.57 pm. If summer totals were disappointing, the winter totals of passengers travelling were depressing and virtually destroyed any argument in favour of retention of services. From Merstone to Ventnor West the maximum loading on any one day was 35 passengers on the 7.35 am, 2 on four other trains and no passengers at all on the 11.27 am and 7.27 pm. In the reverse direction 31 travelled on the 8.12 am, reducing to 1 on the 12 noon train and none on the 5.57 pm on three separate occasions. Compared with the railway the local bus service conveyed an average of 450 passengers daily. The only freight carried by the goods services was sugar beet and coal to local fuel merchants whilst other commodities included a few parcels and occasional churns of milk. With no possibility of development in the area, there was little likelihood of traffic growth and withdrawal of services was the only alternative. The Executive considered closure would result in an estimated annual saving of £16,000.

The matter received widespread coverage in the correspondence columns of the Island newspapers where readers deplored closure and suggested the use of lightweight railcars. Following further representation from Whitwell Parish Council and with full support of the Newport branch of the NUR, members of Ventnor UDC voted at their July meeting to write to the Transport Users Consultative Committee objecting to the closure. Unbeknown to the UDC, the TUCC had taken the decision on 1st July 1952 that 'the proposal was one they could not object to and as the County Council had raised no objection' they had advised the Railway Executive to proceed with arrangements for closure.

The announcement brought immediate response by the Ventnor UDC and other parties anxious to avoid closure. Further letters were sent to the TUCC backed up by a deputation which was told the arguments submitted by British Railways contained no grounds in favour of the retention of services. Despite further correspondence from the protestors there was no change of heart at the TUCC and the inevitable resulted. The *Isle of Wight County Press* reported 'the fact remains, the public use of the line has dwindled over a period of several years and it has now become impossible effectively to resist the argument that no undertaking can continue to run such a service at a loss'.

On 1st August 1952 the closure date for the branch was finally announced as 15th September 1952, bringing to an end the long period of uncertainty which had prevailed since the first rumours of impending closure of the line started following the suggestion of a general scheme of local railway economies. The *Isle of Wight County Press* summed up the thoughts of many when it reported 'the line was little used particularly in winter and for this reason closure could not reasonably be opposed.' Within days notices were posted at the branch stations and throughout the island.

CLOSING OF MERSTONE-VENTNOR WEST BRANCH LINE

On and from Monday September 15 1952 the passenger and freight services will be withdrawn from the above line and stations Godshill, Whitwell, St Lawrence and Ventnor West will be closed.

Alternative services were to be arranged by Southern Vectis Omnibus Company and within days an announcement was made that from Monday, 15th September, additional buses would run on Service 9 from Newport St James Square to Ventnor Town Hall via Merstone, Godshill and Whitwell, an arrangement deemed satisfactory to all parties.

Similar notices were placed in local newspapers and as there was no Sunday service, the last trains were to run on Saturday, 13th September. The final few weeks of operation saw the normal summer holiday loadings increased by railway enthusiasts and local people making last journeys on the branch.

On Saturday, 13th September 1952, Class 'O2' 0–4–4T No. 27 *Merstone* was rostered to the branch in place of one of the push/pull fitted engines Nos 35 and 36 because the locomotive carried a name associated with the branch. This proved a popular choice. The locomotive (not fitted for push/pull working) had to run round the train at Merstone and Ventnor West after each trip. Surprisingly, the authorities at Newport only provided a two-coach set with no strengthening, but the main attraction was No. 27 in spotless condition conveying a headboard bearing the simple inscription 'BR Farewell to

The last train from Merstone to Ventnor West passing over Dean level crossing on 13th September 1952 hauled by 'O2' No. 27 Merstone.
PAMLIN PRINTS

Ventnor West 1900–1952' on the top lamp bracket. Throughout the day local people and enthusiasts crowded the two-coach train to pay their last respects to the 'Wittul Express', and Ventnor West was its busiest for many years. Alec Widger, the booking clerk, received such a demand for tickets that many of the printed stocks were exhausted and he was forced to issue blank card and paper tickets. He also exhibited a notice board at the station entrance advising 'If half the people who are interested in this line today had been as interested in the last two years, we should not be closing'. Before the final up run to Ventnor, No. 27 shunted her train into the siding at Merstone to allow the connecting Sandown to Newport services to cross. The branch train then pulled into the platform for the last time and, to the cheers of spectators, departed over exploding detonators to head south to Ventnor West.

At the terminus passengers and wellwishers had been gathering for nearly an hour before the final train was due to depart. Twenty-five members of Ventnor Jazz Band dressed in period costume and led by Jim White as a drum major, paraded through the town and proceeded to the station where they entertained the crowd on the platform. The train arrived in the gathering dusk, exploding detonators as it entered the platform to the cheers and shouts of the crowd. A BBC television crew recorded the last rites as paper streamers were thrown over No. 27 and the coaches. Fireworks exploded as the throng entered into the spirit of the occasion. After the locomotive had run round and recoupled to the train, the engine whistle was sounded and bells rung. Some four minutes late at 8.01 pm, Michael the 7 year old son of Reg Seaman the guard, waved the green flag and Driver Jack Sewell opened the regulator of No. 27 to set the train in motion. His mate, fireman L. Harris, acknowledged the goodwill cheers as the crowd on the platform sang 'Auld Lang Syne' accompanied by the band. The chorus was drowned by exploding detonators and the engine whistle as the train disappeared into the darkness. Amongst those seeing the train away was S.A. Smith, chairman of Ventnor UDC; Ventnor station master, Mr Harms; the Deputy Assistant for the Island railways, A.L. Wallace, and Inspector H.S. Powers. Also present was G. Thorne of Rookley who as a schoolboy had watched the ceremony of the cutting of the first sod in 1893. On the return run, the oil-lit platforms at St Lawrence, Whitwell and Godshill were crowded with people congregating to see the branch train for the last time. At Whitwell Mr A Western, who occupied the station house, made tea for the engine crew whilst at Godshill the communication cord was pulled, delaying the train for a few minutes. On arrival at Merstone more detonators were exploded as the train pulled into the platform. Passengers then alighted to allow No. 27 and her two coaches to run forward to the siding so the connecting Sandown-Newport line trains could pass. When they had departed the branch train ran light to Newport and into history.

On Monday, 15th September 1952 Southern Vectis Omnibus Company ran two additional buses each way on route 9, departing Newport St James Square at 9.30 am and 4.30 pm, with arrival at Ventnor Town Hall at 10.25 am and 5.25 pm respectively. Return buses departed Ventnor at 10.30 am and 5.30 pm, with arrival at Newport at 11.25 am and 6.25 pm respectively. Monthly return tickets issued by BR to and from stations on the Ventnor West branch prior to closure were accepted for return journeys on the bus until 15th October 1952. After 20th September the winter SVOC timetable fully reflected the replacement bus service on route 9.

The contract for the demolition of the line was awarded to Thomas Ward & Sons of Sheffield. Dismantling began at Ventnor in November 1953 with a gang of seven men cutting rails before loading the scrap and sleepers on to a lorry by aid of a crane. The steel bridge girders were removed last and the work was completed by May 1954. Disposal of the former trackbed and railway land commenced in February 1953 with the sale of a small plot to the south of Dean Crossing to enable the garden of the crossing cottage to be extended. Later in the year almost a mile of formation between St Lawrence station and Underbridge 31, at 10 miles 39 chains, including the quarry, was sold off. Four years elapsed before the next sale in March 1957 when half a mile of formation south of Merstone was sold to a local farmer for extension of farmland. In the summer of 1957 the section north of Godshill station to Bow Bridge was disposed of whilst on 19th November a sale was concluded for Godshill station and yard area. By 8th May 1958 the section from Bow Bridge, north of Godshill, to Merstone was transferred to farmland with the sale of trackbed to local estates.

A year later, on 8th May 1959, almost a mile of the trackbed and formation south of Godshill station was sold to local farmers although much of the line was on an embankment. The substantial area of land of the station site at Ventnor West was sold on 23rd October 1959 to local land agents who resold the land for property development, although the actual station buildings were retained (much altered) as a private residence. Whitwell station and adjoining land remained railway property until 19th December 1960 when the buildings, land and track formation north of the station were sold. Three years later the section from Dean Crossing cottage exclusive to the tunnel was sold to a local landowner in May 1963. The last remaining section of line, that south of Whitwell bridge to Dean Crossing, was disposed of in July 1965. The goods shed at Ventnor West was bought by the proprietors of the Old Park Hotel at St Lawrence and the timbers now form part of their dining room.

Thirty-nine years after the passing of the 'Worthless Railway' some of the former assets are still in evidence to the discerning eye. At Merstone the island platform stands in the IWCC depot yard with the pine trees alongside, but the former junction has disappeared under a 1970s housing development. Godshill, Whitwell and St Lawrence station buildings are all standing in rebuilt form, whilst at Ventnor West housing development has covered the former terminal site with a road running along the former trackbed. Amidst the modern bungalows, however, the investigator will discover the old station house in use as a residential dwelling. Two overbridges have withstood the years, the brick arches of the bridge north of Whitwell and St Lawrence Shute bridge adjacent to the station. The large retaining wall alongside the road west of St Lawrence keeps the downland and former trackbed in place whilst nearby the most tangible reminder of the abortive branch is the tunnel which, after years of disuse, was converted to a mushroom farm in 1982.

The sheer delight of a journey on the Ventnor West branch can be expressed in no better way than by quoting from 'An Islander's Notes' written by Vectensis in the *Isle of Wight County Press* on 27th September 1952.

> It is sad to reflect that no more will travellers have the breathtaking thrill of the view of the Undercliff and the English Channel on emerging from the St Lawrence Tunnel on the Merstone-Ventnor West railway line. It was surely one of the most entrancing views to be seen from a train window anywhere in England. I shall never forget the first time I looked on that wonderful blend of richly wooded undulating country in the Undercliff, with the blue sea in the distance, on coming out of the gloom of the tunnel on a perfect summer day. There must be many many thousands who will remember the experience with abiding pleasure, and regret it may no longer cause the traveller to gasp in amazed delight.

On the last day of operation on 13th September 1952 'O2' No. 27 Merstone, *adorned with special headboard, is shown here at the buffer stops at Ventnor West in the course of running round. The engine was not push/pull fitted yet* Merstone *was chosen to work trains on the last day in preference to the push/pull fitted engines No. 35* Freshwater *and No. 36* Carisbrooke.   PAMLIN PRINTS

MERSTONE – VENTNOR WEST BRIDGES

No. IWCR No. in brackets	Known as	Mileage from Newport M ch	Locality	Public or Private	Crossing under the railway	Carrying over the railway	Type of construction	Spans	Dimensions of Span on square ft in	on skew ft in	Minimum height from ground or rail level To underside of girder ft in	To soffit of arch ft in
13 (36A)	Culvert	4 40	Merstone & Godshill	Private	Stream		Brick arch and culvert	1	6 0	8 10		5 6
14 (51)	Kennerley Bridge	4 45	" "	Private	Road		Wrought iron troughing on brick abutments	1	12 0	12 4	13 4	
15 (52)	Bow Bridge	5 04	" "	Public	Road		Wrought iron girders and parapets, trough decking, brick abutments	1	19 11	21 0	14 11	
16 (53)	Bridge Court Bridge	5 55½	Godshill & Whitwell	Private	Road		Wrought iron troughing on brick abutments	1	12 0	13 3	9 6	
17 (54)	Bridge Court Farm Bridge	5 62	" "	Private	Road		Brick arch abutments and parapets	1	12 0	12 2		18 1
18 (55)	Nodehill Bridge	5 77	" "	Public	Road		Wrought iron girders and trough decking, brick abutments	1	20 0		14 11	
19 (56)	Roud Bridge	6 27	" "	Public	Road		Wrought iron girders and trough decking, brick abutments	1	19 9	20 8	15 0	
20 (57)	Roud Footbridge	6 52	" "	Public		Footpath	Wrought iron girders, timber decking brick abutments	1	35 2		14 9	
21 (58)	Millers Lane Bridge	7 03	" "	Public	Road		Wrought iron decking on brick abutments	1	11 9	11 11	17 10	
22 (59)	Combley Bridge	7 19	" "	Public	Road		Wrought iron girders and parapets, trough decking, brick abutments	1	19 9	25 10	15 0	
23 (60)	Southford Bridge	7 33	" "	Private	Road		Brick arch and abutments	1	12 0			15 2
24 (61)	Whitwell Bridge	7 50½	" "	Private		Cart track	Brick arch and abutments	1	15 2			14 5
25 (62)	Whitwell Cattle Creep	7 65	" "	Private	Cattle Creep		Wrought iron troughing on brick abutments	1	10 0		10 11	
26 (63)	Whitwell Bridge	7 73	Whitwell & St. Lawrence	Public	Road		Wrought iron girders, parapets and trough decking, brick abutments	1	19 8	20 11	14 3	
27 (64)	Dean Bridge	8 40½	" "	Private	Cattle Creep		Wrought iron trough decking, masonry abutments	1	8 0		5 9	
(65)	Dean Crossing Footbridge (Removed to Wroxall 27 August 1926)		" "	Public		Footpath	Wrought iron lattice girders, cast iron columns, timber decking	1	27 7		15 0	
28 (66)	St. Lawrence Tunnel	8 64 to 9 12	" "				Brick semi-circular arch, masonry abutments	1	15 8			15 7
29 (67)	St. Lawrence Bridge	9 32	At St. Lawrence	Public		Road	Brick semi-circular arch, masonry abutments	1	14 11			15 9
30 (68)	Pelham Woods Bridge	9 61	St. Lawrence & Ventnor West	Public	Bridle path		Wrought iron decking, masonry abutments	1	11 11		15 11	
31 (69)	Ventnor Bridge	10 39	St. Lawrence & Ventnor West	Private	Footpath		Wrought iron decking, masonry abutments	1	7 9		10 0	
Also Sandown–Merstone Line		*Miles from Sandown M ch*										
16 (37)	Merstone Subway	5 19	Horringford & Merstone	Private	Railway subway used as a reservoir		Steel trough decking, brick abutments	1	5 11	6 7	6 7	

BIBLIOGRAPHY

General Works
Allen P. C., *The Railways of the Isle of Wight*, Loco Publishing Co.
Allen, P. C. & MacLeod, A. B., *Rails in the Isle of Wight*. Allen and Unwin.
Bradley, D. L., *Locomotive History of the Railways on the Isle of Wight*, RCTS.
Robbins, M., *The Isle of Wight Railways*, Oakwood Press.

Periodicals
Bradshaws Railway Guide
Bradshaws Railway Manual
British Railways (Southern Region) Magazine
Buses
Locomotive Carriage and Wagon Review
Locomotive Magazine
Railway Magazine
Railway World
Railway Year Book
Southern Railway Magazine
Trains Illustrated

Newspapers
Isle of Wight County Press
Isle of Wight Guardian
Isle of Wight Mercury
Isle of Wight Chronicle

Minute Books of Isle of Wight Railway, Isle of Wight Central Railway, Newport Godshill and St. Lawrence Railway, Southern Railway
Working and Public Timetables of IWR, IWCR, SR and BR (SR).
Appendices to Working Timetables of IWCR, SR and BR (SR).

ACKNOWLEDGEMENTS

The publication of this history would not have been possible without the help of many people who have been kind enough to assist. In particular I should like to thank A. Turner, H. Linnington, J. Hunnybun, H. Lacey, W. Miller, E. Pragnell, D. Saunders, H. Watson, E. Joyce, W. Gear, M. Prouten, G. Prouten, N. Parsons, E. Dale, K. West, C. Eason, W. Hayward, O. P. Vallender, W. Vallender, R. Seaman, P. Primmer, M. Jeffries, R. Tewksbury, G. Gardner, A. B. MacLeod, S. W. Baker, H. C. Casserley and W. A. Camwell.

I should also like to thank Tim Cooper, who has made a special study of all the Island Railways, and Dr. John Mackett, both of whom have advised and guided me on finer details and who have been kind enough to check the manuscript. Roger Silsbury and Alan Blackburn have placed their photographic collections at my disposal and provided additional snippets of information, and Mike Christensen has kindly added details about the signalling.

Grateful thanks to the staff of the former motive power depots at Newport and Ryde and many other active and retired railway staff, some of whom worked on the branch.

I should also like to acknowledge the help of the Public Record Office, British Rail (Southern Region), The House of Lords Record Office, The British Museum Newspaper Library, Isle of Wight County Record Office, Isle of Wight County Press, also the Isle of Wight Steam Railway and Wight Locomotive Society.

Last but not least, special thanks to Mavis Herbert and my daughter Ruth for typing the manuscript.